MURDER AT THE
BRIDGE TABLE

Matthew Granovetter

MURDER AT THE BRIDGE TABLE

Master Point Press

Some of the images used herein were obtained from IMSI's MasterClips
collection, 1895 Francisco Blvd. East, San Rafael, CA 94901-5506 USA.

*This is a work of fiction. Except for Roth, Zia, the Mitchells and my
wife, all the characters and events portrayed in this book are fictitious,
and any resemblance to real people or events is purely coincidental.*

> ### If you like this book, don't miss
> ### 'I Shot My Bridge Partner'
> ### also by Matthew Granovetter

Master Point Press
22 Lower Village Gate, Toronto, ON M5P 3L7
(416) 932-9766
www.pathcom.com/~raylee

Distributed in the USA by Barricade Books
50 Fifth Avenue, Suite 700, New York, NY 10011
1-800-59-BOOKS

Canadian Cataloguing In Publication Data
Granovetter, Matthew
        Murder at the bridge table, or, How to improve your
        duplicate game overnight
    2nd edition
    ISBN 1-894154-11-8
1. Duplicate contract Bridge 2. Duplicate contract bridge
— Fiction I. Title II. Title: How to improve your duplicate
game overnight

GV1282.8.D86G72 1999   795.41'5   C99–930831-9

Cover and interior design: Olena S. Sullivan

Printed and bound in Canada
1 2 3 4 5 6 7   07 06 05 04 03 02 01 00 99

FOREWORD
(TO THE FIRST EDITION)

The notion of a murder at the bridge table usually makes people smile. Although the thought of committing such a violent act over something so casual as a card game is funny, it is not unrealistic. Bridge players know how emotionally distraught they can become over a misplayed hand or a horrible bid.

Partners that hope for longevity require both a cool disposition and consistently accurate card play. Quite frankly, they are usually doomed from the start. I have said goodbye to over a dozen 'long-time' partners. The hardest element in such an affair is finding the appropriate technique. One way to end a partnership, like a marriage, is to simply state you want a divorce. This is a rather unpleasant business. Guilty feelings linger and sad remembrances, such as old convention cards, pop up when you clean out drawers. A more efficient way of ending a partnership is murder, which at least has the merit of sparing your ex-partner's feelings.

The most famous bridge murder case is well documented. It occurred in Kansas City, 1931, and involved the Bennetts, a husband and wife playing in a 'friendly' home game. Unable to cope with his last misplay in a four spade contract, Mrs. Bennett called Mr. Bennett 'a bum bridge player' for the umpteenth time that evening. He reached over and slapped her, the game broke up, and

Mrs. Bennett slipped into the bedroom, emerged with a pistol and shot her partner twice through the heart. At the trial (in which she was acquitted for reasons of temporary insanity), bridge experts testified that her husband's pitiful performance that evening would be ample cause to drive a partner crazy. The momentary madness which infects bridge players occurs frequently at rubber bridge and duplicate; and though it rarely results in murder, it often terminates marriages and close friendships (when such couples dare to form bridge partnerships).

I shall never forget my first experience with bridge violence. I was fourteen years old and was playing in the Asbury Park Individual, a duplicate tournament that required each player to partner every other. While I was declaring a hand there was a piercing shriek. It came from two sections away. Some lunatic was standing on top of the table, a chair raised above his head. He was swinging it, attempting to bring it down hard upon his partner's head. The madman was restrained of course, and play resumed briskly. Later we learned that the lunatic was a local clergyman, and his partner had merely pulled a penalty double.

Within the last two years the bridge world has seen vile crimes committed upon three well-known players. One was a kidnapping and two were murders. The most publicized incident was the Los Angeles murder of Barry Crane, (then) the leading ACBL masterpoint holder of all time. He was killed in his home, and to this date the crime remains unsolved. There is no reason to connect the murder with his bridge career; however, the lack of clues certainly leaves bridge as a possible motive. It is not unusual for even the best bridge players to annoy an opponent, upset their partner, or create jealousy by choosing to play with one person rather than another.

If even a good bridge player can do things which cause tempers to flare, one can imagine the extreme emotions that can be provoked by a bad bridge player. As a writer, I imagined such a situation occurring within my circle of friends. The story told in these pages involves Victor and Jacqui Mitchell, Zia Mahmood, Alvin Roth, and my wife, Pamela Granovetter, who all talk, act, and discuss bridge as I know they do in real life. Vic Mitchell was in fact the manager of the Bucket O' Blood Bridge and Chess Club located in Times Square, New York, during World War II. It later moved uptown to the Embassy Hotel. In the book, I meet him for the first time in 1983, while in fact, I've known him since 1975. The bridge hands that appear are also 'true' in spirit — hands similar to these have actually been played, discussed, and analyzed. The bridge lessons are as true as one could want in a book designed to help improve your game.

This brings us to the question: what is this book, a self-help duplicate bridge book or a mystery-detective novel? The answer is 'both'. In the past, there have been novels set in the background of bridge tournaments with a few bridge hands sprinkled in. This book is more like a 'how to improve your duplicate game' with a murder mystery thrown in! The amateur sleuth story line is designed to parallel the bridge lessons (the game is certainly a mystery to most of us). After a few chapters, my investigation of the murder of a bridge player in 1942 begins to intertwine with the lessons. The bridge hands and story become more and more tied together until finally a novel emerges.

Many of my experiences in life have contributed to the make-up of this book. The real-life characters have been dear friends and mentors. Victor Mitchell* has been my friend and adopted godfather for twelve years. His wife Jacqui literally fed me through college when I returned to school at the age of twenty-seven. Al Roth taught me much more about bridge than I ever admitted. Zia Mahmood introduced me to realms of bridge thought I never dreamed of before. My wife, Pamela, is my editor here and co-writer at other times. She crosses out the worst, and helps me correct the best in both my writings and my life.

Two friends who have enriched my life but did not fit into this particular plot (watch out next time) are Jimmy Cayne, a silent, but important partner in Granovetter Books, and Nick Lyons, formerly a professor of creative writing at Hunter College. While I'm at it, I'll thank my parents too. My mother tried her best to get me to write early in life and eventually succeeded. My dad died when I was eighteen, but he played a vital role by teaching me both to pursue the things I love most, and also to play a decent game of bridge.

Matthew Granovetter
May, 1988

* Victor Mitchell passed away in 1994. M.G.

CONTENTS

INTRODUCTION

Overnight success

No one can become a success at bridge overnight. In the chess world we encounter eleven-year-old prodigies because chess is an open game — all the pieces are in view and strategies may be calculated by any capable mind (or computer). Good bridge players usually do not come into their own for at least five to ten years. This is because bridge is a closed game — the pieces (the cards) are hidden (75% during the bidding, 50% during the play). Thus, other elements besides pure analysis are crucial — deduction, psychology, imagination, and the adult attribute of poise.

Although overnight success is almost inconceivable, overnight improvement is easy. Most players are taught bad habits by well-meaning partners. This book is intended to do away with illogical conventions and popular misconceptions. Although you may not be a great bridge player by the time you finish this book, I guarantee you will become a vastly improved player.

What does it take to become a 'bridge player'?

'About ten years of losing your money in a tough rubber bridge game.' This is the answer Alvin Roth would give. The bridge world's greatest theorist, Al has always thought that unless your bad bids cost money you can never learn to stop making them. (One famous psychiatrist agreed with Al, and compared learning bridge to learning to drive a car. Can you imagine how bad one's driving would be if accidents merely cost matchpoints rather than higher insurance premiums and lives?) Still, not all of us have the time or money to spend at rubber bridge clubs. Presumably, if you have bought this book you take your bridge seriously, whether you play for pleasure on a train, for matchpoints at the local duplicate, or for money at the club. As with any other endeavor, you should be able to become a better bridge player through reading and practice.

Are we born with bridge talent or is it something that can be achieved through hard work? The answer is 'both'. The talent to analyze and deduce within a given time period is certainly a natural thing — some are better at it than others. Some of us must work harder at the table to achieve the same results as those lucky people born with 'card sense'.

I used to know a respected surgeon whose hands shook at the bridge table. He was a brilliant man who could not apply his high IQ to the game of bridge. Through constant practice he was able to become a good player, but not an expert. At the same club where he played, a young backgammon expert switched his attention to bridge with stunning success. He was deemed a 'natural' by his peers. He counted the hands without strain and played his cards smoothly. But if I told you his name, you'd say, "Who?" The reason he never realized his full potential was laziness. He didn't care to discuss a bridge hand or study a better approach. He only wanted to play bridge if he could do it without a lot of effort.

The point is this: whether you are a natural or not, you will benefit from a solid foundation. Your future success at the bridge table will always be proportional to the extent of work you are prepared to put into the game.

Constant thought processes on defense

Anyone can become a decent bidder, and most people can become adequate declarers. However it is the person who defends well, that is considered to be 'a bridge player'.

During the course of an evening's duplicate, you will find yourself on defense roughly 50% of the time. It is therefore important to keep the mental juices flowing from trick one to trick thirteen. Average players stop and think on defense only when they have a problem — the good bridge player thinks constantly.

What does this mean? It means that he is ready to play a card in tempo without giving away his hand by hesitating. He can duck an ace smoothly if he has to. But more importantly, by thinking constantly he alleviates mental strain when problems arise late in the hand. At trick twelve, when he has to discard correctly, he doesn't have to sit there with his head in his hands trying to remember who played which card. He remembers the original fifty-two cards and now makes the logical discard in the same way that an actor remembers his lines late in a play — they simply come to him because he's been following the scene throughout.

When dummy comes down, I count. I count points and figure out from the bidding how many points my partner is likely to hold. I count distribution, and with the bidding reviewed in my mind, I try to piece together declarer's shape as quickly as possible. Although at first it might seem like hard work, relentless thought on defense will open up a whole new world. You'll begin to form mental pictures of all the cards around the table. Bridge hands will become double-dummy problems rather than intangible mysteries. You'll take a giant step toward becoming a 'bridge player' — someone who plays the game rather than someone who plays at the game.

A short list of dos and don'ts

Every bridge teacher has their own favorite rules. 'Always lead your partner's suit.' Would you lead your partner's suit if you held A-K-Q-J of another? 'Second hand low.' Should you duck your ace if it is the setting trick? 'A king is worth three high-card points.' But is a king worth three high-card points when the hand on your left overcalls that suit? Yes, these rules are valuable, but they are only generalizations. They are intended to be used in conjunction with the old-fashioned occupation of thinking.

My wife, Pamela, and I did a study of the most serious flaws in the average player's bridge game. Here are the results translated into a short list of dos and don'ts. The rules have nothing to do with our personal preferences — we think all good players will agree with them. Since some of the ideas are generalizations they will not always work but the odds are that, if you take this list to the local club tomorrow and follow this advice on every hand, you'll discover what overnight improvement feels like.

DOs	DON'TS
An A-K combination is your first choice of leads.	Don't lead an ace without the king.
Support partner with three+ trumps whenever you conceivably can.	Don't pass partner's preempt, then later back into the auction.
Open the bidding in your longest suit.	Don't overcall two of a minor with only a five-card suit.
Double them for penalties when you have a nice trump stack, not just points.	Don't pull partner's penalty double.
Defend hands carefully while watching partner's signals.	Don't break suits for declarer when he has to do it himself.
When declaring, study the hand before you call a card from dummy.	Don't call a card from dummy until you have formulated a plan of play.
Concentrate.	Don't criticize partner until the end of the game. *Then* shoot him. (Just kidding.)

Rules must be placed within the context of each hand

Most bridge teachers insist on their favorite methods so strongly that they actually prevent their students from thinking — on purpose! One very popular teacher told me that his students simply *must* follow rules — and are better off for it. It is true that following rules can be a lot easier than thinking, but it doesn't seem right to inhibit the most vital element of a game that requires complex lines of reasoning — thinking. It is best to use rules as a 75% guideline. Rules will never adequately replace thinking.

Why did you duck your A-K-Q, Esther?

You told me 'second hand low' Sam. So I played low.

'Always split two touching honors.'

I had three

You must develop the judgment to put rules into context. For example, you tend to cover an honor with an honor. But when dummy has J-10-9-8, it would be foolish to put the queen on the jack. Here is a more advanced example. I was West playing with one of my better students.

North dealer
Neither vulnerable

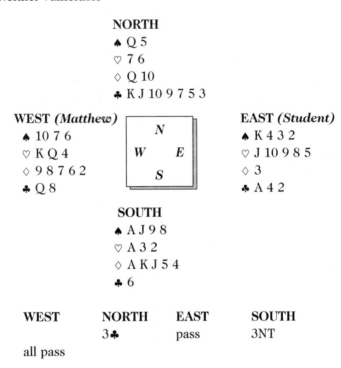

NORTH
♠ Q 5
♡ 7 6
◇ Q 10
♣ K J 10 9 7 5 3

WEST *(Matthew)*
♠ 10 7 6
♡ K Q 4
◇ 9 8 7 6 2
♣ Q 8

EAST *(Student)*
♠ K 4 3 2
♡ J 10 9 8 5
◇ 3
♣ A 4 2

SOUTH
♠ A J 9 8
♡ A 3 2
◇ A K J 5 4
♣ 6

WEST	NORTH	EAST	SOUTH
	3♣	pass	3NT
all pass			

This was a sequence indicating that the opponents might have nine quick tricks. With so little defense in my hand, and the dreaded club queen in front of the club suit, I decided to break the rule of fourth-best leads. Using the clues of the bidding, I tried to find my partner with as little as possible to defeat the hand. That might be ace-fifth of hearts, or jack-fifth and an entry. I led the heart king.

Declarer held off taking his ace of hearts until the third round. Then he led a diamond to the queen and cashed the diamond ten. Next he led dummy's queen of spades and my partner ducked smoothly. This duck gave away the contract because declarer finessed the jack next, making three spade tricks. In all, he made one heart trick, five diamond tricks, and three spade tricks.

The question is, where did my student go wrong? Had he woodenly followed the rule 'cover an honor with an honor', my spade ten would have prevented declarer from making three spade tricks. I felt like offering a stern lecture about the virtue of following simple rules. I had the presence of mind, however, to keep silent and ask him later why he had not covered. His answer was very good. Because he had four cards to the king, and dummy only a doubleton, by not covering, declarer could make only three spade tricks. Whereas, if declarer had A-J-10-9, A-J-9-8-7, or A-J-9-8-7-6, the cover of the king would give away the entire suit.

Yes, this was an accurate assessment with regard to the isolated spade suit. However, within the context of the entire hand it was wrong not to cover. My partner should have counted declarer's tricks. Declarer had taken one heart trick and was known to hold the A-K-J of diamonds at least five times, since the diamond queen-ten had been cashed in dummy. With at least six tricks for sure, declarer needed three tricks at most in spades. Within the context of the hand, partner's objective in the spade suit had changed. He was no longer trying to prevent declarer from making four, five, or six spade tricks — his objective was to stop declarer from scoring three spade tricks. The cover of the king was necessary if I held the ten.

Suddenly seeing a rule like this one in context, a whole new area of analysis opened up before my student's eyes. He was not afraid of the difficulty of putting old ideas into new perspectives. After all, bridge is a great game not because it is simple or because it can be played well (and enjoyed to its fullest) by simply following suit.

Who should be reading this book?

No matter who you are, how much you know about bridge, or how long you've been playing, you can benefit from this book.

1. Beginners who wish to start out on the right foot

If you're just learning the game, this book should be a unique reference guide — a foundation to build on. Although it does not contain such specifics as point-count formulas, it illustrates the major errors that even advanced bridge players sometimes make. Keep this book under your arm, follow its advice, and you'll be off to a great start.

2. Advanced players who wish to get rid of bad habits and gain good ones

If you've been playing for a number of years and are looking for a way to improve your results, this book is perfect for you. No matter what bidding system you play, or which carding methods you use, you have basic tendencies that need checking. We get into bad habits over the years, and sometimes find it difficult to break them. I want you to be introspective about your game. I want you to be open-minded to new ideas, and to thinking and improving.

Some observers claim the level of bridge among club players has vastly improved over the last two decades. I don't believe it. I play against people who don't know what an opening bid looks like. There are so many confusing conventions available in today's high-tech bridge society that many players have adopted methods they don't know how to handle. Remember one thing about all sports — professionals can do unorthodox things and still win; amateurs need to be consistent.

This book should be read in the order it was written, since the plot and the bridge diagrams parallel each other in level of complexity. If you feel you are ready to apply what you've read to your game, review one chapter per sitting and think of the chapter's theme when you go to the next duplicate. But take your time. It is not easy to play bridge with five new ideas in mind and still follow suit at the same time. Even if you bring only one new idea to the table, some other part of your game will suffer. Once, in an effort to get my student to count during a duplicate, I asked her to try and tell me declarer's shape at the end of every hand. I can't tell you how many tricks went away that evening while she was busy counting!

Which is why I suggest you try only one idea per duplicate; eventually all these concepts will sink in and become good habits. Since the book is in a novel form, I've been careful to outline the chapter headings and subheadings with bridge motifs. This will help the serious student keep track of the book's bridge strategies.

3. Experts

Okay, so you're an expert. You bought this book because you collect bridge books. You don't expect to learn anything. After all, you've already won a number of tournaments. Nevertheless, sometimes very good players get into the habit of overplaying. You try for 100% perfection when 75% is all that's needed to win.

The attempt to reach the maximum result on every hand is admirable but not practical. You start to get fancy, which often creates disaster. You begin to lose points, to get more zeros than you did in the past. You try the underlead of your ace through dummy's long suit and declarer wins his singleton king. Your novice rubber bridge partner yells at you, *"Why didn't you lead the unbid suit?"*

You should get back to basics. Perhaps this book will revitalize you or help you remember how well you did when you played 'normally', and won because you were a better analyst or quicker thinker. If you honestly believe there is always room for improvement, you'll use this book to get back in shape.

4. Those reading for enjoyment

This is not just an 'improve your bridge' book. It is a novel about a murder investigation that features many real-life characters who play top-level bridge. For those who have trouble following the bridge diagrams, simply peruse them and note the bidding. The book begins with an introduction to improving your bridge game. Soon a story will unfold. The lessons and story will slowly intertwine, the story taking over at the end. So even if your intention is simply enjoyment, read the discussions of bridge strategies. They will enhance the novel for you by shadowing the dark events of the plot.

How I became involved

In the summer of 1983, after being married for a full year to a mystery novel fan, I took up the sport myself, reading many of the famous whodunits and detective novels from the first half of this century. During that August it was not uncommon for me to be seen reading something from my wife's Agatha Christie collection while turning the dummy for my students at the local bridge club. (Some might think it improper to read at the bridge table, especially when engaged to teach the principal points of the game. I thought it quite appropriate since not only did it help me relax, but it also aesthetically accented my opponents' mysterious bids and plays.)

On the twenty-first of the month, my wife suggested that we do a book with all our lessons in it so that her students could review at their leisure. I absent-mindedly agreed, and stuck my nose back into *Murder on the Orient Express.*

"By the way," she said next, "there's a package for you with no return address."

```
Matthew G.
32 E. 61 St.  Apt. 2B
New York,  NY 10021
```

The anonymous box contained a strange collection of items: a newspaper headline from 1942, some additional clippings of the same period, and a large bundle of photocopies from New York City Police archives. I shoved my Agatha Christie novel into a drawer, and, in my wife's words, 'became transfixed'. The more I read, the more enchanted I became with the notion of an unsolved murder connected to the game of bridge.

I took out a fresh notebook, and began to make a list of clues...

MURDER AT THE
BRIDGE TABLE

1   STOP LEADING ACES

BRIDGE PLAYER FOUND DEAD AFTER LEADING AN ACE

Aces were meant to seize kings

On Friday, January 23, 1942, at 8:35 a.m. a body was found in Room 623 of the old Embassy Hotel. It was a man, in his evening clothes, approximately five feet eight with no great or distinguishing features. His name was Marcel Moskowitz, purported profession: salesman (in truth, a handicapper at New York racetracks, a tout, a bookie, and a swindler in other less acceptable occupations, most notably a con-man of older women's affections and wealth). He had a reputation as a ladies' man, and was thought to be equally adept at handling a deck of cards.

The corpse was clean-shaven, fully dressed, and presumed to have been dead five to six hours, official cause: natural (unofficial rumor: suffocation by pillow). No autopsy was ordered (at least there is no record of one). And though the case most assuredly lies in obscurity at the bottom of municipal records of hotel deaths, certain facts that led to an inquiry at the time (a brief inquiry, leading nowhere) are well worth reviewing forty years later for two reasons. First, there was evidence that the man was smothered: five pillows were found surrounding his head (the chambermaid insisted she had only made up two of them). Nothing had been stolen, and there seemed to be no obvious motive for any crime... except perhaps one clue which the investigator at the time did not fathom. That is, on the northwest corner of the bedspread was a number-two lead pencil, the point broken off. To go with this, in the corpse's hand, clutched to his heart, was a pad of paper with twenty-one funny-looking diagrams in longhand, the first of which was this one (reconstructed here, as best as possible from my photocopy):

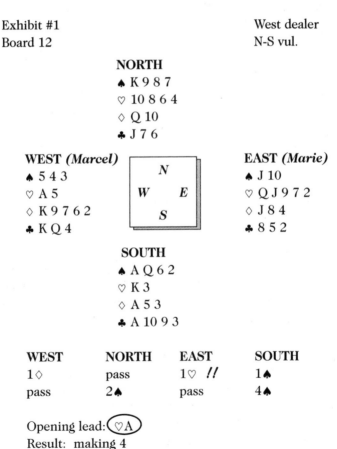

| Exhibit #1 | | West dealer |
| Board 12 | | N-S vul. |

NORTH
♠ K 9 8 7
♡ 10 8 6 4
◇ Q 10
♣ J 7 6

WEST *(Marcel)*
♠ 5 4 3
♡ A 5
◇ K 9 7 6 2
♣ K Q 4

EAST *(Marie)*
♠ J 10
♡ Q J 9 7 2
◇ J 8 4
♣ 8 5 2

SOUTH
♠ A Q 6 2
♡ K 3
◇ A 5 3
♣ A 10 9 3

WEST	NORTH	EAST	SOUTH
1◇	pass	1♡ *!!*	1♠
pass	2♠	pass	4♠

Opening lead: ♡A
Result: making 4

Obviously this strange scribbling — strange to the Chief Inspector at the time — was a list of bridge hands. Exhibit number one showed the dealer as West with North-South vulnerable. This precise combination of dealer/vulnerability matches Board 12 on the convention card, and I have written in that number next to the exhibit number on top. (Board numbers marked on subsequent hands are also my deductions and markings.)

The result of the hand reveals a disaster for Marcel, West, and his partner, a mysterious woman named Marie, East. The reader will note that the contract of four spades is rather precarious. But apparently Marcel led the ace of hearts. He must have felt some satisfaction when dummy came down with so little in hearts and the dreaded club jack; and perhaps Marcel congratulated himself for not leading the club king into declarer's ace. However, after the ace lead, declarer must have made the contract by giving up the diamond king and one club honor, discarding a second club from dummy on the diamond ace, and ruffing out the club suit (losing three tricks: the heart ace, diamond king, and club queen).

Upon further analysis (the sort that was not made by the Inspector at the time), we see that a neutral trump lead or the simplistic lead of the club king would have beaten the contract. After a trump lead declarer must lose two heart tricks and two minor suit tricks. After the lead of the club king, declarer can win, draw trumps, and knock out the queen of clubs, to discard one of dummy's diamonds on his fourth club; but only one diamond can be ruffed in dummy and declarer must lose two heart tricks and two minor suit tricks.

Careful reconstruction of the photocopies also shows a post-mortem argument of a highly emotional nature. The response of one heart to one diamond has two exclamation points next to it. I showed the 'original' photocopies to a handwriting analyst who quickly spotted the beginning of a pattern in which two distinct handwriting tones were established. One person drew circles, the other, exclamation points. Unless human nature was very different forty years ago and bridge players went about pointing out their own mistakes, we can deduce that it was Marie who had circled Marcel's lead of the heart ace, and Marcel who had added exclamation points to Marie's response of one heart.

Nor does it take much imagination to decipher the post-mortem argument. Marcel was accused by his partner of making a dreadful lead. Marcel defended himself by pointing out Marie's one over one response on only five points. Had she not responded one heart, Marcel would never have led the ace; and if she held the heart king instead of the queen (to get up to six points), his ace of hearts lead would have been successful.

Had Marcel really put up such a futile argument? (Futile because if Marie held the heart king it wouldn't have mattered what he led.) I don't know the answer. I do know that professional analysis of the deal, both the handwriting and the bridge, indicate that something had occurred to cause an argument, and that an argument had indeed taken place, just minutes after the scene of the crime (the crime of leading the heart ace).

As long as we're on the subject of leads, let's continue. I'll get back to the case of Marcel's death (murder?) in a few pages, while I leave you with one other piece of evidence that the Inspector — his name was Gardner, and he did not play bridge — did in fact discover in his incomplete investigation. (I say incomplete because this pad of bridge evidence must have been gathered up with the other articles in the room and taken to the precinct along with the corpse's personal belongings; yet it was never mentioned in any newspaper account.) The other piece of evidence was that the Embassy Hotel, during the war years, rented out the east wing of its penthouse floor to a bridge and chess club nicknamed 'The Bucket O' Blood'.

Make normal and safe leads

Contract bridge is usually portrayed to the public eye as a social and genteel pastime. The truth is that the game resembles war; this is why people love it so much. It allows us to fulfill our darker competitive desires without really hurting our fellow human being. Even in the afternoon duplicate, blood is spilled on every trick; on every hand a battle is won or lost.

The opening lead is the initial assault on a contract, but it is never a surprise. Declarer knows it's coming and partner is wary of it. Attacking declarer can be very much like attacking a fortified position on the battlefield without knowing whether your ally (your partner) is there to back you up or not; you may have the advantage of making the first move, but your success depends on making a perfect hit. More often than not you will miss the target, and you will lose much more than you hoped to gain. This is because in bridge, as in war, the person who goes last gets to see both the direction and strength of his enemy's attack. On the battlefield, the soldier inside the fortress has the advantage. At the bridge table, declarer has the edge.

Look at this ordinary combination of cards:

NORTH
♠ 10 3 2

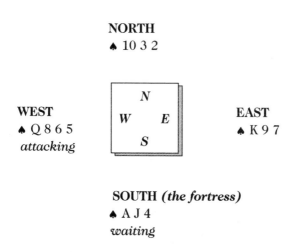

WEST
♠ Q 8 6 5
attacking

EAST
♠ K 9 7

SOUTH *(the fortress)*
♠ A J 4
waiting

If West leads a low spade, South gains the advantage by being last to play. Dummy plays low. If East puts up the king, South wins the ace and plays back the suit, eventually winning two tricks. If East plays the nine, South wins the jack and ace, again for two winners. But if South is left to attack the suit himself from his hand or dummy, he cannot score more than one trick.

Try to give nothing away

Stinginess is hardly an admirable trait. But when you're careful with your grocery budget at the local supermarket you come home with more money. And when you're careful about giving away your assets on opening lead during a local duplicate, you take more tricks, and come home with more masterpoints. Stinginess at the bridge table is a good trait when you are being stingy to 'the enemy'.

Some players seem to think that the opening lead is a reflection of their courage, the lead of an ace being the bravest blow for the defense. (The lead of an ace is a blow all right.) Bob Hamman once compared bridge to a boxing match. This is an interesting analogy because if you know anything about boxing you know that the best boxers do not come flying out at the sound of the bell, their arms flailing wildly in an attempt to score a first round knockout. On the contrary. Muhammad Ali used to come out dancing, avoiding his opponent until an opportunity was presented to him. When a boxer swings and misses, his opponent usually counter-punches and connects. When a bridge player tries to attack on opening lead he often blows not just a trick, but the whole contract. When a bridge player comes out dancing like Ali, looks around to study the opponents' cards, and then seizes the offensive at an opportune moment, he often ends up winning.

Let's sum up with a simple, irrefutable analysis. During the course of a hand, fifty-two cards are placed face up on the bridge table, thirteen by each player. Fifty-one out of those fifty-two cards will be played by players who can see half the deck (their hand and dummy). One of those fifty-two cards is placed on the table by a player who sees only his own hand; that card is the opening lead. And that is why the opening leader must be careful: he is at a big disadvantage.

List of good choices

This book is not meant to teach you to be a great opening leader. To do that you would have to analyze the bidding, and know your opponents' methods and styles. But I can help you to stop making suicidal leads, and to stop giving away tricks before you're even into the hand. At the top of the next page is a list of good choices for opening leads against suit contracts. (Fourth best against notrump contracts is so powerful that we won't go into choices there.) I list the very best holding you can lead from down to the very worst.

The list is easy to remember this way: the two best leads are from an ace-king or a singleton. Otherwise, look for two touching honors. Next, look to lead from weakness. If you must lead from an honor, try a low one in preference to a high one. But don't lead an ace (except from ace-king or singleton ace).

This may sound like elementary stuff, but you would be surprised how many 'good' players give away points in this area. As a teacher, I give this list to my students. It doesn't always help. Jack, a stubborn fellow, examined my list, burned it, and led out his aces

> **Opening leads against suit contracts, in order of preference**
>
> A-K
> a singleton (non-trump)
> K-Q
> Q-J
> J-10
> 10-9
> x-x
> x-x-x or longer
> weak trumps
> 10-x or longer
> J-x or longer
> Q-x or longer
> K-x or longer
> a singleton trump
> the disastrous A-x or longer

for one month straight. On his fourteenth try he defeated a contract by leading an ace, looked up at me and said, "There!" Audrey, an emotional student who takes every word I say as gospel, pasted it to the front of her pocketbook which she rests on her lap during the game. One night we played together at the duplicate. On the second board, Audrey's right-hand opponent opened four spades and Audrey doubled. This became the final contract and two minutes went by without an opening lead. The opponents were getting annoyed and started to stare at her. At one point she looked up, her cheeks a bit red, then went back to her cards. Another few minutes went by. Finally I pleaded, "Audrey, lead."

She burst out crying, "I can't!" Poor Audrey had four unsupported aces in her hand.

"It's all right," I said, "lead anything." She did. That ace got ruffed and they made four.

Exceptions: against slams and five of a minor

When the opponents are playing at the five-level or higher, the lead of an ace rises quickly in merit. It's worth noting these exceptional cases because of the amount of points that can be lost when leading against a high-level contract.

Let's begin with slams. Here I also adhere to the rule 'give nothing away'. Sometimes a slam is bid when only eleven tricks are available, and the twelfth trick is often presented to the declarer by the clever means of underleading a queen or king. (Yes, the attacking lead might work one out of ten times. But do you want nine bottoms for one top?) However, contrary to my advice for leads against other contracts, the lead of an ace against a slam (except six notrump) is the most attractive lead you can make! This is because here you need only two tricks and slams often succeed if the defenders don't take them immediately. There is a possibility that partner will have the king in the suit where you have the ace, or, just as good, a singleton. Also, by cashing one trick, and waiting for another, you may defeat the slam. If you fail to lead your ace, declarer might discard that suit, and you won't see your ace take a trick.

Against five of a minor, the lead of an ace is so-so. It's not as bad as an ace lead against a lower contract, but not as good as against a slam. A happy medium that works nicely against five-level contracts is an attacking lead from a king or queen. In fact, leading from an honor at the five level should be on top of your opening lead list. The fact that the opponents have avoided three notrump to play five of a minor is unusual. It means that either they lack a stopper in one suit (so you should attack it) or they have misbid.

Let's list these two exceptions again:

1) The best lead against a slam in a trump suit is an ace.

2) The best lead against five of a minor is from strength.

When to attack

As I said, five of a minor calls for an aggressive lead even if it means taking a chance and leading away from an honor. When the contract is at the four-level or lower, passivity wins most of the time. However, there are some exceptions where attacking against a low-level suit contract is right. These cases must be judged by listening carefully to the bidding.

Case 1. It sounds like the opponents were looking for notrump and avoided it. You should figure out which suit they are weak in and attack it.

Case 2. Leading your partner's overcalled suit. Usually,

although not always, a safe bet.

Case 3. Attacking the unbid suit. This is not a bad idea in any auction.

Don't always lead partner's bid suit

Believe it or not, partner does not always enter the auction so that he can help you out with your opening lead. Opening leaders too often think that's why partner bid. It's a good excuse for a lead, and it rarely loses the post-mortem argument. "If you didn't want me to lead it, why'd you bid it?" is about as dumb a comment as any you might hear at your local duplicate. But you do hear it a lot.

I usually bid a suit I have some length in, but that is not a very strong basis for an opening lead. When I'm dealt:

♠ A Q 3   ♡ J 8 7 5 3   ◇ K Q J 2   ♣ Q

I open the bidding one heart, not one spade or one diamond, because I'm hoping that our side will play the contract somewhere. I am not opening the bidding because I think my left-hand opponent will play the contract and I must help my partner find the best lead. Yet this absurd thought is the basis for most bridge players' opening leads! (There are even some people, often beginners, who will go so far as to lead partner's suit when looking at K-Q-J-10 of their own. This is scary.)

A good opening leader looks at his own hand first. The bidding is important and often provides clues, but it shouldn't outweigh the evidence of your own eyes. When my partner opens the bidding one spade and I have the king-queen of clubs, I lead the king of clubs. Not only does this philosophy help me win, it keeps me sane besides.

Be disciplined on lead

It is easier to memorize rules and apply them than it is to interpret rules and recognize *when* to apply them. The obvious danger in thinking for yourself is that you might think the wrong thoughts. You learn to ride by falling off a bike, not by keeping the training wheels on. If you actually felt the concrete on your rear end every time you made an undisciplined lead, I'm sure you would quickly learn to be a better player by trial and error. But the pain of a bottom score is fleeting, which is why experimentation at the bridge table has little value (although it does help you lose partners).

Does this mean you should become a robot? In general, no, but on opening lead, to some extent, yes! This is because the best opening lead is rarely arrived at through in-depth analysis. Assuming you are given the correct set of rules — which you are here — the edge you have over a robot is your ability to interpret the bidding. The edge the robot has over you is its lack of imagination. Discipline is required, and discipline means restraining your imagination. It's sad but true — the mundane lead is usually the best lead.

There's a story about a mad scientist who was never satisfied with her partner at the bridge table. So she built a robot, and programmed him to bid in a disciplined fashion, make leads according to formula, signal perfectly on defense, and play the hand according to Watson. Two weeks later, they had won six out of seven duplicates and she was considering marrying the fellow! From time to time a bid would not be perfect, or a reasonable line of play would backfire; but on opening leads their record was phenomenal. Add to that the fact that he never talked back when she called him a 'stupid robot', and you'll see how a wonderful partner can behave.

During the third week, she decided to improve matters by teaching him an exception to a rule. He was reprogrammed to lead his king doubleton when partner opened the bidding in that suit. A hand came up in which she had to open one heart on a 10-8-6-5-3 suit. The next hand bid one notrump. Robot passed and fourth hand bid two clubs, Stayman. This was fortunate since our scientist also held the K-Q-J-9-8 of clubs and doubled the Stayman bid. The opponents ended up in three notrump and Robot led the heart king. "You stupid robot," she muttered under her breath.

Robot lit up. "Exception to rule... beep... exception to rule... beep."

That night, she improved her programming. Robot was taught to prefer leading the suit partner doubled. Needless to say, the next duplicate found our heroine making a takeout double on the very first hand. Robot led the opponents' best suit, and before she could mutter one curse he said: "Exception to the exception... beep... exception to the exception... beep." She flung a cup of decaf at him and he revoked.

Recognize when partner has bid for the lead or has simply bid his length

In bridge, the value of a hand or a specific card changes from bid to bid, trick to trick. When I pick up:

♠ 5 4 3   ♡ A 8 6   ◇ 9 7 5   ♣ 8 4 3 2

I say to myself, "What a boring hand." However, if I find myself on lead against seven notrump, I love this hand. The value of the hand depends on the opponents' final contract.

Robots can't distinguish the context of a bid, or the context of a play. Yet it is paramount that you, a human being, understand bids and plays within their timely framework. For example, the play of a deuce. What does it mean? "You don't like that suit," someone says. Okay. Try to explain this to a beginner, when in the middle of a hand his partner shifts to a deuce. "Aha, he doesn't like this suit."

"No, this deuce means that he likes the suit. He is *initiating* the lead of the suit. He doesn't like it if he follows to partner's lead with the deuce."

"What if the opponents start the suit? What does the deuce mean then?" asks the bright beginner.

"Count," says the teacher, "an odd number of cards." Whereupon the ace is led off dummy and with K-2 the student drops the king. "No, no. The deuce could also mean you have nothing else to play. You see, well, its message could be... meaningless." The student looks aghast.

On the next deal diamonds are trumps. Partner leads the heart king, then the ace, and then the cursed deuce, which the student ruffs. The student now has a choice between returning a spade or a club and starts to return a spade. "What are you doing?" asks the teacher. "Partner returned the deuce for you to ruff."

"What?" asks the student.

"Don't 'what' me. That deuce is obviously suit preference and asks you to return the lower-ranking suit, clubs."

Easy game. The play of the deuce can mean: discouraging, encouraging, odd number, suit preference, or nothing at all. The only way to determine the meaning is to place the card in context of the whole hand.

Now let's get back to leads. Partner has bid a suit. Is there any way we can tell whether he was bidding to help us with the lead or whether he was merely bidding his length? Perhaps by studying the bidding we can place his bid in context. If he opens the bidding or responds, we cannot judge whether he is bidding for a lead. If he has thirteen points he has to open; if he has six points he has to respond. But let's take the overcall. Suppose you are South and the auction has gone:

WEST	NORTH	EAST	SOUTH
1♣	1♠	1NT	pass
2NT	pass	3NT	all pass

♠ 4 3   ♡ K J 10 5 2   ◇ 10 5 4   ♣ 7 4 3

Partner has *overcalled* one spade, so it certainly can't be wrong to lead a spade. However, it wouldn't surprise me if a heart were the only lead to defeat the contract. East has bid one notrump and probably has two stoppers in the spade suit. He might easily take the first nine tricks when a heart lead to partner's ace would have taken the first five tricks for the defense. But how is one to know?

The bidding suggests that the opponents are not loaded in high-card points since they struggled to game. Add your four points to their total and you get about 28-30. If partner has 10-12 points, his overcall is not necessarily lead-directing. It might have been made on almost any decent hand with five spades to an honor. His high-card strength could be mostly in spades, but there is no reason to believe it isn't scattered among the other suits as well. Therefore, a heart lead is a reasonable shot here.

A heart lead, in fact, has a better chance of defeating the contract than a spade lead, because it requires less from partner to be successful. To defeat the contract with a spade lead requires partner to have a very strong spade suit, as well as the necessary entries to regain the lead. To defeat the contract with a heart lead requires that partner hold the ace of hearts, while the queen is in declarer's hand or doubleton in dummy.

Now let's look at a slightly different hand. We will simply add a king to our hand and it looks like this:

WEST	NORTH	EAST	SOUTH
1♣	1♠	1NT	pass
2NT	pass	3NT	all pass

♠ 4 3   ♡ K J 10 5 2   ◇ K 10 4   ♣ 7 4 3

With the same auction, this time I would lead a spade. The reasoning goes like this: I now have seven points. Add that to the twenty-five or so the opponents have and subtract from forty — the result is that partner has overcalled with about eight points. He would not do that unless he had a very good reason, which is that his spade suit is very strong. By examining his overcall in context of the bidding and our hand we can conclude he was making a lead-directing overcall as opposed to simply bidding his long suit in an effort to compete or reach game.

Stop trying to get in the newspaper

Everybody loves to read their name in the morning bridge column. The easiest route into a bridge column is the same as the easiest route into any newspaper column — do something dramatic and make it work. I'm sure if you drown your father-in-law in a goldfish bowl or walk to work on your hands, you'll get into the newspaper. Unfortunately, at the bridge table, your partner is less than appreciative when you bid and play upside down in your chair.

Yet there are players who lead low from doubletons, lay down aces on opening lead from A-Q, and lead queens from Q-x-x. They get bottom after bottom (which we never hear about), and one day it works and they get a top. Then they call the local bridge reporter and we have to read about it the next day at breakfast:

Contract Bridge
by Charles Goren

NORTH
- ♠ 6 2
- ♡ A J 6 3
- ◊ Q 9 6 4
- ♣ A 4 3

WEST
- ♠ K J 5 4 3
- ♡ Q 7 4
- ◊ K 10 7
- ♣ Q 8

```
        N
    W       E
        S
```

EAST
- ♠ 9 8 7
- ♡ 9 8 5 2
- ◊ A J 8 5 3
- ♣ J

SOUTH
- ♠ A Q 10
- ♡ K 10
- ◊ 2
- ♣ K 10 9 7 6 5 2

A brilliant lead of the ten of diamonds from K-10-7 was the only lead to defeat the three notrump contract. Mr. Shmigeggie, sitting West, deduced from the bidding that the Q-9 fourth would be on his left. His partner, whom he had just met that evening

(Of course he just met the partner that evening; he's lost every other partner he's ever had! M. G.)

was surprised when the ten held the trick. Shmigeggie continued with the king and seven to East's A-J fifth. The choice of the diamond suit was remarkable. Even more outstanding was the choice of the ten-spot. In order to appreciate this, readers will note the ill effect of the king lead. Declarer may cover the ten on the second round...

Lead your singleton, Mr. Brilliant

Brilliancy may get you an occasional top at the local duplicate and your name in the newspaper, but most of the time, attempts to be brilliant will earn bottoms (and lose friends as well). Partners of brilliant players chew Tylenol for snacks.

Early in my bridge career I had the good fortune to play with the great Italian Blue Team star Benito Garozzo, winner of countless world championships. We were in Las Vegas for a money tournament, and there was a side game at 1:00 p.m. It was my twenty-first birthday and I got all dressed up in tie and jacket (I even combed my hair). Heading through the casino to the bridge room my heart was pounding with excitement. We started play and went on to have a decent game. Near the end of the session the opponents reached a four heart contract and I had the choice of leading from the Q-J-10-9-8 of spades or leading my singleton diamond. With four small trumps on the side as a nuisance, I cleverly deduced the value of pumping declarer in my long suit while promoting trump tricks with my short suit. Therefore, I led the queen of spades. This was the full deal:

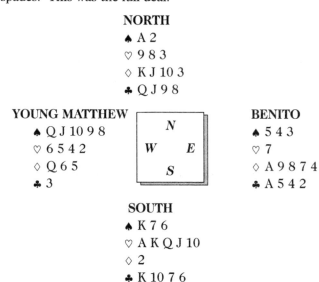

NORTH
♠ A 2
♡ 9 8 3
◇ K J 10 3
♣ Q J 9 8

YOUNG MATTHEW
♠ Q J 10 9 8
♡ 6 5 4 2
◇ Q 6 5
♣ 3

BENITO
♠ 5 4 3
♡ 7
◇ A 9 8 7 4
♣ A 5 4 2

SOUTH
♠ K 7 6
♡ A K Q J 10
◇ 2
♣ K 10 7 6

Declarer won the spade lead with the ace, cashed the king and ruffed a spade in dummy. Then, after making short work of my so-called four nuisance trumps, he led clubs, claiming an overtrick. I

was distraught. If I had led my singleton club, my partner would have won the ace, given me a ruff, back to his diamond ace, and another ruff to beat the hand. Benito was kind to me when he called me over near a slot machine for consultation.

"Listen to me, young Matchu. Your lead — it stinks."

"I was going for the pump. The pump and... "

"Pump shmump," he wisely interrupted. "Take the advice of one who knows these things. Always lead your singleton."

"Always?"

"I use to think like you. I would figure out when it was smart not to lead it. But after a while I lose so many games and slams, my head — it starts to spin. So now I am older and wiser. I go back to my beginnings and always lead my singleton."

Underlead your ace in the post-mortem only

Finally we come to the most stubborn among you who say, "Oh yeah? I shouldn't lead my aces? Okay, then I'll underlead them."

I have to admit one thing. The *underlead* of an ace is better than the *lead* of an ace. But then, poison is a better suicide than stabbing oneself to death. (This is merely conjecture, but poison is probably less painful, and you even have a better chance of survival.) Underleading an ace may also permit you a second chance, whereas the ace itself does not. For example, if declarer holds the K-Q-x, the lead of the ace sets up two tricks for him, while the underlead of the ace still allows partner a chance to lead the suit back through an unsupported honor.

A negative difference between leading an ace or underleading one is the inclusion of an unwilling partner in the perpetration of a crime. Whereas the lead of an ace does not involve partner and is thus strictly suicidal, the underlead of an ace brings partner into the dangerous scenario, and may eventually lead to your getting murdered when he fails to figure out what you've done. The following scene is common after the underlead of an ace:

NORTH
♠ K J 8 4

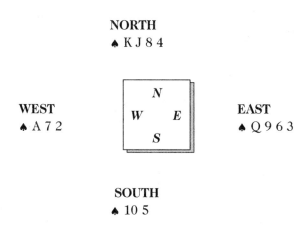

WEST
♠ A 7 2

EAST
♠ Q 9 6 3

SOUTH
♠ 10 5

West leads the two of spades against a four heart game. Declarer, completely fooled, plays low from dummy. East hesitates. Who has the ten? The play of the queen looks fatal to him. After all, declarer must have the ace. But if the two was led from the 10-7-2, the nine will now force the ace. East puts in the nine. Declarer wins the ten. West becomes furious. Another brilliant lead spoiled by his idiot partner! Declarer agrees with West at the end of the hand, and the two of them can't imagine how East could fail to put up his queen. East, if carrying a loaded revolver, completes the post-mortem.

DON'T WITHHOLD SUPPORT, PLEASE

Partner has risked bidding in order to find a fit

When Inspector Gardner entered the premises of the Bucket O' Blood Bridge and Chess Club at ten o'clock in the morning of January 23, 1942, he did not expect it to be doing business. Gray clouds of tobacco permeated the air despite two open windows. Four tables were still in play. I say 'still in play' because these people were not early risers who had dropped in at the club on their way to work. This *was* their work. The fact that they had been there all night could be detected from their open collars, rolled-up sleeves, and one local cop's uniform hanging on a coat-rack near the sofa. This particular city servant was down to his T-shirt, entranced in a chess position, at the time of the Inspector's arrival. (He was disciplined sharply of course, and did not have the nerve to reappear until the next night, whereupon he was hustled into a two-handed kaluki match that lasted the rest of the week.)

The name of the club, 'Bucket O' Blood', originated from this type of all-night ritual. An ordinary human who arrived at the club for one hour of friendly diversion might be seduced into staying for a long weekend (until such time as his blood had been sapped by the other players, exhaustion had set in and he was forced to leave, his clothes rumpled and wallet empty).

What seems to have made a marked impression on the inspector, judging from his written report, was the total lack of response when he blurted out for all to hear, "Holy mackerel, are you not aware there's been a murder in the building?" (By the way, this is the only mention of murder in his entire report, and apparently it was a professional ruse to see if any of the players, considered suspects, would reveal some sign of panic.) However, no one flinched. No one asked who had been murdered. In fact, the games went on as if a murder in the building was an everyday occurrence.

When the inspector asked to see the proprietor of the joint, a tall, skinny, young man with thick glasses told him the 'p-p-proprietor' was out. For the record (his stutter included), the statement was, "He d-d-does'nt come in... after d-d-duplicate nights."

When asked the name of the proprietor, the dummy from the bridge game near the radio, an elderly woman by the name of Little Lulu, blurted out, "Don't tell the copper!"

This angered the inspector to no small extent, and he put on a show of force by stopping all the activity (including a high-stake gin rummy game) to disclose his badge and point out that a serious investigation was currently in progress. I believe this is when the cop who had been studying a chessboard in his undergarments realized a superior was in the room, jumped up, retrieved his pistol

from the coat-rack, and, waving it about the room, declared he was undercover all the while and none of them were to move if they valued their lives. "Sit down Harry!" rang out all across the room, including one, "You ain't gettin' outta your debts dis way." The inspector sent Harry back to the precinct and took down everyone's name, address, and phone number (only a few of these appear in the photostats sent to me).

Then he asked who could go for coffee. Everyone yelled "Jinks!" and the skinny kid was given ninety cents to buy coffee for twelve at a local deli called Hector's. While he was out, the inspector copied the positions of the games in progress: the chess game, the gin rummy hand, the solitaire position (Jinks's game), and the bridge hand. When a fellow by the name of Dr. X. suggested he also jot down the bidding of the hand, the inspector, who didn't play bridge, appeared a bit confused. However, Dr. X. (who was merely a kibitzer) insisted that the bidding was interesting and might shed some light on the type of people who 'frequent these premises of late (sneer).' For the record, here is the hand in progress that the inspector stopped at approximately 10:10 a.m., January 23, 1942:

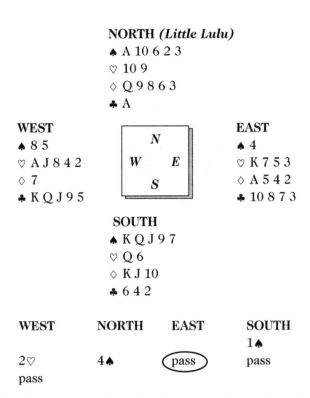

NORTH *(Little Lulu)*
♠ A 10 6 2 3
♡ 10 9
♢ Q 9 8 6 3
♣ A

WEST
♠ 8 5
♡ A J 8 4 2
♢ 7
♣ K Q J 9 5

EAST
♠ 4
♡ K 7 5 3
♢ A 5 4 2
♣ 10 8 7 3

SOUTH
♠ K Q J 9 7
♡ Q 6
♢ K J 10
♣ 6 4 2

WEST	NORTH	EAST	SOUTH
			1♠
2♡	4♠	pass	pass
pass			

For the purposes of our study, there is the curious fact that East, with excellent support for partner, a singleton in the opponents' suit and an outside ace, never took a bid. This is the crime to which Dr. X. wanted to call attention. West had taken a chance overcalling at the two-level on a rather poor suit, hoping to find partner with a fit, found that fit, yet never heard from partner about it! The vulnerability does not come with the auction, but does it really matter? To allow South to declare four spades (which would only go down if West led his singleton) hurt the doctor's sense of proprieties. Was East in a comatose state when he passed four spades? Did West want to murder him when he saw the failure to raise? Was it worth murdering a player who was already bidding like a corpse anyway? Who knows? The point is that Dr. X., chief kibitzer of the Bucket O' Blood, found this type of error grievous to his soul (so much so that he found it necessary to tell a detective on a murder case about it when it surely had very little to do with his investigation).

Readers will note the inverted three and deuce of spades in the North hand. The room number of the late Marcel Moskowitz was 623. Was this a clue left by the dummy, Little Lulu? Unlikely. The deceased's room number was a well-known fact. Was this a clue left by Dr. X. that Little Lulu was the murderer? Also unlikely. If Dr. X. had wanted to name Little Lulu as the murderer, he could merely have told Inspector Gardner in private. More than likely these switched spot cards were a joke of some sort — yet who could have such a weird sense of humor?

Readers should also note the oval drawn around East's timid pass. It is clearly the handwriting of Dr. X., yet resembles those egg-shaped circles drawn by the woman named Marie in the list of diagrams found in the deceased's hands earlier that morning. This suggests that Dr. X. had some connection with both Marcel and Marie, perhaps helping Marie in some way with her post-mortem analysis. More on this later.

The other important item is the similarity of this hand to exhibit number two on the notepad from Marcel's deathbed:

Exhibit #2   South dealer
Board 11   Neither vulnerable

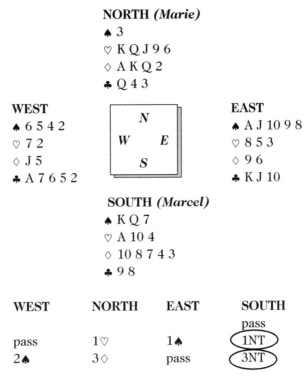

NORTH *(Marie)*
♠ 3
♡ K Q J 9 6
♢ A K Q 2
♣ Q 4 3

WEST   EAST
♠ 6 5 4 2   ♠ A J 10 9 8
♡ 7 2   ♡ 8 5 3
♢ J 5   ♢ 9 6
♣ A 7 6 5 2   ♣ K J 10

SOUTH *(Marcel)*
♠ K Q 7
♡ A 10 4
♢ 10 8 7 4 3
♣ 9 8

WEST	NORTH	EAST	SOUTH
			pass
pass	1♡	1♠	1NT
2♠	3♢	pass	3NT

Opening lead: ♣5 *!*
Result: down 2

The lead of the club five doomed the contract. Apparently Marcel had put his exclamation point on the lead is an attempt to defend his position of bidding notrump twice, thus never — *never* — supporting partner's hearts. The circles around both his bids (drawn by Marie? by Dr. X.?) indicate disapproval.

It seems that West knew more about the game than most players, raising his partner immediately with a weak hand and four trumps, then leading a club rather than a spade into the South hand that obviously had spades double-stopped.

Another clue is the fact that this time Marie and Marcel were North-South rather than East-West. Does this mean that they had been playing some kind of Howell movement, and were moving around the table? Probably not. You don't change positions after every hand. The dealer and vulnerability match Board 11, however, and is circumstantial evidence that they were playing some form of duplicate — perhaps they had played Board 12 first, then 11. This fits in with another clue overlooked by the Inspector (probably because of his lack of bridge knowledge). When he asked for the proprietor of the club, Jinks had replied that he did not come in after duplicate nights. (Did the Inspector think Jinks meant two nights in a row?) A later remark by Dr. X. revealed that duplicate night at the Bucket O' Blood had been the same night as Marcel's demise.

It doesn't take too much detective work to put these pieces together from the evidence we have gathered so far:

(1) Marcel and Marie played duplicate (Howell movement probably) on the night of January 22.

(2) After the game Marie consulted Dr. X. on some of the hands and wrote them up on a pad, circling Marcel's mistakes.

(3) She later went to Marcel's hotel room to review his errors.

(4) He added his own defenses via exclamation points.

(5) Marcel was found dead in bed Friday morning, the pad and pillows beside him, a victim of murder by smothering.

The eventual appearance of the proprietor would shed further light on the matter. His name was Victor Mitchell (a man who in later years was to become a legendary figure in the world of bridge). However, until his arrival on the scene, not one more important clue was uncovered. Inspector Gardner, efficient as he was, grilled the entire group of suspects, yet failed to raise the key issue: who in the club knew a woman by the name of Marie? The inspector's error in omitting this question allowed the culprit (whoever she was) to escape.

Perhaps the Inspector forgot about the notepad. Maybe, for some reason, he was content to report the murder as a natural death. (The fact that he did not order an autopsy is suspicious.) Certainly, a bridge-related motive was beyond his comprehension. But for us duplicate players, who know the passions that withholding support can ignite, any single bridge hand could have been motive enough.

Raise partner's preempt immediately

Moving the subject to today's world of light preempts and ultra-weak Weak Two-bids, weak jump overcalls and weak jump responses, it is no mystery to me why players are reluctant to raise their partner: fear.

The concept of trusting your partner to have his bid may be archaic, but is still very useful. *For even if partner does not have the values for his bid, it pays to raise!* That's what people don't understand. Trumps are more important than points. I say this at least once a night to my students. The effect of partner's preempt is voided when you don't give him a boost with support.

Don't let the preempt go to waste

Consider the tap shot in basketball. Your teammate shoots the ball, it hits the rim, circles, but won't go in. If you are near the basket and can reach the ball with your fingertips, you may be able to tap it in. This partnership basketball ploy is analogous to a bridge pre-empt (the shot) followed by the raise (the tap).

Many preempts are squandered by partners who won't raise with three trumps. The fact is, you should always raise partner's preempt with three-card support, regardless of the strength of your hand! It is really that simple. Yet many players sit at the bridge table like spectators in front of their television sets, watching and not participating. They pass their partner with support, and permit the opponents to enter the auction at a lower level. These players are tired, mean, or just plain scared of 'the bad bid' their partner might have made.

Don't pass, then raise later!

One of the worst ploys in competitive bidding is to pass partner's preempt, then re-enter later with what is called a 'delayed raise'. Here is an example:

North dealer   Neither vulnerable

NORTH
♠ A J 10 9 6 5 2
♡ 10 7
◇ 2
♣ 10 5 3

WEST
♠ 3
♡ K J 9 6 5 2
◇ A 10 8 5
♣ K 9

```
      N
  W       E
      S
```

EAST
♠ K 4
♡ A 3
◇ K Q 4 3
♣ J 8 7 6 4

SOUTH
♠ Q 8 7
♡ Q 8 4
◇ J 9 7 6
♣ A Q 2

WEST	NORTH	EAST	SOUTH
	3♠	pass	pass
4♡	pass	pass	4♠
pass	pass	*fielder's choice*	

South passes on the first round, then comes back to the land of
the living on the second round. This permits East and West to team
up. West has room to bid four hearts on the first round. Later he
can pass the delayed four spade bid and leave things up to partner
(having already described his hand). East ends up with what in
baseball is called a 'fielder's choice'. He may throw the ball to any
base for the put-out: double four spades for a juicy penalty or bid
five hearts or five diamonds and make a game. No matter what he
does, he emerges a winner.

If East is a winner no matter what he does, then South must be
a loser. South has made that dreadful blunder — the delayed raise,
a bid that almost never works. I have one question to ask South:
where was he the round before? Was he sleeping? Was he scared?
Was he actually expecting three spades to buy the contract?
Because if he was, he is in the habit of playing against very poor
players.

Now let's look at the effect of a direct raise to four spades with the South hand. After all, he does hold three trumps for his partner.

WEST			EAST
♠ 3			♠ K 4
♡ K J 9 6 5 2			♡ A 3
◇ A 10 8 5			◇ K Q 4 3
♣ K 9			♣ J 8 7 6 4

WEST	NORTH	EAST	SOUTH
	3♠	pass	4♠
?	pass	?	

Isn't it likely that four spades will buy the pot? West can hardly venture to the five-level on such a weak suit. Neither hand can double four spades with the strength of the high cards equally divided. Neither opponent knows whether South has a good hand or a bad hand for his raise. It doesn't matter to a smart South. He's got trumps. And when you've got trumps, you can get away with murder (as they say).

Exception: defensive hand

The delayed raise has merit occasionally as a tactical move. When you pass and later back in with a delayed raise, you should have a good defensive hand (as well as support). With good defense you don't mind passing the first round and allowing the opponents to find a fit, since, if they do, they will be walking into trouble. For example, partner opens two hearts, weak, and you hold:

♠ J 10 8 7   ♡ K J   ◇ K J 3 2   ♣ Q J 10

The auction proceeds with a pass on your right, and you pass. Fourth seat balances with double and partner passes. Your right-hand opponent bids two spades. Here is a review:

PARTNER	OPP.	YOU	OPP.
2♡	pass	pass	dbl
pass	2♠	?	

Now for that rare bird, 'the delayed raise'. The bid of three hearts is safe because you have enough values to make three hearts a reasonable chance, while you also do not mind if the opponents bid up to three spades, where you are fairly certain they will fail.

When delighted by partner's bid, let him know it

When my partner makes a bid that shocks me because I have so many trumps for him, I let him know it — either by jump raising, or by making a simple raise when I had no intention of bidding at all before he shocked me.

WEST		EAST
♠ 9 8 4 3		♠ 2
♡ A 5 2	N	♡ Q J 10 4
◇ K Q 9 8 3	W E	◇ 10 7 6 5 4
♣ 2	S	♣ A J 7

WEST	NORTH	EAST	SOUTH
			1♠
pass	2♠	pass	pass
3◇	3♠	?	

Recently I was playing with a student who believes in the theory of pushing opponents to the three-level whenever they stop at two. On this hand, I was the pusher in the West position, and when two spades was being passed out I ventured a balancing bid of three diamonds. North bid three spades, and my student passed without even pausing. They made their three spade contract, while we were on a finesse for five diamonds.

My student explained to me that he could not consider bidding because, in theory, I had done the work for the partnership by balancing (essentially, I was bidding both hands). He further claimed that in cases such as this, it's best to pass without even looking at one's hand. I thought about it for a while

INVOICE

Bridge lesson
---------- $$

Thank you

and decided to charge him double my usual playing-lesson fee. When it came time to pay me, he objected to the amount on the revised bill. "Why even think about it?" I asked. "In cases like this it's best to pay without even looking."

He stared at me in amazement. Then he told me to stop kidding around, that in all truth, he was shocked by the balance on the bill. I suggested to him that he should have been equally shocked by my earlier balance of three diamonds.

Points-shmoints; trumps are more important

The sad fact remains, players place too much emphasis on high-card points and not nearly enough emphasis on trump length. How many times have you heard someone say, "Points-shmoints!" This less than subtle expression refers to bidding on the basis of points when a misfit should have warned you to stop.

Let's say you pick up this nice eighteen-point hand:

♠ — ♡ K Q J 6 4 ◇ A K J 2 ♣ K J 9 4

Partner opens the bidding with three spades. You could now take your eighteen-point hand to the Chase Manhattan Bank and get three cents for it. Yet many so-called bridge players will not give in. They study the cards furiously, then plunge to the depths of ineptitude by bellowing three notrump. When this terrible contract goes down three or four tricks, they are amazed.

"But I had eighteen points!"

"Points-shmoints. Where are your spades?"

Jumps in trumps show good trumps when non-jump raises are forcing

The fewer trumps you have, the more conservative you should be. On the contrary, the more trumps you have, the more you should bid. In the delicate area of slam bidding, long strong trump support is often the key to partner's slam hopes. One way to help partner in the bidding is to jump in the trump suit when you have good support, and to bid slowly in the trump suit when you have weak support. For example, let's look at an opening bid of one spade with two different responding hands, one with bad trumps and one with good trumps.

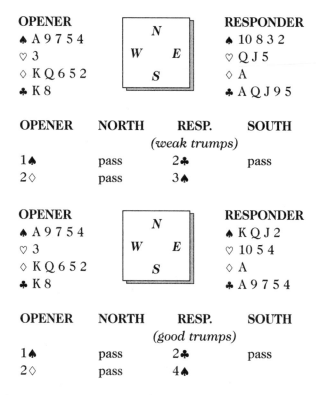

OPENER			RESPONDER
♠ A 9 7 5 4			♠ 10 8 3 2
♡ 3			♡ Q J 5
◊ K Q 6 5 2			◊ A
♣ K 8			♣ A Q J 9 5

OPENER	NORTH	RESP.	SOUTH
		(weak trumps)	
1♠	pass	2♣	pass
2◊	pass	3♠	

OPENER			RESPONDER
♠ A 9 7 5 4			♠ K Q J 2
♡ 3			♡ 10 5 4
◊ K Q 6 5 2			◊ A
♣ K 8			♣ A 9 7 5 4

OPENER	NORTH	RESP.	SOUTH
		(good trumps)	
1♠	pass	2♣	pass
2◊	pass	4♠	

The auctions are identical for the first three bids: opener bids one spade, responder two clubs, and opener rebids two diamonds. Now responder, who both times has fourteen high-card points and definite slam interest, wants to let partner know about his strength and support. The responder with weak trumps should content himself with a bid of three spades.

The responder with strong trumps can make a 'picture bid' of four spades. This magnificent jump says to partner that he is interested in slam and has great trumps, but only enough points to bid game at the moment. If a good trump holding relieves opener's concerns about slam, he may continue on, in this case via four notrump to check for aces.

The difference between strong and weak jumps

Players at all levels get confused over which jumps to game show strong trumps and which jumps are merely a desire to play game. Many experienced partnerships use a principle known as 'fast arrival', in which a jump to game is always weak. This concept makes life easy on many hands, but it strikes me as illogical. If a jump to game shows weakness, it is possible you would rather not get to game in the first place. If the jump to game can be made on weak trumps, it is possible you belong in another suit or notrump.

I like to use an approach in which a bid is what it sounds like. If you jump to game in a suit, you have a good trump holding — otherwise you shouldn't be jumping. The only exception to this 'bid what you got' rule occurs when partner has made a limited bid and therefore is not going to be heard from again. For example:

OPENER	NORTH	RESP.	SOUTH
1♡	pass	1♠	pass
2♡	pass	4♡	

Although four hearts is a jump, it has no special meaning. It does not promise good trumps, nor is it a slam try, because opener has limited his hand with the two heart rebid, and is not going to be heard from again.

Another example of a well known 'shut-out' jump is this:

OPENER	NORTH	RESP.	SOUTH
1NT	pass	2♣	pass
2♡	pass	4♡	

Again, four hearts is a shut-out bid because that is the only way to bid hearts and get to game — three hearts by responder would be invitational and not forcing. This demonstrates two important principles of shut-out jumps to game that all players should memorize.

A jump to game means shut-out bid when:

(1) A bid in the same suit below game would not have been forcing — *and*

(2) Partner has limited his hand.

You may of course think of it in reverse. A jump to game is a 'picture jump' with good trumps when:

(1) A bid in the same suit below game would have been forcing — *and*

(2) Partner is unlimited.

Let's take a most common auction: 1♠ — 4♠. Although this is not a slam try, and is in fact a very weak sequence, it still falls into the category of a 'picture jump' since partner has not limited his hand with his one spade opening — opener can have a distributional monster such as:

♠ A J 7 6 3   ♡ —   ◇ A K Q 3 2   ♣ K J 3

that needs only trump help to make a slam. This common picture jump to the four level shows good trumps and little else (good trumps can of course simply mean lots of them).

Here are two further examples. See if you can figure out whether responder's jump to game is 'shut-out' or a 'picture jump' before looking at the analysis below each sequence.

OPENER	NORTH	RESP.	SOUTH
1◇	pass	2♣	pass
2♡	pass	4♡	

Here four hearts is a picture jump, and promises good trumps because:
(1) opener did not limit his hand with two hearts and,
(2) responder could have raised to three hearts, forcing.

OPENER	NORTH	RESP.	SOUTH
1◇	pass	1♡	pass
2♣	pass	2♡	pass
4♡			

Here four hearts is merely a sign-off. Why? This time:
(1) responder has limited his hand, *and*
(2) a raise to three hearts by opener would not be forcing.

Understanding these principles may require a constant review and can be murder on the brain. Every time you hear a jump to game, you must decide which type it is. Is there still a possible future in the auction or is the game bid the auction's demise? When partner jumps to game, remember *your last bid*. If you haven't yet described your hand, there might still be life to the bidding. If you have limited your hand, consider partner's game bid the final nail in the coffin.

THE BEST BID IS PASS

Searching for support

I got Victor Mitchell's telephone number from New York City Information. It might as well have been unlisted. No matter how many times I let it ring, there was never an answer. Sometimes the number would be busy. I'd call back in two minutes and get no answer (very frustrating). Once a maid answered, "Mr. Mitchell will be back later." He was alive and living on 97th Street. That much was for sure.

Once I got lucky — his wife answered. This was at five in the afternoon. "Victor? He's at the track. He'll be back later."

"That's what the maid said."

"Then why are you bothering me?" Click.

But he never was back later when I called. There was never an answer later. One day I went out to Belmont to look for him. This was where Marcel Moskowitz, the racetrack tout, must have spent his days. Not only didn't I find Mitchell, I didn't find anyone else. Belmont is closed in August. That was enough for me. I certainly wasn't traveling two hundred miles up to Saratoga.

So I decided to try the bridge clubs. The Regency Club hadn't seen him in seven years. The Cavendish had his name on file, but none of the afternoon players admitted to having seen him for many months. At the Mayfair Club downtown at Gramercy Park, I met Al Roth. One of the great theorists of the game, he's been running a bridge and backgammon establishment for twenty-five years, and though he didn't seem to have a lot to say about Victor, he did recollect an 'incident' in 1942 at the Embassy Hotel. Only it wasn't the incident of murder.

"I remember that night because the bridge became so atrocious I left in the middle of the game."

"But what about the murder?"

"He was an overbidder."

"Who was an overbidder?" I had to ask, since to Al, everybody is an overbidder.

"The bookie — Marcel Moskowitz. He never had his bid. That's why he lost so much."

Al knew Marcel? Now I was getting somewhere. "Was he murdered? Can you tell me what actually happened that night? I heard he had quite a reputation."

"What that guy did to the game of bridge shouldn't happen to a side of beef."

"Never mind his bridge game, Al. Were you there the night he played his last duplicate? Did you know a woman by the name of Marie?"

"He butchered every hand he played." Al swept his wide palm across my face missing me by half an inch. "But his bidding made his play of the hand look good. Every ten-point hand he opened. A real wise guy. I warned him but he wouldn't listen to me. Big shot. Always held good hands. *I* never get dealt a good hand, you know. My whole life I've had to do what I can with lousy cards. He always picked up monsters. Never knew what he was doing. Always was two tricks too high anyway."

I waited until Al let off some more steam. Al has always been a proponent of solid opening bids, and the recollection of Marcel's light openings set Al off on a rampage. Just then a young, skinny

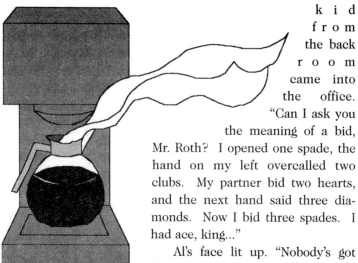

k i d
f r o m
the back
r o o m
came into
the office. "Can I ask you the meaning of a bid, Mr. Roth? I opened one spade, the hand on my left overcalled two clubs. My partner bid two hearts, and the next hand said three diamonds. Now I bid three spades. I had ace, king..."

Al's face lit up. "Nobody's got their bid," he squawked with delight. "I'll lay you three to one right now. Not one person has their call in this auction." He started to chuckle as the young fellow kept us abreast of the bidding as it snaked its way up to the five-level.

"Finally," he said, "I bid five notrump."

"What happened?" I asked.

"Everybody passed! Now Mr. Roth, ain't that forcing? It must mean pick a slam, right? I mean, I bid spades three times. I got no intention of playing five notrump."

Al took my elbow and led me into the dining room, leaving the kid standing there talking to an empty chair. "Aren't you going to answer him, Al?"

"If I answer him he'll be back with another insane auction. Come on, we'll have some coffee, and you'll show me the list of hands. Besides, the air conditioning is cooler in there."

We sat down and I took the photostats out of my jacket pocket. Al examined a couple and without looking up, mumbled, "These are from a duplicate. I remember." He remembered?

How could he remember hands from forty years ago? "In those days I was very enthusiastic. There was a Winter Nationals coming up, and I was practicing that night. I can't remember who my partner was. But I remember this hand very well." He was pointing to deal number three.

Exhibit #3
Board 10

East dealer
Both vulnerable

NORTH (Marie)
♠ 2
♡ A Q 10 8 5
◇ K Q 7
♣ A J 10 8

WEST			EAST
♠ A Q 9	N		♠ 8 4
♡ 4	W E		♡ 9 7 6 3 2
◇ 8 6 3	S		◇ A J 10 9 4 2
♣ K 9 7 6 5 4			♣ —— **!!**

SOUTH (Marcel)
♠ K J 10 7 6 5 3
♡ K J
◇ 5
♣ Q 3 2

WEST	NORTH	EAST	SOUTH
		pass	1♠
2♣	2♡	3◇	3♠
4◇	dbl	pass	4♠
double	all pass		

Opening lead: ♡4
Result: down 2

"This is the worst auction I've seen in fifteen years," Al remarked. The sequence rang a familiar note. Wasn't the first round of bidding the same as the skinny kid's?

Al got excited again. "Look at that opening bid of one spade. He deserves whatever he got. The only person who comes close to having his bid is North. See that four spade bid by Marcel? He pulls his partner's double out of fear. He opens the bidding out of fear of being passed out. He rebids three spades out of fear of not showing his extra length. Then he pulls the double because he fears his partner might be counting on him for something. Four spades doubled went down two. I know this hand — when I played it I was South."

Stop bidding so much

I took a slow sip of coffee. It was illuminating to hear Al analyze the bidding of a hand that took place so many years ago. It was even more incredible that he could recollect his own auction on the hand. I asked him how he had bid the South cards.

"How did I bid it? I didn't. I never took a call."

"What? How is that possible? You must have bid your spades somewhere along the line."

Al looked at me like I was a novice. "We weren't playing weak two bids yet in those days, so I passed and listened to the auction. Before I knew it, spades became the final contract; only it was West who was declarer, not me." Al jotted down the amazing auction:

WEST	NORTH	EAST	AL
			pass
1♣	1♡	2◇	pass
2♠	all pass		

"I passed. I had no qualms about passing for two reasons. One, I didn't have two quick tricks. I expected the auction would get competitive, and I didn't want my partner to count on me defensively. Two, I had the spade suit. I could always enter the auction later at a convenient level. If I ended up declarer I would play the hand two tricks better than anyone else because I was listening to the auction." Al looked up. "I remember now — I passed out of turn! But West was so anxious to bid, he accepted my pass and opened one club."

"He had two quick tricks and a rebid," I noted.

"You should take up another game if you think the West hand is an opening bid. Before you know it you're going to be in trouble, and that's just what happened. My partner overcalled one heart and East, another overbidder, couldn't resist bidding his diamonds. All he had to do was say the word 'pass', then later bid his diamonds. That way his partner would have known that he held nothing but diamonds. But like most players, he thought the world was going to come to an end before the auction got back to him, so he had to bid his suit now."

"Why didn't you bid two spades over two diamonds?"

Al gave me another one of those looks. "Two diamonds was forcing. It sounded like we were using a pinochle deck. If I passed,

I couldn't lose anything. I would force West to take another call. If I bid two spades, West could weasel his way out of the auction by passing. So I checked the backs of the cards and passed. Well, you see what happened. West, out of fear of raising the auction another level, bid his three-card spade suit. East, out of fear of a misfit took the easy way out of the auction by passing. And there I was defending two spades with seven of them."

'When in doubt, bid' is ridiculous advice

I didn't comment on Al's failure to double two spades. It was obvious that the opponents had a superior contract. And though I knew from experience that the popular advice, "When in doubt, bid" is not correct, I hadn't really understood how easy it could be to say the word 'pass' and learn something about a hand before sticking your neck on the butcher's block.

The reasons people bid too much are a subject for analysis in themselves. Let's face it; most players enjoy bidding — it's more fun than passing, more risky, more adventurous. But it's also fun to win. Does this mean you have to be a boring, conservative bidder to win? Can passing ever be deemed an aggressive action? Can passing offer an aesthetic pleasure equal to that of bidding your head off? Maybe, if you use the word 'pass' as an intelligent tactic.

A noted psychiatrist of the 1930s reflected on this issue in a thesis about the fear of death. "Contract bridge players demonstrate a similar anxiety (or fear) that time is running out. In the auction of a hand, the player feels he must bid a suit at any cost, even vulnerable, or risk losing the opportunity. In the same way, players of life feel they must enter into every avenue of temptation that comes their way, out of fear of missing that one great miraculous moment. 'Is life passing me by?' their subconscious asks. Likewise, the contract player, with little to risk but a poor score, enters the bidding on risky values in the fear of missing that one great miracle trump-fit."

Bidding does not equal virility

Later, the psychiatrist goes on to equate the plunge into an auction on questionable values with a show of virility. Al Roth's examination of hand number four from the post-mortem note pad of Marcel Moskowitz falls into this psychotic vein.

To Observatory

WISDOM PASS

OVERBIDDERS ROAD

DO NOT ENTER

DANGER AHEAD

-200

Gold Mine 1 mile

620

-1100

Exhibit #4
Board 14

East dealer
Neither vulnerable

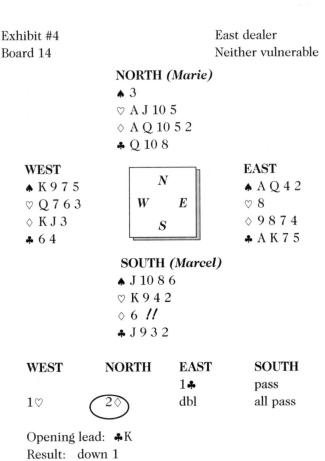

NORTH *(Marie)*
- ♠ 3
- ♡ A J 10 5
- ◇ A Q 10 5 2
- ♣ Q 10 8

WEST
- ♠ K 9 7 5
- ♡ Q 7 6 3
- ◇ K J 3
- ♣ 6 4

EAST
- ♠ A Q 4 2
- ♡ 8
- ◇ 9 8 7 4
- ♣ A K 7 5

SOUTH *(Marcel)*
- ♠ J 10 8 6
- ♡ K 9 4 2
- ◇ 6 *!!*
- ♣ J 9 3 2

WEST	NORTH	EAST	SOUTH
		1♣	pass
1♡	(2◇)	dbl	all pass

Opening lead: ♣K
Result: down 1

The auction seemed innocent enough. East had opened one club and West responded one heart. Marcel, in the North position, stuck in a two diamond overcall, and East made a dubious business double. It worked though, Marcel going down one. Marcel and Marie must have received a poor matchpoint score on the board because (without the overcall) most East-West pairs would have reached their 4-4 spade fit at the three- or four-level, and gone minus.

The critical circle around Marcel's overcall seemed a bit harsh, but Al had no pity. "There are a million things wrong with that two diamond overcall. Never mind that he's bidding a five-card minor suit at the two level, which is very dangerous. Look, he's also jumping in between two bidders. You gotta watch yourself like a hawk when there's bidding on your left and on your right. It shouldn't shock you when partner comes down with a Yarborough."

I suggested to Al the theory that the overcall was made in the psychotic spirit of trying to prove one's virility at the bridge table. He gave me another look. "There's virility and senility. This is senility. He's bidding when it's not necessary. West's response to the opening bid is forcing. That means North can always pass, listen, and decide to come in later." Al pointed to North's heart holding. "Look at this. It's a baby clue as to when to keep your mouth shut. The hand to your right bids one of your best suits; your best tactic is to pass." His arm waved across my nose. "Nobody knows this any more. In the old days when bridge hadn't deteriorated to the groping-in-the-dark bidding of today's young players, the art of trapping was common strategy."

The lost arts of passing, trapping and scouting

I think most reasonable players know that when your opponent opens the bidding in your strongest suit, it's best to pass without showing too much concern. Only a rank beginner doubles the opening bid of one heart with long hearts. Nor should you overcall when you hold the opponents' suit. You don't want to do anything to impede their bidding when you are looking at a robust trump stack, and the potential for a juicy penalty. Well, here was a case that resembled the trap pass in second seat, only this time it was in fourth seat.

Al went on to demonstrate why passing with their suit can work on an even higher level of strategy. "I also sat North on this hand. Here was my auction:"

WEST	AL	EAST	SOUTH
		1♣	pass
1♡	pass	1♠	pass
2♠	dbl		

I jotted it down for future reference.

"The second I heard West bid hearts, I shut up," said Al. "I was very happy if they continued in that suit. Furthermore, the last thing I wanted to do was stop them from finding a spade fit, since with my singleton, it was obvious my partner held at least four

NORTH (Al)
♠ 3
♡ A J 10 5
◇ A Q 10 5 2
♣ Q 10 8

WEST
♠ K 9 7 5
♡ Q 7 6 3
◇ K J 3
♣ 6 4

	N	
W		E
	S	

EAST
♠ A Q 4 2
♡ 8
◇ 9 8 7 4
♣ A K 7 5

SOUTH (Jinks)
♠ J 10 8 6
♡ K 9 4 2
◇ 6
♣ J 9 3 2

spades. This is another point of interest for your readers. When you start overcalling and bidding with singletons, you often succeed in preventing the opponents from finding a fit in a suit where your partner is loaded! Anyway, I passed one heart, knowing I could come in later if I judged the auction to be dying out. When East bid one spade and West raised to two spades, it sounded like it might end there, and, more importantly, they had located a fit. So I balanced with a double."

This is where I stopped Al. Why hadn't he simply bid his diamonds? What was this double in the middle of an auction? How could it be takeout for the unbid suits when only one suit was unbid?

Al held up his index finger. "The first double, in the middle of any auction in which partner has yet to act, is takeout. That's a rule of competitive bidding. The hand that's short in the last-bid suit is the hand that should strive to get in the bidding. I often pass for a while on a good hand until their auction hits my singleton; then I double. The double is takeout of the suit most recently bid. In other words, forget about the suits that have been bid along the way. I don't care if they've bid seven suits and then I double two spades — it means takeout of spades."

Actually I have used this delayed takeout double myself (sometimes to my partner's confusion). I was happy to hear somebody express the theory in a way that made it sound easy. Double means takeout of whatever suit was just bid. When you think about it, why *should* Al bid his diamonds with adequate support for two other suits? It was quite possible that North-South's best contract was a suit that had already been mentioned by the opponents! The one club opening bid certainly could have been on a three-card suit. And the one heart response, though it showed four cards in hearts, could have been made on a poor suit. In fact, this was the case. Look at the rest of the auction:

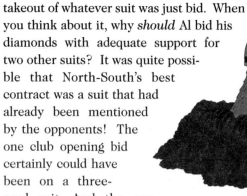

WEST	AL	EAST	SOUTH
		1♣	pass
1♡	pass	1♠	pass
2♠	dbl	pass	3♡
dbl	all pass		

"I understand your double, Al. But many players would have been confused."

"Only a child would be confused. Come to think of it, I was playing with a child, and he understood me perfectly. His name was Jinks, Jinks Barkowsky. He was the gofer of the club."

"Gopher?"

"Yeah, go for this, go for that. He was a nervous kid with a stutter. But he was a real whiz. Quick to learn. He not only understood my double as takeout, but realized that one of my best suits must be hearts because I had passed the one heart response the round before.

"Now look how he played the hand. Never mind the double of three hearts which was foolish on only queen-fourth of trumps. After East cashed the ace-king of clubs, and gave partner a ruff, West led a spade to East's ace. A spade return to West's king, trumped in dummy, left this position:

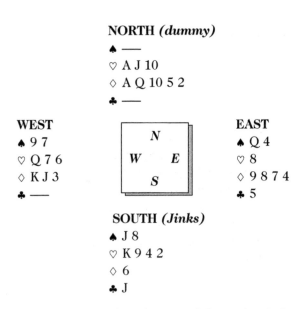

NORTH *(dummy)*
♠ —
♡ A J 10
◇ A Q 10 5 2
♣ —

WEST
♠ 9 7
♡ Q 7 6
◇ K J 3
♣ —

EAST
♠ Q 4
♡ 8
◇ 9 8 7 4
♣ 5

SOUTH *(Jinks)*
♠ J 8
♡ K 9 4 2
◇ 6
♣ J

"In dummy, and needing the rest of the tricks, Jinks counted East for the spade ace-queen and club ace-king, thirteen points. West had shown the king of spades and must have originally held four hearts to the queen for his one heart response. The greedy double and East's failure to bid up to three spades indicated that West had one more king. Jinks, with a good mental picture of the opposing hands, led the ten of hearts to his king, finessed the diamond king, cashed the ace, and trumped a diamond in his hand. When the jack fell, he finessed the heart queen and drew the last trump, dummy's diamonds being high."

It was a well-played hand, indeed. Three hearts doubled making three by North-South was a phenomenal result considering that the first person to bid the suit was West. The main point was that if East-West had never bid, Jinks, South, would never have been able to place all the cards and make nine tricks. Al's pass of one heart not only enabled his side to reach the best contract, but also gave Jinks the opportunity to listen to the bidding before playing the hand.

You might call this silence by Al on the first round 'scouting'. When his partner finally got to be declarer, he was aided by a wealth of information gathered from the opponents' bidding. After East won the first two club tricks and gave West a ruff, Jinks could call the shape of the East-West hands. East had shown up with four cards in clubs and West had bid hearts showing at least four. Thus, East could hold at most one heart; in fact, he must have exactly one because, with a heart void, he would have had a five-card suit to bid instead of his four-card club suit. Indeed, if East had four clubs and one heart, and opened the bidding one club, he could not have a five-card diamond or spade suit, so his shape had to be exactly 4-1-4-4. This left West with precisely 4-4-3-2.

You might find all this counting difficult at first, but the strategy of scouting before bidding to your best contract can often make a difference between a top and a bottom.

Al had time to look at one more hand from Marcel's list. This one also showed how a little investigative work can be accomplished by hiding in the bushes while the opponents reveal their distribution. The fact is, most bridge players don't have the patience to pass forcing bids and listen. Yet animals with much less intelligence do it quite naturally. Take the cagey Tibetan mountain lion; he stalks behind the bushes up to three hours waiting for his

prey to arrive. Some stakeouts last longer. The stakeout of a detective often lasts all night as the exhausted scout waits in a car for some sign of his suspect. The stakeout of a bridge player is easy in comparison. Does it take much endurance to pass and wait for a few seconds until the bidding comes back around the table?

| Exhibit #5 | North dealer |
| Board 13 | Both vulnerable |

NORTH *(Marcel)*
♠ A J 5 4 3
♡ J 8 7 4
◇ 10
♣ A 6 3

WEST		EAST
♠ K Q 9 8 6		♠ 10 7 2
♡ 3		♡ Q 10 5
◇ A K J 6 3		◇ Q 8 2
♣ 9 7		♣ J 10 8 4

N W E S

SOUTH *(Marie)*
♠ ——
♡ A K 9 6 2
◇ 9 7 5 4
♣ K Q 5 2

WEST	NORTH	EAST	SOUTH
	pass	pass	1♡
dbl	redbl	pass	pass
1♠	dbl	all pass	

Opening lead: ◇ 10
Result: down 1

North scores three ruffs, underleading club ace twice!!

"Ridiculous bidding by North," Al commented. "To double the opponents in a partscore holding four-card support for partner's long suit bears no relationship to the game of bridge." I showed Al the circle already marked around Marcel's double. The exclamation points (marked by Marcel himself, and usually reserved for criticism of others) must have been egotistical compliments of his own defense, his double underlead of the club ace to reach Marie's hand for two ruffs. Nevertheless, Marcel's so-called excellent defense (wouldn't tapping the West hand also hold declarer to six tricks?) was no excuse for his failure to raise partner to game with four trumps, two aces, and a singleton.

I asked Al if he remembered playing the hand. "I was also North," he answered rubbing his temple. "Though it's funny, my recollection is that I was playing with a woman by the name of Little Lulu. But why I was playing with her on this hand I have no idea. I remember because I made a good pass on the first round of the auction which helped Little Lulu play the hand."

Al had passed again? Here was the auction at his table:

WEST	AL	EAST	LITTLE LULU
	pass	pass	1♡
dbl	pass	1NT	pass
2♠	4♡	all pass	

Indeed, Al had passed West's takeout double. Since he knew he was going to game in hearts, he decided to take advantage of any gratuitous bidding the opponents might engage in. He craftily allowed East to reveal something about his hand; whatever East bid would help South read the shape and high cards when she eventually declared four hearts. Al explained this scouting maneuver, and had critical words to say about West's takeout double as well.

"West's double was wrong, but was the sort of double made in those days. A takeout double is supposed to show support for three suits, not two. Today's young bridge players make a different mistake with the West cards. They cuebid two hearts, the Michaels convention, to show 5-5 in spades and a minor. This bid backfires when South becomes declarer and takes all the finesses in clubs and hearts through the East hand. The correct bid over one heart is a simple one spade overcall. When you have a five-card major you should just overcall and hope to find three-card support from partner." Al stared at me like he was waiting for an answer. I nodded in agreement. Who wouldn't?

"Anyway, getting back to the actual auction, I passed the takeout double because it was forcing. The next two bids by the opponents gave Little Lulu a good picture of the whole deal."

NORTH (Al)
♠ A J 5 4 3
♡ J 8 7 4
◇ 10
♣ A 6 3

WEST
♠ K Q 9 8 6
♡ 3
◇ A K J 6 3
♣ 9 7

EAST
♠ 10 7 2
♡ Q 10 5
◇ Q 8 2
♣ J 10 8 4

```
        N
    W       E
        S
```

SOUTH (Little Lulu)
♠ ——
♡ A K 9 6 2
◇ 9 7 5 4
♣ K Q 5 2

Contract: 4♡
Opening lead: ◇ K

"After the opening diamond lead, West switched to the spade king and Little Lulu, not wanting to commit herself, trumped in her hand."

"She couldn't be sure which minor to pitch from," I commented.

"Lulu was an underrated player because she was a quiet, elderly little woman. But as you'll see, she was a declarer who worked hard at counting the opponents' hands. She ruffed a diamond in dummy and led the jack of hearts forcing the cover of the queen from East. The one notrump bid had helped her figure the 3-1 heart break.

Then she ruffed a second diamond. Here's where most declarers would go wrong. But Little Lulu had the advantage of hearing the opponents' bidding for one full round."

I jotted down the position with Little Lulu on play in dummy:

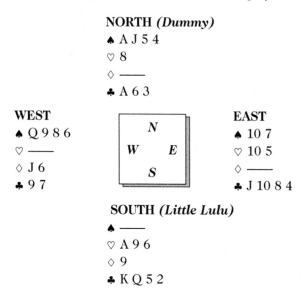

NORTH *(Dummy)*
♠ A J 5 4
♡ 8
◊ ——
♣ A 6 3

WEST
♠ Q 9 8 6
♡ ——
◊ J 6
♣ 9 7

EAST
♠ 10 7
♡ 10 5
◊ ——
♣ J 10 8 4

SOUTH *(Little Lulu)*
♠ ——
♡ A 9 6
◊ 9
♣ K Q 5 2

Al went on to explain how Lulu counted East's hand. East was known to hold three hearts and less than four spades because of his failure to bid one spade over West's takeout double. This left East with at least seven minor-suit cards. East's choice of one notrump made the chances of his holding a five-card minor very slim. After a takeout double, he would be much more likely to bid a five-card suit if he had one than to bid one notrump.

This meant that East held either 4-4 in the minors or 4-3 one way or the other. With a sure diamond loser and a possible club loser (if clubs did not divide 3-3), Lulu discarded her last diamond on dummy's spade ace, but did not finesse against East's heart ten just yet. If East held four clubs, she would still have to ruff one. Since she had counted East's hand, and knew he had at least three clubs originally, it was safe to test that suit before wasting dummy's last trump. Little Lulu led out three rounds of clubs ending in dummy. When East *did* show up with four of them, the position looked like this:

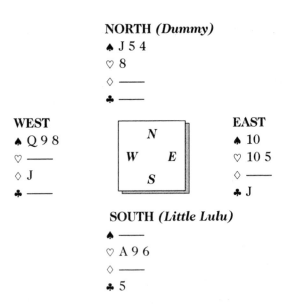

NORTH *(Dummy)*
♠ J 5 4
♡ 8
◊ ——
♣ ——

WEST
♠ Q 9 8
♡ ——
◊ J
♣ ——

EAST
♠ 10
♡ 10 5
◊ ——
♣ J

SOUTH *(Little Lulu)*
♠ ——
♡ A 9 6
◊ ——
♣ 5

Little Lulu trumped a spade in her hand, and trumped her five of clubs in dummy. Not only had she got rid of all her losers, but she ended up leading a spade off dummy at trick twelve through East's ten-five of trumps. She overruffed the heart five with the nine, and scored the last trick with the trump ace. Making twelve tricks was a top.

I had to ask Al why I had never heard of this exceptional Little Lulu who declared hands so well. He told me she was one of his first students and had taken up the game late in life. "Any average player who listens to the auction, and does some elementary counting can ruff out their losers and pick up finesses that the opponents reveal in the bidding."

I heard the office phone ring and Al was paged. Suddenly it occurred to me that both Little Lulu and Jinks were at the Bucket O' Blood on the morning following Marcel's death. Yet instead of asking questions about the case, I had been listening to bridge hands. Was there a connection between them and the murder? What about Marcel's partner, Marie?

By now Al had to be a bit off his guard, and any incriminating question could be cloaked in further small talk. So, when he returned I rose to shake his hand and say goodbye. Then, as nonchalantly as I could, I asked him if he had ever met this woman named Marie.

His answer left me deeper in the dark than before. "I don't remember ever meeting any woman player by that name."

I shook my head in disbelief. How could he not recall the chief suspect of my investigation, yet remember three bridge hands played over forty years ago — from the very same night that she had partnered Marcel?

Avoid opening one notrump so much

I left the club, turned right into Gramercy Park and sat on a bench in front of the fountain. The late afternoon sun was still hot, and children were running through the spray. Although I had learned next to nothing from Roth about the death of Marcel, I had got some insight into the many opportunities bridge players miss in competitive bidding. The failure of Marcel to raise his partner with four trumps was tantamount to keeping an important secret from your best friend. But wasn't it typical of so many duplicate players today? Maybe this explains why people like to open one notrump so much. Why bother bidding your long suit if partner is reluctant to raise you?

I got up and started to pace. Avoiding a puddle, I couldn't help but wonder if I had stumbled on a new theory to explain bad bidding. Numerous errors in bidding must stem from the frustration of players who cannot elicit support from their stingy partners. For example, why do players open one notrump when they have a perfectly good suit and rebid? Take this hand:

♠ K J 8 3　♡ A 2　♢ A Q 9 8 5　♣ Q 10

Deal this hand out to ten experienced duplicate players and I'll bet at least four open the bidding one notrump. Yes, it falls into the strong notrump point range, and it is fairly balanced. But the nature of the hand is suit-oriented because you have most of your length and strength in two suits. If you bid your two suits you are far more likely to arrive at the best contract than if you hide them — that is, if you have a partner who will raise you. And bidding two suits has never stopped anyone from eventually playing notrump in the end.

If you open one notrump however, your partner becomes captain. He directs the auction. You may never get a chance to bid either diamonds or spades, and may easily miss a good fit.

I know someone will argue, "How can you miss the spade fit over one notrump? Partner can always use Stayman." When this hand was dealt in real life, those who opened one notrump did miss a good spade fit.

OPENER		RESPONDER
♠ K J 8 3		♠ Q 9 6 5
♡ A 2		♡ 10 8 7
◇ A Q 9 8 5		◇ 3
♣ Q 10		♣ K J 9 4 2

N			
W	E		
S			

OPENER	NORTH	RESP.	SOUTH
1NT	all pass		

After one notrump, responder did not have enough points to use Stayman safely and had to pass. One notrump made exactly one at four tables and went down at two others. Those who played in spades after opening the bidding one diamond, made ten tricks! One pair actually bid to four spades for +420.

Good bidding is often rewarded with good scores. There are some players that defend their bad bids by arguing that the rest of the field will do the same. They may be right, but why not earn some points by bidding better than the rest of the field? For example, the modern trend is for the strong notrump to head downward on the point-count scale. A strong notrump used to be 16-18. Then it became 15+ and 18-. Then it fell to 15-17. Presently, some players are using 14+ and 17. At this rate the strong notrump will soon become the weak notrump.

Why has this happened? The answer is that the 16-18 point range was a little too strict. There are some eighteen-point hands that are so powerful in trick-taking potential they will produce game opposite a six-point hand. There are some excellent fifteen-point hands that may miss a game if you open them in a suit and rebid one notrump.

A great 18	*A poor 18*
♠ A K 2	♠ K J 8
♡ K 6	♡ A Q 8
◇ A 10 5	◇ K Q 6 3
♣ A 10 7 6 3	♣ Q J 2

A great 15	A poor 15
♠ J 10 9 6	♠ Q J 5 3
♡ A K 9 8	♡ A Q 6 4
◊ K 3	◊ J 6
♣ A 9 8	♣ K Q 6

So the adjustment of the 16-18 point notrump to 15+ and 18- was well reasoned. It was an advancement of a sound structure to a range that permitted more judgment. Then, as often happens when modifications of existing formulae are made, further changes that were not to the advancement of good bidding began to sneak their way in. Bridge teachers deemed all these pluses and minuses too complex for their students and the range was leveled off to a simple 15-17 — not for any sound reason mind you, but for the idiotic reason that judgment was for experts only!

There's no question that players enjoy opening one notrump on 15-17-point hands because that range comes up more often. Also, most players are more secure with their structure of responses over one notrump than over one of a suit. Ease of use has merit, but who said winning bridge is easy?

At the same time, a popular and mistaken theory sprang up among duplicate players that one notrump is a great matchpoint contract. Quite frankly, two of a major has always been a better scoring contract than one notrump, especially when one suit is wide open and you are vulnerable. Still, the rush to open one notrump went on, sometimes helped along by the popularity of the Jacoby Transfer convention (in which responder transfers to opener in any long suit, so the strong hand is still on play). Players who liked to be declarer and steal the hand from partner began to open a 'strong' one notrump on fourteen points. Did you ever play with any of these hand hogs? Only once I hope.

Many players are now copying these bad habits to 'stay even with the field'. Lowering yourself to the poor standards of others doesn't make much sense to me. In the case of the strong notrump, I suggest you and your partner stick to the rational, judgmental (and winning) 15+ to 18- range.

Start with your longest suit

The choice of your opening bid is important because it is the bid that initiates the auction. A constructive bidding sequence is akin to the structure of a building: if the frame is shaky or crooked, the rest of the building may collapse. When your opening bid is light, don't be surprised if catastrophe befalls you later on. Likewise, when you open in a short suit, you risk playing in that suit at a higher level than you ever intended.

An architect of good bidding waits for a solid opening bid before he starts to build. And when he does, he starts off in his longest suit. The more points you have and the more trumps you hold, the better positioned you are in a competitive auction. Yet players continue to open light hands, and worse, open in their short suits. We have already seen that passing a questionable hand may be a virtue later on in the auction (when you can bid your crazy head off without partner thinking you have more than twelve points). The virtue of opening in your longest suit is that no matter what you do later on in a competitive auction, partner knows where your greatest length is, and can better evaluate his cards.

The short minor

If you play five-card majors, you often find yourself forced to open a three-card minor on a hand that does not fit your opening one notrump range. Although I personally prefer opening four-card majors, I do not expect or advise most duplicate players to switch at this stage. Opening four-card majors is a drastic step and one that may be approached when you have a partner who is equally ready to venture into the sophisticated world of pure, natural bidding. In the meantime, most players will open the following hand with one club:

♠ A K 3 2   ♡ K Q 9 8   ◇ J 9   ♣ 4 3 2

Playing five-card majors, there is nothing you can do about it. However, some people who are forced to open three-card minors make two mistakes in their choice of opening bids.

♠ Q 7 5   ♡ K J 9 8   ◇ A Q 3   ♣ Q 7 6

Open 1♣, not 1◇

Error number one is that they open their better minor with equal length. This is not best. You do not open the bidding to get the lead — you open to build an auction between you and your partner with the intention of buying the contract. If you open the above hand with one diamond, you make it more difficult to bid the hand. You take away a one diamond response from partner, and you make it impossible for partner to show a weak hand with clubs. You should always open one club with three-card length in clubs and diamonds.

♠ Q 7 5 3   ♡ K J 9 8   ◇ A Q 3   ♣ Q 7

Open 1◇, not 1♣

Error number two is more extreme. Since 4-4-3-2 shape is the only distribution where five-card major players must open one diamond on a three-card suit, some partnerships open one club anyway (one diamond always promises four cards in their methods). This is going too far. If you open two-card suits you will either play in lots of six- and seven-card minor-suit fits or worse, miss a lot of eight- or nine-card fits because partner fails to support you out of fear that you have opened on a doubleton. Many Precision players who play that a one-diamond opening can be short have this problem and are constantly staggering in the dark in competitive auctions, responder always confused as to which minor suit opener really holds. Avoid this headache by not opening a two-card suit.

Don't open one diamond on 2-2-4-5

When you hold two suits and one is longer than the other, it is almost always right to open in your longer. A typically misbid hand is one with four diamonds and five clubs:

♠ 10   ♡ A J 7   ◇ A 9 8 6   ♣ K J 8 5 2

Open 1♣, not 1◇

Many players open this type of hand with one diamond. They argue that if they begin with one club, they cannot bid their diamonds next because a rebid of two diamonds would constitute a reverse (17+ points). So they open one diamond and rebid two clubs. There is no question that bidding both your suits gives you the best chance to locate a fit with partner. However, if you bid suits in a haphazard order (such as starting this hand with one diamond and rebidding two clubs), how will your partner know which suit is longer?

Artistic readers will note the pyramid shape of the example hand, the longest suit resting on bottom, the shortest on top.

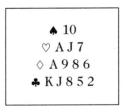

Aesthetically
speaking, doesn't
one club look like the
best choice of opening bid?

Using the one notrump rebid as a harbor

Students are easily influenced by the methods of top-flight players. However even experts can get mired in bad habits picked up in their early 'education'. Take this example from the finals of the 1980 World Championships in Valkenburg, Holland. The United States team lost to the French by a small margin, a famous pair of American experts contributing to the loss with this auction:

WEST		EAST
♠ K Q 6 2		♠ J 8 5
♡ 4		♡ A Q 10 9 2
◇ Q 7 3 2		◇ 5 4
♣ K J 7 6		♣ 10 8 3

WEST	NORTH	EAST	SOUTH
	pass	pass	pass
1◇	pass	1♡	pass
1♠	pass	1NT	pass
2♣	pass	2◇	all pass

West must have been very proud of the manner in which he organized his bids: he was able to mention all three of his suits. However, when dummy appeared his pride became that of a pigeon, not a peacock.

East, believing that West held 4-0-5-4 shape, gave preference to two diamonds, a contract which was not a good example to the rest of the world.

Where did West go wrong? Just because he had three suits it did not mean that his partner would match up with him nicely. Yes, you should look for a trump fit, but within reasonable space. If you start in a minor, and haven't found a fit by the time you bid up to one notrump, maybe you should stop looking. It follows that if one notrump is to be your harbor when no fit is located, you should start your search for support in the lowest suit, not the middle one. (Obviously with 5-5 you should open the higher ranking and rebid the lower. This time the odds favor a fit.) But with two four-card suits, never open the higher and rebid the lower, even if you have to rebid one notrump with a singleton in partner's suit.

♠ 5   ♡ K Q 8 6   ◇ K J 9 8   ♣ A J 8 6

OPENER	NORTH	RESP	SOUTH
1◇	pass	1♠	pass
?			

Players often make the mistake of opening this hand one diamond and, over partner's one spade response, rebidding two clubs. This is poor planning because:

1) there is no guarantee that responder will have a fit in either minor, and

2) the heart suit will be lost because partner's two heart rebid would be a conventional fourth-suit forcing bid rather than natural.

If you open one diamond (I prefer one club), and partner responds one spade, you should rebid one notrump. This limits the point count, and permits partner to continue on with two of any suit, naturally. Here is a real nightmare for the player who opens one diamond and rebids two clubs:

The wrong auction:

WEST			EAST
♠ 5			♠ K Q 10 6 4
♡ K Q 8 6			♡ J 10 7 3
◇ K J 9 8			◇ 5 4
♣ A J 8 6			♣ 5 4

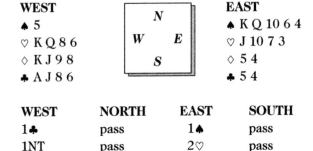

WEST	NORTH	EAST	SOUTH
1◇	pass	1♠	pass
2♣	pass	2◇	all pass

Responder takes a preference because he is not nearly strong enough to bid two hearts, fourth-suit forcing. Opener, with a minimum, can hardly venture on and the partnership lands in the nightmarish contract of two diamonds instead of two or three hearts.

The right auction:

WEST			EAST
♠ 5			♠ K Q 10 6 4
♡ K Q 8 6			♡ J 10 7 3
◇ K J 9 8			◇ 5 4
♣ A J 8 6			♣ 5 4

WEST	NORTH	EAST	SOUTH
1♣	pass	1♠	pass
1NT	pass	2♡	pass
3♡	all pass		

Here opener rebids one notrump to slow down the auction, limiting his hand to fifteen points maximum. Responder can now bid two hearts, not forcing! (If you did not know that this auction is not forcing, it is worth reviewing. After a one spade response and a one notrump rebid, responder's two hearts call shows less than ten points. This allows the partnership to explore the best major-suit fit without getting too high.)

Don't open one diamond with 4-4 in the minors

When I returned to my apartment, there was a message on my answering machine from a Ms. Marie Gardner. She instructed me to meet her at a coffee shop with an orange canopy on 34th Street between Second and Third Avenue. I didn't know a Ms. Gardner, but an alarm went off in my head, and I couldn't help but get excited at the thought that this could be the same Marie from our mystery of forty years ago.

I hailed a cab and drove down towards 34th Street. The driver turned on Second Avenue towards Third, and asked me where I wanted off. Looking for the orange canopy, but still thinking about opening bids, it struck me as funny that bridge is very much a mirror of life. I have always opened one club with four cards in both diamonds and clubs, contrary to the popular 'style'. It has always worked well, but until this precise moment I had never realized why it has always worked so well. Finding a trump fit is like finding an address. Here I was searching for an orange canopy between two avenues; it would be silly to start in the middle of the block and walk to one end, then if it is not there, walk all the way back to the other corner. Similarly, if I'm looking for a trump fit between two minor suits, it would be silly to start with diamonds, bid up the one level, then if a fit is not found, restart at the two level! So I told the cabbie to let me off at the corner, and like a good bidder, I limited my search to a one block walk.

Rebid of suit usually equals six-card length

The idea that bidding a bridge hand mirrors our journey through life stayed with me all evening. For example, I wondered if the orange canopy I was looking for was a coffee shop haven for bridge players who liked to play 'canapé', opening their shorter suit first?

A Greek host with a handlebar mustache led me to a quiet booth in the rear where a very young blonde woman of startling beauty was drinking a cup of coffee. Ms. Marie Gardner was certainly not the same Marie who had partnered Marcel Moskowitz forty years ago.

"Sit down," she said in a less than seductive tone. I remained upright, observing her wide, wet dark eyes. "Do I have to repeat myself?" she said softly. "I said sit down."

"If I sit down, my wife will kill me."

"If you continue this investigation, she won't have to."

I sat down. Suddenly my head felt very hot and I was dizzy. "C-could you tell me what you mean by that?"

She looked at me very much like Roth had looked at me earlier in the day, like I was a bad bridge

player who had failed to understand my partner's bids the first round and had made him repeat them on the second round. This is probably why players rebid five-card suits. They think their partner wasn't listening the first time. I'm always scolding my own students for opening the bidding in a suit and rebidding it with only five cards. "If I had three-card support you would have heard from me. The rebid of a suit shows six, how many times do I have to tell you six, six, SIX!"

• • •

The Greek was standing over me, a wet washcloth hanging on his apron string. "I theenk he's a-okay now." Marie took the washcloth and bent over me, pressing the cloth to my temple. Her silky hand wiping the sweat off my brow did nothing to dispel the hot, dizzy feeling that had prefaced my faint. I got a whiff of her perfume. It was strong stuff, French no doubt.

"You're overreacting," she whispered. "I didn't say you were going to be killed. I simply wanted to warn you that a certain party would prefer that you drop your investigation."

I lifted my head and took a sip of coffee as she sat back staring bluntly into my eyes. The Greek dropped a plate of 'Sara Lee' donuts on the table. She continued, "My name is not a coincidence. My father was Detective Gardner, Mr. Granovetti. He died seven years ago." She lowered her eyelids. "He worked for the force at a time when corruption was more or less an acceptable and necessary part of his job." She looked around and leaned forward, lowering her whisper even further. "The circumstances behind the death of Marcel Moskowitz are embarrassing to friends of his who are still living, and who have enormous influence in a certain dangerous organization that I need not identify. Eat your donut."

I picked up my donut, making a good effort not to let my hand shake, and dunked it into the hot coffee. It wasn't bad, but I preferred fresh baked. Then I answered her threats with two remarks, one a flat contradiction, the other a key question.

"In the first place, Ms. Gardner, my name is Granovetter, not Granovetti." She did not flinch at this. I don't think she really cared. "Secondly, I have here in my pocket a list of bridge hands written by the late Marcel Moskowitz and a woman who identified herself as Marie. Do you have any clue as to whether or not these hands are connected to the death of Marcel Moskowitz?"

She got up from the booth and headed directly toward the door. "Wait a second," I said, grabbing her arm. She spun around like a greeting card stand.

"If I'd had any idea you had those photostats with you, I would never have come. So long as you keep that list in your possession, you are vulnerable, mister. You better watch out."

I followed Marie Gardner out of the coffee shop, the Greek running after me into the street waving a bill for four dollars and thirty-nine cents. For some reason, I imagined it was a gun that he was waving, and I ran like a petty thief into a nearby subway entrance.

COMPETITIVE BIDDING

Watch the vulnerability

When I got home, I told my wife the whole story, for some reason recalling the canopy as red, not orange, and changing, ever-so-slightly, my description of Marie Gardner's physical appearance. "Isn't it funny," I said, "how in mystery novels you would never meet a woman as unattractive as she was." My wife did not think it was so funny. She directed me to open a large package that had been delivered by UPS that afternoon. I picked it up, listened for ticking, ran to the window, and threw it into the courtyard.

"You've gone berserk," she said. "That was the new kitchen clock I ordered from Macy's. You're vulnerable to every goofy story you hear. Nobody is interested in your stupid investigation. You're losing touch with reality, fainting in a coffee shop. You've been wasting time running all over town with bridge hands from forty years ago. You haven't walked your dog in three days. Your bridge game has gone downhill."

"My bridge game?"

"Yes," she insisted, her hands on her hips. "Your bidding has suffered. You think about too many extraneous things. Look at this hand in today's *Times*." She went over to the kitchen table and handed me the column from the late edition. "You opened three spades vulnerable against not on ace-jack seventh and out. How could you? A wife is always the last to know."

Vulnerable preempts are different animals

I took the newspaper into the living room and switched on the lamp. My eyes went straight for the diagram:

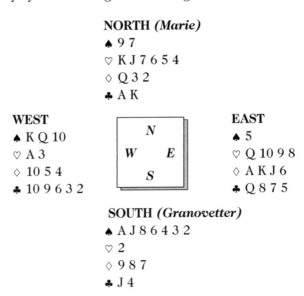

NORTH *(Marie)*
♠ 9 7
♡ K J 7 6 5 4
◇ Q 3 2
♣ A K

WEST
♠ K Q 10
♡ A 3
◇ 10 5 4
♣ 10 9 6 3 2

EAST
♠ 5
♡ Q 10 9 8
◇ A K J 6
♣ Q 8 7 5

SOUTH *(Granovetter)*
♠ A J 8 6 4 3 2
♡ 2
◇ 9 8 7
♣ J 4

Indeed, there it was in black and white: a deal reported in the *New York Times* bridge column in which I had committed a grievous bridge crime. Supposedly I had opened three spades with the South hand at adverse vulnerability. The complete bidding was in a box under the diagram. I read it, aghast.

WEST	MARIE	EAST	MATTY
			3♠
pass	pass	dbl	all pass

Need I say that my hands began to shake when I read the name of the North player? My wife sat down in the love seat, took out her needlepoint, and spoke to the cushion in her hands, never once looking up. "I don't know which I'm more upset about. The fact that you snuck off to some local duplicate to play with your so-called ugly duckling, Marie Gardner, or that you embarrassed the family name with your loose preempt vulnerable against not. Good Lord. Vulnerable against not! How could you... *Matty*?"

Matty? What is this Matty? My wife never called me 'Matty.' Was I hearing things? I looked back at the paper to see if I was also seeing things and took a deep breath. I didn't want to faint twice in one day. Yes, there it was. Just like the cursed notepad in my pocket, except this time it read 'Matty' and 'Marie' instead of 'Marcel' and 'Marie'. The column's heading was: 'Revival of New York Club'. It went on like this:

Vulnerability plays a large part in the scoring of games, slams, and doubled contracts. At duplicate, in particular, down two tricks undoubled (-200) can mean a zero on a board, and players of experience are usually more careful in competitive bidding when vulnerable.

Today's modern tendency towards light preempts is often misused by beginners

---

Beginners!

---

who fail to note the vulnerability on the hand before they open the bidding. That this can lead to disastrous conse-quences is demonstrated in the diagram deal played at the newly-renovated Embassy Bridge Club, 406 West 48th Street, which runs Open games on Monday through Saturday at 7:15 p.m. along with low-stake rubber bridge and backgammon.

As reported by the player in the West seat, South, a prominent New York expert, opened with a bid of three spades, a preempt that most good players would make only when not vulnerable. Part of the blame was that Matthew Granovetter of Manhattan did not notice the vulnerability because the Embassy Club was using new duplicate boards without the customary red box slotted in the vulnerable positions. West, quite humorously, also reports that the missed check of vulnerability could easily have been attributed to the uncommon beauty

Oh, no!

of Granovetter's partner, Ms. Marie Gardner of Brooklyn, a rising young bridge starlet.

As readers will note from the bidding, East made an excellent balancing double influenced by his singleton spade, and West converted the double to penalties with his strong trump holding. West started a passive club, but when Granovetter came to his hand with the trump ace to lead his singleton heart, West rose with the ace, cashed his two trump tricks, and shifted to a diamond. The net result was down two vulnerable, or minus 500 for North-South.

When the hand was over the dangers of bidding too much when vulnerable became more acute as Granovetter was heard to mutter sheepishly, "Believe me, this hurts me more than it hurts you." Whereupon Ms. Gardner answered sprightly, "You're just lucky, Matty, that I don't carry a gun."

My wife sat there working her needlepoint like Madame Defarge, stitching into her pillow cover the names of 'Matty' and 'Marie', heads that were due to roll. How was I to explain that you can't always believe everything you read in the *New York Times*? The truth was I had never set foot in the Embassy Hotel. I had never played bridge with Ms. Marie Gardner. And more importantly, I had never opened a vulnerable preempt like that in my life.

I telephoned the *Times*, but the bridge editor was on vacation. Who had reported this hand? Was it Marie Gardner, again warning me to stop my investigation? Or was it that unknown player in the West seat drawing an analogy of dangerous preempts at the bridge table to sticking one's nose into dangerous matters such as the busi-

ness of murder?

In either case, it was a stern warning, and under normal conditions there would be no way for a guy in my slippers to convince his wife that he was seriously in trouble, not foolishly flaunting himself about town playing bad bridge with beautiful women. However, as luck would have it (if a bomb going off under your courtyard window can be deemed luck), the clock from Macy's turned out not to be a clock from Macy's.

It wasn't a huge explosion; in fact, it was hardly an explosion at all. It was mostly smoke and a little firecracker. Perhaps it too was meant only as a warning. However, it was enough to patch up any small differences between a husband and wife very quickly. We embraced each other while neighbors opened their windows and screamed, "Smoke!" (New Yorkers tend to wait for red flames before calling the fire department.) I stuck my head out and assured everyone it was only the toaster. Then, after struggling to convince my dog to come out of the closet, my wife and I double-locked the door and climbed into bed, shivering on a hot August night.

We decided not to discuss the case until morning, concerned that the apartment might be bugged. (Calling the police was out of the question. It was very probable that it was some person or persons in the police force who wanted me to stop my murder investigation.)

Normally, there's nothing like an outside danger to heat up

the inside passions of romance. But the truth is we were too upset to think about anything but that list of bridge hands in my jacket pocket. So I retrieved it from the living room, came back to bed, and reached for my book-light. Then, turning on the radio to drown out our whispers, we examined the photostats. I was convinced that whatever incriminating evidence existed would come to light through a detailed analysis.

You don't need six points to respond, especially at favorable vulnerability

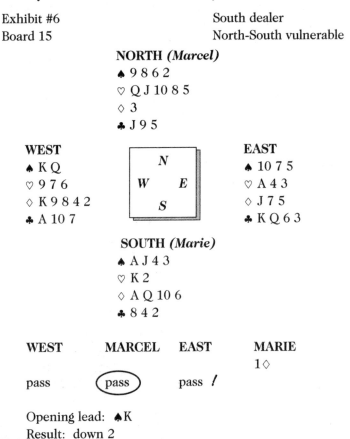

Exhibit #6
Board 15

South dealer
North-South vulnerable

NORTH (Marcel)
♠ 9 8 6 2
♡ Q J 10 8 5
◇ 3
♣ J 9 5

WEST
♠ K Q
♡ 9 7 6
◇ K 9 8 4 2
♣ A 10 7

EAST
♠ 10 7 5
♡ A 4 3
◇ J 7 5
♣ K Q 6 3

SOUTH (Marie)
♠ A J 4 3
♡ K 2
◇ A Q 10 6
♣ 8 4 2

WEST	MARCEL	EAST	MARIE
			1◇
pass	pass	pass /	

Opening lead: ♠K
Result: down 2

On the sixth deal from Marcel's notes, we came across a well-known rule in bidding theory that is not very smart practice. Most bridge books say you need six points to respond to an opening bid.

In 1942, before the Goren point count was prominent, requirements for a response to an opening bid were hazy. There were various honor-trick systems, but no universal rule. If your hand looked like a response, you made one. If it didn't, you passed. Judgment was often a better guideline than point count.

Criticism of Marcel's pass over one diamond is noted by the circle around his bid. Marcel (as can be seen by the exclamation point next to East's final pass) must have complained that his side was fixed by East's failure to balance with a double. Had West converted a balancing double of one diamond to penalties (by passing the double), Marcel could then have rescued to one heart without fear of Marie thinking he had more than four points. The problem of the analysts was to decide if Marcel really was fixed by East's failure to balance, or had caused his own bad result by passing the one diamond opening.

Pamela was adamant. "You don't need six points to respond. That's a silly rule designed for players who can't think for themselves." I pointed out that the vulnerability probably inhibited Marcel from responding. Marcel was worried that the next bid from Marie would be three diamonds.

"You shouldn't worry about partner's rebid," she replied. "Although vulnerability should inhibit you from entering the auction

YOU SHOULD RESPOND NOT JUST WHEN YOU MIGHT MAKE A GAME, BUT WHEN THEY MIGHT MAKE A GAME!

when the opponents are bidding, it has nothing to do with responding to partner when the opponents are silent. There are many rebids partner might make over your one heart response. Only a couple of them are bad for your side. But if you pass, you may play one diamond — with a singleton in partner's suit, you know this contract will play poorly. Sure, fourth hand might rescue you by balancing; but fourth hand is likely to hold length in diamonds when you're short. And the more diamonds he holds, the less likely it is that he'll balance."

I agreed. Why go down without a fight? What if partner jumped to four hearts over one heart? You would probably make a game. It's basic bridge philosophy that any time you could possibly have a game, you must keep the bidding open. This concept applies to duplicate as well as teams or rubber bridge, since game bonuses score many extra matchpoints.

Then Pamela sprung a new theory on me. "In my rubber games at the Cavendish, we don't respond only when we might make a game, but also when we think *they* might make a game. Ira taught us that." Ira Rubin, known as 'The Beast' for his less than calm composure at the table, has been a successful money and duplicate player for over thirty years. It's never a mistake to pick up a lesson from a veteran master, so I asked Pamela to give an example.

"Well, it's usually done at favorable vulnerability. I was at the club this afternoon and picked up one of my usual hands:

♠ 8 5 4 3　♡ 9 2　♢ Q 9 7　♣ 8 7 6 2

"We were not vulnerable, and they were. My partner opened the bidding one club and the next hand passed. I responded one spade without flinching. This wasn't a psyche — it was a tactical bid. Obviously from my hand I could imagine the opponents scoring a vulnerable game. If I passed, it would be easy for them to get together. So I made a forcing response. Maybe this would inhibit my left-hand opponent from bidding.

"This is what happened. He had a good hand with four spades himself. Not wanting to risk a vulnerable one notrump overcall between two bidders, he passed. My partner raised to two spades with three-card support. This was the final contract, down four undoubled, minus 200, a small price to pay for keeping the opponents from scoring 600 points."

<table>
<tr><td>Rubber Bridge (Chicago)</td><td>North dealer</td></tr>
<tr><td>Third deal</td><td>East-West vulnerable</td></tr>
</table>

NORTH
♠ K 10 7
♡ K Q J 3
◇ J 8
♣ K J 10 9

WEST
♠ Q J 9 2
♡ A 8 4
◇ A 10 6
♣ A 4 3

```
        N
    W       E
        S
```

EAST
♠ A 6
♡ 10 7 6 5
◇ K 5 4 3 2
♣ Q 5

SOUTH *(Pamela)*
♠ 8 5 4 3
♡ 9 2
◇ Q 9 7
♣ 8 7 6 2

WEST	NORTH	EAST	SOUTH
	1♣	pass	1♠
pass	2♠	all pass	

Opening lead: ♣3
Result: down 4 (Here down four *is* good bridge)

Push 'em up when you're not vulnerable

At duplicate, the advantages of being not vulnerable against vulnerable are greatest in an auction in which both sides are fighting for the part-score. Marcel's next blunder was not obvious, since it was again a failure to make a good bid rather than an egregious misbid.

Exhibit #7
Board 16

West dealer
East-West vulnerable

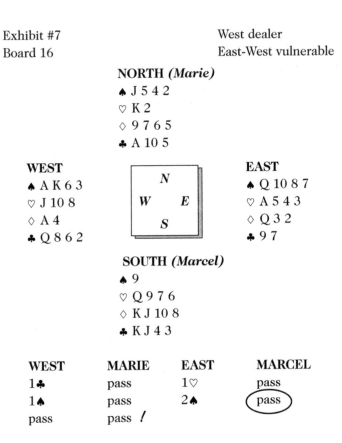

NORTH (Marie)
♠ J 5 4 2
♡ K 2
♢ 9 7 6 5
♣ A 10 5

WEST
♠ A K 6 3
♡ J 10 8
♢ A 4
♣ Q 8 6 2

EAST
♠ Q 10 8 7
♡ A 5 4 3
♢ Q 3 2
♣ 9 7

SOUTH (Marcel)
♠ 9
♡ Q 9 7 6
♢ K J 10 8
♣ K J 4 3

WEST	MARIE	EAST	MARCEL
1♣	pass	1♡	pass
1♠	pass	2♠	pass
pass	pass /		

Opening lead: ♢ 5
Result: making 2

It was a typical matchpoint disaster. Marie and Marcel sold out to a two spade contract which made exactly two. Who should have bid, North or South? The circle around Marcel's second pass certainly seems like harsh criticism. The opponents were in the middle of an auction in which they had bid three suits. Still, Marcel had been chastised for not taking action. With his singleton spade and support for all the other suits, he could have doubled.

In return, Marcel points to Marie's final pass. She was in the pass-out seat, and he felt it was *her* duty to push the opponents up since, until West passed, no-one knew how far East-West would go. One glance at Marie's horrible hand seems to exonerate her from

I was balancing, Martha.
Whaddya want me to do,
go down on my knees?

George, I don't understand. If
you went down three, I think I
would understand. But down
five, George, down *five*!

For crying out loud! I
was short in their suit.
Granovetter said I *had* to
balance if I was short. I
read it in his new book.

You had one jack, George.
Does Granovetter know
you had one jack?

any wrongdoing. Even though it's considered a crime by many good
duplicate players to allow the opponents to rest in a partscore at the
two level, her final pass looks like the only rational action. The
unbid suit was diamonds, and her four small diamonds were certainly not tempting. Yet somehow North-South should have been
in the auction.

Shortness acts

Pamela blamed Marcel. "He didn't balance live."

"Balance live?"

"Yes. Because he was short in spades, he was the player who
had to bend over backwards to get in the bidding. Once the auction
sounded like it might die, he should have doubled rather than leave
it up to his partner, who was known to have length in spades and
therefore would be unable to compete."

The live seat

You are sitting in the 'live seat' when the opponent to your right makes a bid — not a pass. The bidding is still 'alive' since your partner still has a chance to act if you pass and your left-hand opponent passes. When you balance in the 'live seat', you presume left-hand opponent is about to pass and partner holds a hand unsuitable for balancing.

The idea of pushing the opponents up has six elements worth reviewing. Here are the six in order of importance:

When to push them up

1) The opponents have found a fit.
2) The auction has died out, or it sounds like it will at any moment.
3) You are short in the suit in which the opponents have found a fit.
4) You are not vulnerable.
5) They are vulnerable.
6) You hold some high cards.

When short in their suit, try to get in the auction

You will note that that four out of the six elements have nothing to do with the thirteen cards you hold! (I suppose if it weren't for numbers (3) and (6), on certain auctions you could balance without even looking at your hand!) Number (3) does involve your hand, yet it does not address point-count. It points to a more important facet of your hand: shape. Shortness acts, length remains silent.

Element number (6) refers to having some points when you bid. It's not a bad idea, but remember: it's less important than shape when trying to push them up.

No heroics in the bidding

Bridge is such a fascinating game that by midnight Pamela and I were no longer thinking about Marcel Moskowitz's murder and related threats. We were thinking about competitive bidding, and wondering why in forty years it has not taken any major step forward. I blamed bad bridge on the nature of mankind. People are flawed, not bidding methods. She agreed that mankind was at fault. "Women are steadier and more reliable in general, and at the bridge table they tend to be more disciplined." The next hand from the list did little to dampen that theory.

Once you've shown your hand, let partner decide

Exhibit #8   North dealer
Board 17   Neither vulnerable

            NORTH *(Marie)*
            ♠ Q J 9 7
            ♡ J
            ◇ J 9 6
            ♣ 9 8 5 4 2

WEST   **EAST**
♠ A K 5 4 3   ♠ 10 8 6
♡ 8 7 6 4   ♡ K 10 3
◇ A 10 8 5   ◇ Q 7 4 2
♣ —   ♣ A J 3

            SOUTH *(Marcel)*
            ♠ 2
            ♡ A Q 9 5 2
            ◇ K 3
            ♣ K Q 10 7 6

WEST	NORTH	EAST	SOUTH
	pass	pass	1♡
1♠	pass	2♠	3♣
3◇	4♣ *!!*	4♠	5♣
pass	pass	double	all pass

Opening lead: ♠K
Result: down 1

Marcel, South, opened one heart and West overcalled one spade. Marie passed and East raised to two spades. Marcel competed with three clubs, and since he was bidding completely by himself, this probably showed 5-5 distribution. West bid three diamonds, a game try in spades, as opposed to three spades which would have been merely competitive. It was at this point that the post-mortem argument began.

Marie's four club bid was criticized by Marcel, presumably because of her spade stack. One can almost hear the man cry out, "Why encourage me in clubs if you don't want to hear me bid again?"

Pamela sniffed. "You must be joking. If my partner didn't raise me with five-card trump support, I'd shoot her."

I'd have preferred her to have used a different expression. I saw her point, however. With five-card support you usually jump the bidding. It was because of her spade stack that Marie held back and bid only four clubs. Marcel wanted her to hold back altogether. If the opponents got to game she could double. If they stopped in three spades, she could venture four clubs, and he would know it was merely an attempt to push them to four spades. I believe that this was Marcel's thinking.

"That was Marcel's excuse," corrected Pamela. "When East bid four spades, Marcel should have passed. His bid of five clubs screams of machismo — the big hero is going to carry the world upon his shoulders. I hate one-man-army acts. Clearly he had already shown his hand. To bid in front of partner was to exclude her from the proceedings as if she were an idiot."

True, true. Marcel's five club call was certainly a blunder. But was it so obviously wrong? Many players would fall from grace in this sequence, which makes it a bid worth reviewing. Here is a list of the things that were wrong with bidding five clubs:

1) He had exactly what he already described in his previous bidding; therefore, it was not necessary to bid his hand again.

2) Since his partner knew more about his hand than he knew about his partner's, he should have let her make the final decision.

3) He bid in the direct seat, in front of a partner who might easily have had a trump stack.

4) He got caught up in the rhythm of the auction. Just because

everybody else keeps bidding doesn't mean you should keep bidding.

Rescuing partner when she is doubled

Personally, I think if you don't trust your partner enough to allow her to make her share of the decisions, you shouldn't be playing with her. Partnership bridge is based on trust in all areas of the game, but most particularly in competitive bidding.

Still, there are exceptions in which you should trust your eyes more than your ears. Let's take the case when partner gets doubled for penalties. For example:

WEST	NORTH	EAST	SOUTH
1NT	2♡	double	?

Never mind what your hand is for now. Your heart support is lacking — either you have a singleton or void for partner. You can't help but wonder if there isn't a better contract. On the other hand, your partner may have a very strong suit and no support for any of your suits. The question you must resolve is this: should you rescue him or should you let him stew in his own juice?

Most bridge authorities say that you should be wary of rescuing partner. This is a generalization and it has the merit of being simple: never rescue partner — end of argument. Most astute readers will note immediately the illogic of this rule. Obviously you must look at your own hand and review the bidding in each case. Even if you take the attitude 'rarely rescue partner', you'll often be looking at a hand that screams for a bid when partner is doubled. That is because when partner is doubled you are often short in his suit. How do you decide whether to send for a lifeboat or not?

One way of answering this is to look at your hand and see if you have a suit that is likely to be better than partner's. I was playing with a student once who never liked to play the hand if he could help it. He held:

♠ Q J 10 9 7 6 5   ♡ —   ◊ J 10 9 8   ♣ 4 2

His left-hand opponent opened one notrump. I overcalled two hearts and the next hand made a booming double. He passed in a flash. He was happy to be dummy, I suppose; but I wanted to hit him for his remark as he put down his cards: "I trust you partner." Trust me? Trust that I also have a solid seven-card suit? An overcall is always based on the hope of finding some small token support. When a business double is made, you should think about alternative contracts rather than taking the coward's way out by passing automatically, and blaming partner if things go wrong.

Contrary to popular belief, you should be less inclined to save partner when he is vulnerable than when he is not. For example, say once again the bidding goes:

WEST	NORTH	EAST	SOUTH
1NT	2♡	double	?

You hold the following hand:

♠ Q 10 9 8 6   ♡ 2   ◇ A 10 4 3 2   ♣ J 10

There is no way to be certain of what to do. Two spades could be making while two hearts is going down. Or the converse could be true — two hearts doubled could be your best score while two spades will be a disaster.

When in doubt, I look at the vulnerability. If we are not vulnerable, partner is more likely to be taking a chance with his overcall, and I am more inclined to rescue him. If we are vulnerable, partner is more careful with his overcall, so I would trust him to have a good heart suit, and let him play it there.

Don't overcall two of a minor on a five-card suit

Another factor to consider is whether or not partner has overcalled a major or a minor. A penalty double of two of a major is more risky than a double of two of a minor for the simple reason that two of a major doubled equals game. Therefore, doubles of two hearts or two spades tend to be more solid than doubles of two clubs or two diamonds.

I'm more inclined to rescue my partner from two of a major doubled than two of a minor doubled for both that reason and one more — partner's two-level overcall in a minor should almost always be on a six-card suit, while partner's two-level overcall in a major can easily be on five.

The reason for this latitude in the case of majors is that it's easier to score game in a major than a minor. One should therefore be more careful about overcalling a minor, the rewards being smaller. Also, since opponents double minor-suit partscores faster than major-suit contracts, the minor-suit overcall should be more fortified.

Hearts is another story

A two-heart overcall after a one spade opening bid is the exception to the rule of six-card-suit overcalls at the two level. This is because hearts is a major suit, so there is more to gain, and again, it is less likely the opponents will double.

Here are three hands that look similar:

WEST	NORTH	EAST	SOUTH
	1♠	?	

I — bid 2♡	*II — pass*	*III — double*
♠ A J 2	♠ A J 2	♠ 6 5
♡ K 10 9 4 2	♡ K Q 4	♡ K Q 4
◇ K Q 4	◇ K 10 9 4 2	◇ A J 2
♣ 6 5	♣ 6 5	♣ K 10 9 4 2

Understanding why you would choose three different bids with these hands will help you enormously in future competitive decisions.

I: The two-level overcall is justified because the suit is hearts.

II: You should not overcall at the two-level in a five-card minor, and you cannot double for takeout without support for clubs.

III: Again, you should not overcall two clubs with only a five-bagger, but double is fine since you hold support for three suits.

To overcall or pass

Had Hamlet played bridge he might have pondered, "To bid or not to bid, that is the question." Certainly this is the question second seat asks himself many times during a duplicate session.

Bidding is full of possibilities. Like a forest in which you must take the best path, your first call will often be instrumental in leading your side to the best contract. When your right-hand opponent opens the bidding and you have a good hand, there are three routes to choose from: overcall, double, or pass.

The simplest competitive action is the overcall. If you can make it at the one-level, all the better (all the safer). The two-level overcall is dangerous. There's strength to your right and there could be a trump stack on your left. That's why I have already suggested that you be careful with two-level overcalls.

If the bidding goes one spade on your right and you hold:

♠ 4 2   ♡ K 10 8   ◇ A Q 8 6 4   ♣ A J 2

you do not overcall since your minor suit is only five cards in length. Instead, you choose between pass and double. On this hand I would double because I have support for all three unbid suits. However, reverse the hearts and spades:

♠ K 10 8   ♡ 4 2   ◇ A Q 8 6 4   ♣ A J 2

and I would pass one spade, even though I have 14 high-card points.

If your hand does not meet the requirements for an overcall or a double, you can always pass, wait, and listen. The auction may be far from over, and passing on the first round does not prohibit you from entering the bidding later should the sound of the auction make it safer. You might ask: how can it be safer to bid later in the auction and at a higher level? Here's how:

♠ K 10 8   ♡ 4 2   ◇ A Q 8 6 4   ♣ A J 2

Auction A

WEST	NORTH	EAST	SOUTH
			1♠
2◇			

Auction B

WEST	NORTH	EAST	SOUTH
			1♠
pass	2♠	pass	pass
3◇			

The three diamond balance in Auction B is far safer than the two diamond overcall in Auction A. There are two reasons for this. First, and most obvious, your left-hand opponent in Auction B is limited in strength and has support for his partner. In Auction A his shape and strength are unknown, and he may be sitting with a string of diamonds and a singleton spade. Secondly, in Auction A partner can have any number of spades, and so is less likely to have diamond support. In Auction B, you can infer from the North-South bidding, that partner has no more than two spades (five and three for the opening and response, and three in your hand equals eleven); thus partner is very likely to hold a few diamonds.

The takeout double shows willingness to compete in three suits, not two

The most restrictive competitive action is the takeout double. Players tend to overuse and misuse this bid. Remember this: *99% of the time the takeout double includes at least three-card support for every unbid suit.* When you hold a good hand with two doubletons, and your right-hand opponent opens the bidding, you should not make a takeout double — you should overcall or pass. For example, right-hand opponent opens one spade. You hold:

♠ A 2   ♡ K J 8 7   ◊ J 4   ♣ A 10 8 5 3

You should not double because you have support for only two suits. If you double and partner bids diamonds (and gets doubled for penalties), you will have to leave the room rather than put down dummy.

I knew a guy who made a bid like this in a high-stake rubber bridge game at the Cavendish Club in New York. After one spade, double, two spades, his partner bid three diamonds. This got doubled, and when the opening lead was made, he refused to put down dummy. He was playing with a notorious expert (in fact it was 'The Beast') who was prone to scream at the top of his lungs when his partner did anything peculiar in the bidding. My guy knew that he had been wrong to double one spade, and he was deathly afraid of the shriek that the sight of his dummy would elicit. His infamous partner (who, by the way, held the Q-8-6-3-2 of diamonds and was about to go for 1100 big ones) gently insisted he put the dummy down.

"Don't worry, my friend," The Beast said sweetly, "whatever you've done can't be that bad." After a few prayers, dummy was laid down as slowly as possible. "Aaaiii!!!!!" The shriek reached new heights in volume as the takeout doubler sank beneath the table.

So what should the poor fellow have bid over one spade? Some players would overcall two clubs. This is also a poor call because the club suit is only five cards in length, and you might miss your heart fit. The best bid over one spade is pass, for the simple reason that the other bids are wrong.

Let's look at the hand again and see what the right bid is after a one diamond opening, instead:

♠ A 2   ♡ K J 8 7   ◇ J 4   ♣ A 10 8 5 3

Again the best call is pass. If you bid two clubs you run the risk of a huge penalty. If you overcall one heart, partner will think you have a five-card suit. If you double for takeout, partner's next call may be a jump in spades.

It's important to remember that if you pass, you are not out of the auction. For example, if the next hand bids one spade and this is raised to two spades, you are in a position to make a delayed double for takeout. An even better scenario after passing the initial round is:

WEST	NORTH	EAST	SOUTH
			1◇
pass	1♠	pass	2◇
dbl			

This double shows the two unbid suits, hearts and clubs. Since you failed to double one diamond, you can't have spades as well. It's merely a question of having the courage and patience to pass on the first round when your hand does not fit well into the category of double or overcall.

Some critics will say I'm being too cautious. However, when I have a hand with support for the other three suits, I'll double on fewer values than anybody. Say the bidding starts with one diamond on your right, and you are vulnerable. Your hand is:

♠ A 7 5 4   ♡ K Q 6 2   ◇ 2   ♣ J 9 7 6

I recommend a double. After all my talk about passing and waiting, why do I suggest a double with only ten high-card points? Because here you have great support for three suits, and shortness in their suit. Aggressive competitive bidding will win you matchpoints when you judge your initial actions on the basis of shape, not merely strength.

There are, of course, exceptions to every rule. There are hands that come up which are so strong — 17+ points — that you must take some kind of action without necessarily having the proper shape, such as overcalling with a five-card minor or doubling without support for one of the minors. Remember, what I'm really discussing here are the vast majority of hands that resemble minimum opening bids, hands that the majority of players feel compelled to act on, when they should feel compelled to pass!

Overcall with five-card majors, don't double

Any time you hold a minimum opening bid with a five-card major, you should overcall in preference to doubling. In tennis a player sometimes tries to 'do too much with the ball' and should merely try to return it; in bridge, the player who doubles for takeout with a five-card major and support for the other suits is also trying to do too much with one bid. If you hold:

♠ Q 8 6   ♡ A J 7 4 3   ◇ 6   ♣ K Q 8 2

and the hand on your right opens one diamond, you should bid one heart. Otherwise you will never locate that 5-3 heart fit.

Even if you held four spades on this hand instead of four clubs, you should overcall one heart. Remember this very important rule of competitive bidding: *a takeout double followed by the bid of a new suit shows a very big hand.*

It is rare these days for an overcall to get passed out. When I'm dealt a big two-suiter and my right-hand opponent opens the bidding, I usually take a calculated risk with a simple overcall, hoping to get another chance to complete the picture of my hand. For example, with:

♠ 2   ♡ K Q J 9 6   ◇ A 2   ♣ A K 10 6 5

I overcall a one diamond opening with one heart. My expectations are that one of the three players at the table will keep the auction alive, and on my next turn I'll be able to jump in clubs.

If you double with this type of hand, you risk hitting partner with a spade suit. And believe me, he'll never shut up when you try to correct his insistent spade calls.

The only times I recommend doubling first on a big hand is

either when :

    1) you don't have a suit to overcall, or

    2) your suit is six or more cards in length, so you know where you are heading.

If right-hand opponent opens one club, I recommend double with these exceptional hands:

$$♠ A K \quad ♡ K Q J 5 \quad ◇ A Q 10 \quad ♣ 7 6 5 4$$

$$♠ A K J 10 8 6 \quad ♡ A 7 5 2 \quad ◇ A J \quad ♣ 2$$

On the first hand, I double because I have too many points to risk passing — I may not get a second chance to bid. On the second hand, I double because I know exactly where I'm going, and I am strong enough to out-bid my partner's dreaded diamond calls.

Take a calculated risk to make life easy: overcall, then double

Although my wife and I were totally exhausted with the exciting proceedings of the day (and the long discussions of competitive bidding), we found the strength to examine one more hand on Marcel's list. It made a deep impression on me because it exemplified the differ-ence between 1940s bridge and 1980s.

In those early days, a take-out double was mandatory on any strong hand. The over-call was thought to be a lim-ited bid. Today, overcalls are more flexible and, as I have suggested, the idea of overcalling on a huge hand is not taboo.

Exhibit #9
Board 18

East dealer
North-South vulnerable

NORTH (Marie)
♠ 5 4
♡ 9 7
◊ Q 10 8 6
♣ Q 10 6 4 2

WEST
♠ 10 9 7 2
♡ Q 10 4 3 2
◊ 9 7 4
♣ 9

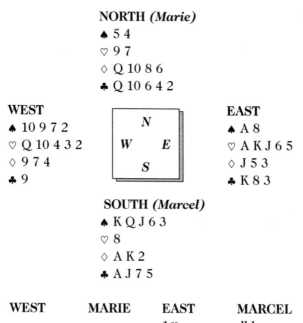

EAST
♠ A 8
♡ A K J 6 5
◊ J 5 3
♣ K 8 3

SOUTH (Marcel)
♠ K Q J 6 3
♡ 8
◊ A K 2
♣ A J 7 5

WEST	MARIE	EAST	MARCEL
		1♡	dbl
4♡	pass	pass	4♠
pass	pass	double	all pass

Opening lead: ♣9
Result: down 1

Astute readers will note immediately the lack of any circles or exclamation points in the bidding. Apparently this was a hand that caused no controversy and Marcel and Marie achieved their usual poor result without blame being placed on either side.

Only in today's bridge world can we see what went astray. No one in 1942 thought that doubling one heart with Marcel's hand was wrong. But in the 1980s, more players are willing to start slowly for the sake of finding a 5-3 fit. Their strategy is to make a simple overcall with the South cards. If and when the bidding comes back around, then they say double.

The overcall followed by the double is the most effective (and elegant) way of competing over an opening bid. Why it wasn't practiced during the War years is strange considering its resemblance to a then-popular dance, the 'two-step'. In the bridge version of the two-step, you first put your best foot forward by bidding your long suit. Then you complete the picture by making a takeout double for whatever suits are still unbid (with the additional vigorish that partner may leave in the double, converting it to penalties).

The old-fashioned two-step could have helped Marcel and Marie achieve either one of two good results. The auction might have gone:

NORTH *(Marie)*
♠ 5 4
♡ 9 7
◇ Q 10 8 6
♣ Q 10 6 4 2

WEST
♠ 10 9 7 2
♡ Q 10 4 3 2
◇ 9 7 4
♣ 9

	N	
W		E
	S	

EAST
♠ A 8
♡ A K J 6 5
◇ J 5 3
♣ K 8 3

SOUTH *(Marcel)*
♠ K Q J 6 3
♡ 8
◇ A K 2
♣ A J 7 5

WEST	MARIE	EAST	MARCEL
		1♡	1♠ *(step one)*
4♡	pass	pass	dbl *(step two)*
pass	pass, 5♣ *or* 4NT		

Here we see a nice little dance number perpetrated by North and South. Marcel leads the way by showing the main feature of his hand first, his spade suit. This calculated risk is rewarded when the bidding returns to him, since he easily completes the picture by doubling for takeout.

The delayed double allows Marie literally to glide across the bridge table in his arms. Whether she passes (and collects a penalty), bids her longest suit (and scores a game) or makes the scientific call of four notrump (asking Marcel to pick a minor, again scoring a game), the partnership comes out ahead.

The problem with Marcel's actual strategy on the hand (doubling the opening bid with a five-card major) is that when he doubled first, he had not shown his suit. So when the auction came back around to him he had the poor options of bidding his suit for the first time at the four level or making a second double and never showing the spades. It must have been painful for Marie to be the wallflower of the auction (her partner not bringing her into the act). Or had it felt more like he had stepped on her toes?

The fact that the hand was recorded shows that Marie was irritated by the result. The failure to criticize Marcel's bidding, however, demonstrates that the problem with the inversion of his bids (double and then four spades) was not understood. The lesson is clear today: with a five-card major and support for the other two suits, don't double and then bid your suit — first bid your suit, then double later.

WHEN COMPETITION GETS FIERCE

Don't sacrifice

Pamela was sound asleep. I shut off the book-light and rested my head on the pillow. Why should I continue this investigation? Solving the murder of a man killed forty years ago could not be worth risking my life. Why not use the same advice I give my readers: sit, wait, and listen? Instead of plunging my head into a noose, why not play a waiting game, and see if any more information is passed to me?

I closed my eyes. Dark, vulnerable images swept passed my restless mind. Orange canopies and black-suit pips. Yellow taxi-cabs and white sheets blotted with bloody-red heart honors. Dripping diamond Jacks and Queens, Dr. X., Marie... Marie.

The murderer seemed to appear to me in a vision as I lay half asleep in bed with the same list of hands that Marcel held so tightly to his chest. A shadow was there, then it wasn't. My subconscious slipped into lighter places; relief came in happy picture cards of blue and green.

Then a strange mixture engulfed my half-doze. I was consumed by both the murder of Marcel and the mysteries of bridge. I made a discovery play at trick two and a bomb went off under the table. Auctions reeled clockwise and counter-clockwise. One auction began with a bid of six spades. The next hand overcalled five hearts, third seat made a negative double, and fourth hand leapt to three diamonds!

WEST	NORTH	EAST	SOUTH
6♠	5♡	dbl	3♢
?			

Guns were pointed at me as I considered passing. Feet kicked me under the table. Messages were passed into my shoes. Dare I bid below the one-level? My wife, kibitzing from the next table, gave me a warning glance. I passed. The entire club rose in applause. Millions began writing lists of my bad bids, squeezing me into a corner of the room. A window that led to a fire escape was opened. We were not that high above the pavement. I tried to throw the list out but it stuck to my hand. "Give it to me," someone said. I held on. "Give it to me."

• • •

I woke up. I had been asleep less than four hours. The sky outside was lighter. My photostats were still on the edge of the bedspread. I got up, wrote a note to my wife, took a quick shower, and packed a small suitcase. I was willing to sacrifice my own safety for the sake of learning the truth, but not hers.

Leaving the note on the kitchen table, I slipped into my summer trench coat and crept silently out into the sun's early rays. It was Saturday and the street was empty. Eventually, I managed to hail a cab and told the driver to take me to the Embassy Hotel, where I checked in under the name of Marcel Moskowitz.

You might defeat their game

More players lose points sacrificing against beatable games than through any other losing strategy at the bridge table. When you are not vulnerable versus vulnerable it can be rewarding to give up only

300 or 500 points instead of 620. But it's so difficult to judge:

1) when your sacrifice will be down only two or three, and
2) when the opponents are, in fact, cold for their game,

that if there is any doubt, you should not sacrifice. Let's look again at Exhibit #8:

Exhibit #8   North dealer
Board 17   Neither vulnerable

NORTH *(Marie)*
- ♠ Q J 9 7
- ♡ J
- ◊ J 9 6
- ♣ 9 8 5 4 2

WEST
- ♠ A K 5 4 3
- ♡ 8 7 6 4
- ◊ A 10 8 5
- ♣ —

```
      N
   W     E
      S
```

EAST
- ♠ 10 8 6
- ♡ K 10 3
- ◊ Q 7 4 2
- ♣ A J 3

SOUTH *(Marcel)*
- ♠ 2
- ♡ A Q 9 5 2
- ◊ K 3
- ♣ K Q 10 7 6

WEST	NORTH	EAST	SOUTH
	pass	pass	1♡
1♠	pass	2♠	3♣
3◊	4♣ *!!*	4♠	5♣
pass	pass	dbl	all pass

Opening lead: ♠K
Result: down 1

It occurred to me that maybe Marcel thought he was favorable when he bid five clubs. More to the point, maybe he thought he was sacrificing. If Marie's four club bid with a spade stack on the side provoked Marcel into his phantom sacrifice, I wondered what might have happened if Marie had not had a spade stack.

Let's experiment. Change the vulnerability to favorable for North-South. Then switch spade holdings between East and Marie (and add one of East's diamonds to Marie's hand). Here's the new picture:

Exhibit #8 (modified)   North dealer
Board 17   East-West vulnerable

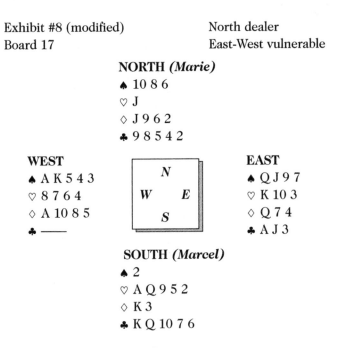

NORTH (Marie)
♠ 10 8 6
♡ J
◊ J 9 6 2
♣ 9 8 5 4 2

WEST
♠ A K 5 4 3
♡ 8 7 6 4
◊ A 10 8 5
♣ ——

EAST
♠ Q J 9 7
♡ K 10 3
◊ Q 7 4
♣ A J 3

SOUTH (Marcel)
♠ 2
♡ A Q 9 5 2
◊ K 3
♣ K Q 10 7 6

Four spades by West is still a hopeless contract. Marie would lead her singleton heart, and after losing two heart tricks and a ruff, declarer would have to guess diamonds to go down only one. The sacrifice in five clubs by North-South is still a phantom. Instead of collecting 100 or 200 points, North-South lose 100, and a bushel of matchpoints as well.

When you go minus it's rarely a good score

The worst thing about sacrifices at duplicate is that they often win the battle but lose the war. In other words, the sacrifice works grandly, but when you open up the score slip, you get a bottom anyway because no other pair in the other direction reached game.

I remember a hand early in my career in which my partner opened two hearts at favorable vulnerability and the next hand bid two spades. I held:

♠ K 7　♡ K 10 8 2　◇ Q J 8 7 6　♣ 5 2

I jumped to four hearts and heard four spades on my left. This was passed around to me, and I considered the auction:

YOUNG M.G.	NORTH	EAST	SOUTH
		2♡	2♠
4♡	4♠	pass	pass
?			

It was possible we were defeating four spades, but rather improbable, so I took the plunge and sacrificed in five hearts. This was the whole layout:

NORTH
♠ Q 10 8 5
♡ 6
◇ A 9 5 4 2
♣ A J 8

NAIVE M.G.
♠ K 7
♡ K 10 8 2
◇ Q J 8 7 6
♣ 5 2

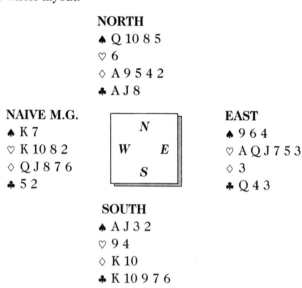

EAST
♠ 9 6 4
♡ A Q J 7 5 3
◇ 3
♣ Q 4 3

SOUTH
♠ A J 3 2
♡ 9 4
◇ K 10
♣ K 10 9 7 6

Five hearts turned out to be an excellent sacrifice. We went down only 300 points against the 620 we would have lost defending four spades. I congratulated myself, as North took out the score slip from the board. This was the last round of the night, and what we saw was deflating: only one worse score than ours. One North-South pair had bid and made four spades. One other pair had bid four spades and gone down. The rest of the field played in hearts our way, down one at the four level, doubled and undoubled.

Partner took out the North-South cards to analyze whether their four spade contract would indeed have succeeded. I was right on top of things. "Of course it makes. Even with a heart lead to your ace and a diamond switch. I score the spade king and give you a ruff for three tricks. But declarer now knows your shape, 3-6-1-3, so he will play the odds and finesse you for the queen of clubs."

My partner was impressed with my fast analysis. So was the South player who had made the successful two spade overcall on a four-card suit. He chimed in, "Yeth, I would have finethed my diamond ten through the notrumpth bidder." Then he drooled.

Don't open Weak Two-bids on five-card suits

One of the fastest growing modern trends towards the obliteration of sound competitive bidding is the opening of Weak Two-bids on five-card suits. These bids are very popular because they are exciting adventures that often achieve tops and bottoms. Like the 10-12 notrump opening that was an integral part of a system invented in the 70s called 'EHAA' (Every Hand An Adventure), the five-card suit Weak Two-bid propels the bidding quickly to a higher level than the opening bidder cares to reach.

But be forewarned — people who open five-card Weak Twos never get raised (their partners are so afraid). But perhaps they are people who never got raised in the past, so they tried opening five-card suits at the two-level in order to locate 5-3 fits all by themselves. Some are merely deluded into thinking they get better results because the bid comes up more frequently than traditional six-card suit Weak Two-bids.

There are three types of Weak Two-bids played today:

1) Traditional: 6-12 HCP, good suit, no side suit, and at most one ace or king outside.

♠ A Q J 6 5 3   ♡ 10 7   ♢ Q 10 3   ♣ 6 2

2) Ultra-Modern (destructive): 5-10 HCP, any 5- or 6-card suit.

♠ K Q 5 3 2   ♡ 10 7 3   ♢ Q 10 3   ♣ 6 2

3) Constructive: 7-12 HCP, any 6- or 7-card suit, could have wild distribution, any number of outside high cards; in short, a good playing hand.

♠ K 9 7 5 4 2   ♡ 10 7   ♢ A Q 10 3   ♣ 6

The best bidders are compromisers. If you are too conservative and wait for the perfect hand before you make a call, you may never make a call. If you are too liberal and bid on anything, you'll run into plenty of disasters. The winning approach is to emulate Goldilocks. If she were to read this book and choose for herself, she would try Number 1, Traditional, and find that although it gave partner a perfect description of her hand, and was also relatively safe to open at the two-level, it simply didn't come up at the table very much. Trying Number 2, Ultra-Modern, she would see that her partners always played her to have a five-card suit; she would find lots of use for the bid, but she would be rather disappointed at the frequent number of disasters. Then she would try the third style. This would combine frequency and safety with a reasonable amount of description. Number 3, Constructive, would be 'just right'.

Use Weak Two-bids constructively

The more trumps I have the happier I am, which is one reason I despise the five-card suit Weak Two-bid — I would rather open a Weak Two-bid on a seven-card suit. I like the protection. I also like the idea that my partner knows I have a lot of trumps for my bid — he can raise on a doubleton honor if he likes. Mostly, I like the constructive style of Weak Two-bids because they get me off on the right path for what might become a dangerous, competitive auction.

There are many other advantages to a constructive style:

1) Not only does partner know you have a good playing hand with at least six trumps, but if the opponents start competing, he knows you have at least a trick on defense.

2) You get to describe a good hand with a long suit immediately, preempting the opponents with a high degree of safety. For example, holding:

♠ J 10 7 6 4 3   ♡ 7   ◇ A K   ♣ Q 10 8 5

you can open two spades. Playing other styles of Weak Two-bids you would have to choose between pass and one spade, neither of which goes very far towards describing a six-card suit and a good ten-point hand.

3) If you can locate that eight-, nine-, or ten-card fit immediately, you may be able to wipe the opponents out of the auction (thereby eliminating the competitive auction altogether) with one the best one-two punches in bridge: 2♠ – 4♠.

Third seat: the seat of sin!

I recently played in a club game where a 'pro' opened two spades in third seat on a four-card suit! His partner couldn't take a joke and raised to game with four trumps. I doubled the final contract and declarer went down four tricks. The fellow screamed at his student (who, under normal conditions, should have been praised for his raise). It was a pitiful scene, illustrating for the umpteenth time that players sitting in third seat are haunted by a devil.

When I preempt in third seat I am extra careful. Since partner has already passed, I have lost one of the main advantages of pre-empting: sometimes the opponents go for a number when they come in and partner is strong. When the overcall of a preempt can be doubled by partner, you often reap huge rewards. For example, if you open three clubs and the next hand overcalls three spades, an unpassed partner might be looking at a spade stack and nineteen points. Double, he'll say, and your preempt will have earned a top. A passed-hand partner is considerably less likely to be able to penalize the overcall. Thus, the third seat preempt is not as useful.

Quite the opposite view is taken by most players. They go out of their way to preempt on bad hands in third seat, thinking they can keep opponents out of the auction. But looking at it from the flip side, a preempt often goads the opponents into reaching a contract that they would never have reached on their own power — a contract that is likely to make only because of the preempt!

If the auction goes pass - pass to you, and your hand is so weak that you think the opponents have a good chance for game, the last thing you want to do is describe your shape. You wouldn't think it smart to turn your hand face up to your opponents, but in essence that is what players do when they open bad preempts in third seat.

Two-bids and three-bids in third seat should be constructive. Let's review this again:

Two-bids are always constructive.

Three bids are constructive only after two passes.

The one time you should open a five-card weak two-bid in third seat is when the suit is good and you hold a singleton in the other major. This is because you will have a difficult time rebidding if you open a one-bid on the hand. For example:

♠ 3   ♡ Q J 10 6 2   ◇ A 10 8 4   ♣ K 3 2

If you open one heart in third seat and partner responds one spade, you are in trouble. You open the hand with the faint hope of reaching four hearts; but when partner does not have heart support you want to quit as soon as possible. You cannot open one heart and pass one spade with a singleton; partner may have as few as four spades, and you provide him with a legal motive for murder.

The best solution is to open two hearts. Although you lie about your heart length by one card, you tell partner that your hand is just under the strength for an opening bid. Since the hand is a closer approximation of a weak two-bid than a one-bid, the two-bid is preferable.

You might ask, then why not open this hand two hearts in first or second seat if it's so close to a weak two-bid? The answer is that if you pass in first or second seat, your partner can still open the bidding and you will miss nothing. If you pass in third seat, however, the hand might be passed out.

Don't semi-psyche in third seat

Semi-psyches are smart-aleck opening one-bids in third seat that lose more matchpoints than they win. They are made on hands with seven to ten points, and though designed to fool the opponents, it is often partner who is made to look like the fool.

The term 'semi-psyche' is accurate. It is not a total psyche (0 points), nor a light opening bid (10–12 points). It is *almost* a psyche and thus has the disadvantage of being too strong to be effective as a defensive measure (since the opponents will often not have the strength to make a game), and too weak to be constructive as an offensive measure (since your side will be too weak to make a contract).

A typical semi-psyche:

♠ J 7   ♡ A Q 8 5   ◇ 10 9 8 7   ♣ 5 4 2

After two passes, a typical semi-psycher opens one heart because he is not vulnerable. He will get a heart lead if his partner ends up on lead, and at the same time confuse the opponents. He is out to steal. He thinks that the opponents will listen to his bid rather than look at their own cards. In the long run he does steal a few hands, some of which, however, are hands where the opponents cannot make a darn thing.

Open to play the hand, not to get a lead

The player who semi-psyches argues that even if he fails to confuse the opponents, he will at least get partner off to the best lead. This is questionable. For one thing, half the time he will be on lead. For another, if (on the example hand) his partner leads a doubleton heart against three notrump, this will only assist declarer (who has the majority of hearts).

If the opponents reach a game in a suit or even a slam from the wrong side, the lead-directing opening bid may work spectacularly well. Unfortunately, there are many more ordinary hands in which partner is fooled long before the opening lead. Pity poor partner on a hand like this:

POOR PARTNER		YOU
♠ K 6 4 3	N	♠ J 7
♡ J 2	W E	♡ A Q 8 5
◇ A 5 4 2	S	◇ 10 9 8 7
♣ K 10 7		♣ 5 4 2

POOR PARTNER	NORTH	YOU	SOUTH
pass	pass	1♡	2♣
2NT	all pass		

In this scenario, the opening lead is a club. You put the dummy down and rush out of the room (one hopes never to return, thinks partner).

Beware of partner who may never stop bidding

PARTNER		POOR YOU
♠ K 6 4 3	N	♠ J 7
♡ J 2	W E	♡ A Q 8 5
◇ A 5 4 2	S	◇ 10 9 8 7
♣ K 10 7		♣ 5 4 2

PARTNER	NORTH	POOR YOU	SOUTH
pass	pass	1♡	2♣
dbl	pass	2◇	pass
3◇	dbl	all pass	

This time, justice is more appropriately served as you become declarer after getting a chance to bid both your suits. This is really a lovely auction, and if he were alive today, Vanderbilt would probably consider hiring a hit man to wipe out the creature who deforms the game he so cherished.

Open four-card majors in third seat

When you open the bidding legitimately, but light, in third seat, your partner does not know how light you are. One way you can improve your score is to open the bidding in a major (the most profitable trump suit), then pass partner's response. Even if you open the bidding on a full thirteen points, it is better to start off on the right track by opening in the major.

I advocate opening the four-card major on any balanced 11+ to 15-point hand in third position.

Some experts believe it is only right to open the four-card major on eleven- or twelve-point hands. I don't see the point in arguing over whether you have twelve or fourteen points. Points-shmoints. When partner is a passed hand it is to your advantage to use that information. If you have less than a one notrump opening bid, slam is virtually impossible and game is not very likely. The partscore becomes most critical. If you've played duplicate for more than a few months, you know by now that major-suit part-scores are better matchpoint contracts than minor-suit part-scores.

Regardless of quality

Let me repeat: the purpose of the opening bid is to reach game. Modify that slightly in third seat and it translates to 'reach the best partscore'. The idea of opening the bidding to direct an opening lead is a losing strategy. The sooner you and your partner get together on this, the sooner you will begin picking up matchpoints. The sooner you can trust that partner, when on lead, will use his brain rather than lead your opening-bid suit blindly, the sooner you will be able to open the bidding in third seat on weak major suits. After all, we are not always dealt the perfect four-card holding: A-K-x-x. Sometimes our major is headed by the jack. Here are four examples of third-seat opening bids taken from real life:

A — bid 1♠	B — bid 1♡
♠ J 10 7 2	♠ 5 2
♡ K 2	♡ K 8 6 3
◇ Q J 10 4	◇ K Q 5
♣ A Q 6	♣ K Q 4 2

C — bid 1♡	D — bid 1♣
♠ A 10 9 5	♠ K Q J 5
♡ 10 8 6 3	♡ 4 2
◇ A 4	◇ A 5
♣ A 4 2	♣ Q 10 8 7 6

A) When this hand was dealt at the local duplicate, the player who opened one spade got a cold top! Her partner raised to two spades, and that made exactly two. Why was +110 a top? Because fourth seat held five hearts and eight points. The other players in third seat opened one diamond, and fourth seat was able to slip in a one heart overcall. The opponents then competed to three hearts, which was sometimes down one and sometimes making.

The one spade opening blocked that heart overcall and knocked the opponents right out of the auction. Major-suit openings are difficult to compete against. Although fourth seat might have balanced after two spades was passed around to him, it was not as easy as slipping in a one-level overcall after a minor-suit opening.

B) In a sectional tournament the person who opened one heart on this hand received next to top for a very funny reason — his left-hand opponent had a better heart suit than he did! Can you imagine the poor guy who held the A-Q-J-9-7 of hearts and heard his suit opened in front of him? Our hero ended up in three clubs from partner's side, making three (partner had six clubs to the ace-jack and queen fourth of spades). Four hearts was cold in the other direction!

C) I opened this hand one heart just last week. Why one heart rather than one spade? Simple. If I open one heart partner can raise hearts or easily bid one spade. If I open one spade, a 4-4 heart fit will be difficult to locate. After my one heart opening partner raised to two hearts with three-card support to the queen. Most 4-3 major fits are usually good contracts at the two level. However, this particular 4-3 fit was heading for a bottom (the suit broke 5-1). That is, until the opponent with a singleton heart balanced with two spades. This pleased me immensely since I am not one to argue the virtue of being assisted by an opponent.

D) The correct opening here is one club because the clubs are longer than the spades. It's possible that a one spade opening might work very well, but it pays in the long run to open your longest suit first. With equal length, of course, start with the major.

Perhaps you think these hands are just lucky examples, and that it's too risky to open a weak four-card major. Perhaps you don't like the idea of declaring in a weak 4-3 fit. Well, you don't have to play everything my way. Try a compromise. Open any decent looking four-card major in third seat. Even if you're a five-card major lover, you simply must branch out in third position.

Take the push with four-card trump support

Listen. The fear of the 4-3 fit is common to many players, but if you want to improve your score significantly, you must learn to cope with the occasional 4-3 trump contract. The last thing you ever want to do is inhibit partner from raising you directly with three-card trump support. Competitive bidding is won by the partnership which locates their trump fit early and diagnoses how big that fit is later in the auction (when the decision must be made to bid one more or let the opponents have it).

WEST	NORTH	EAST	SOUTH
			1♢
pass	1♡	pass	2♡
pass	pass	2♠	?

South opens one diamond and North responds one heart. South raises to two hearts (with three- or four-card support). East makes a balancing two spade call. North-South must now deal with the issue of whether to compete further. The biggest factor in making this choice is the number of trumps North-South hold. A four-three fit is adequate at the two level. But at the three level, eight or even nine trumps are necessary.

The first thing South should look at is his heart holding — not his strength in hearts, but his length. With only three cards in hearts, South should pass. With four cards in hearts, South can consider bidding on.

Similarly, if this auction is passed around to North, he should take the push to the three level only with five or more hearts, never with only four. This is important to remember. Even when the opponents are not competing, the direct raise by opener is frequently made on three-card support. It is therefore imperative that responder does not go leaping to game with only a four-card suit.

WEST	NORTH	EAST	SOUTH
			1♣
pass	1♡	pass	2♡
pass	4♡		

This four heart bid should never be made on a four-card suit. South has promised only three trumps. If North wishes to bid game and has only four hearts, he should bid a new suit or three notrump. This allows opener to raise hearts again with four.

When both sides are bidding, trumps are key

Another example of trump priority occurs when both sides are fighting for the three-level. Nine tricks are not easy when both pairs have equal strength. To determine whether to bid on (rather than let the opponents buy the contract), look at the number of combined trumps you and your partner hold (this is based on a principle known as the Law of Total Tricks). Here is a partscore battle which occurs every night at the duplicate:

WEST	NORTH	EAST	SOUTH
			1♡
1♠	2♡	2♠	pass
pass	3♡	?	

In simplest terms, North is pushing; will East-West let themselves be pushed or not? One easy and effective formula for East is to go with four trumps, stop with three. The strength of your hand is not as relevant. High cards are useful for defense as well as offense. Trump length is useful only for offense, and can be detrimental to the defense. The more trumps you hold, the more you want to declare. The fewer trumps you hold, the more you want to defend.

Don't let them push you around

No one likes to be pushed around. In real life people sometimes threaten other people to get what they want; it is not a nice thing to do. In the world of games and sports, however, pushing your opponents around is common strategy. The defensive linemen of a football team are out to sack the quarterback. The baseball pitcher brushes back the batter with an intimidating inside fastball. The hockey player throws a bodycheck with the intent of knocking his opponent to the ice.

Bridge players push other bridge players around by bidding one more in competitive auctions. They are not bidding to make their contract, but instead, to push you to a level where you may fail. The thing to remember is that this 'evil' ploy is prevalent. Sometimes it is masked in a 'you're not gonna outbid me' threat. But what happens too often is that you out-bid them anyway, and now you go down when they were also going down. Remember this: bids designed to push the opponents higher are often made on flimsy values.

Winning players in all these games are prepared to fight back. Fighting back, however, does not necessarily mean resorting to the same tactics. Such tactics depend on timing and should be used at the right moment to be effective. For example, pushing the opponents up in a competitive auction is much smarter when done at favorable vulnerability than at unfavorable. If you are not vulnerable, and the opponents double you instead of bidding one more, a one-trick defeat will not cost much. A two-trick set undoubled will also be okay. But vulnerable, you have to be more careful. Good matchpoint players are like bulls in a bullring — when they see red, they come after you.

The most successful manner of fighting off the push in competitive bidding is to duck out of the way. The pusher often lands on his fanny, and when he comes up for air, you may be at an overwhelming advantage. Blitzing the quarterback backfires when one fewer offensive player is covered, and he dashes downfield with the football, unimpeded. The baseball hitter who is brushed back by the pitcher gets a free ball for his trouble. The hockey player on the receiving end of a mighty bodycheck may be agile enough to dodge; the aggressor ends up out of position, and perhaps flat on the ice himself. The bridge player who is being pushed higher in a competitive auction, can pass the decision around to partner who may be able to double the opponents.

I have played with students who get caught up in the tempo of the auction. The fact that the opponents bid one more does not mean you must bid one more. In this sequence:

WEST	NORTH	EAST	SOUTH
1♠	2♦	2♠	3♦
3♠	4♦	4♠	all pass
			(from exhaustion)

East may have his bid, but I doubt it. It sounds like East was caught up in the fast-paced tempo. To begin with, West was probably competing rather than making a game try (a new suit at the three level can be used as an artificial game try rather than as a natural call; in this case, three hearts would be a game try in spades).

Even if West were making a game try by bidding 3♠, East should only bid game if he would have done so regardless of North's call. If East was going to reject a game try, he should not allow himself to be goaded into four spades by North's four diamond bid. Let North push. West may be ready to clobber him; or maybe West was the pusher and North has fallen for it!

• • •

Competitive bidding is filled with pushy situations of this type. In this way, the game of bridge reflects the game of life. While I was determined to solve a murder mystery, others were bent on stopping the investigation. They threatened me verbally, they warned me in print, they sent a smoke bomb to frighten me. But I was stubborn; I was not going to allow myself to be pushed around. Perhaps I was making a mistake. Perhaps I should have passed, and let them have it their way. After all, wasn't I more vulnerable than they were? Maybe. But I wasn't so certain they had the values to push. Were they merely trying to intimidate me? Or were they truly ready to back up their threats? I didn't know. I was about to find out. I had allowed myself to be caught up in the tempo. They doubled. I redoubled. Talk about over-bidding!

6 DON'T PULL PENALTY DOUBLES OUT OF GUILT FOR NOT HAVING YOUR BID

I woke up in a sweat. There was no air conditioner in Room 625 of the Embassy Hotel. The clerk must have thought it strange when I insisted on one of the rooms in the old section that had not yet been renovated. I wanted Room 623 of course. I told him that it held romantic memories for me. He thought I was nuts. Anyway, it was a moot point; Room 623 was occupied. Number 625 was next door, and had the merit of a private bath.

There were seven rooms on this end of the building. Mine had a fire escape overlooking a Pakistani restaurant. I could hole up here for quite a while, dining on lamb vindaloo and vegetable samosas to go. My wife would kill me when she found out that I had Indian food without her (it's her favorite), but this was risky business all around.

When I checked in, it was 6:00 a.m. I don't think anyone saw me. I had left my calling card on the desk register by signing the name 'Marcel Moskowitz'. Somebody would find me eventually; with luck, that somebody would agree to answer questions first and shoot later.

It was certainly a hazy plan, and I had completely forgotten that the bridge club on the top floor would be filled with people who knew me by sight. The last thing I wanted was for innocent friends to get involved. Nor did I wish to bother with anyone who could not lead me to the solution of Marcel's death (and this included my wife, for her safety of course).

There had been no bellhop to show me to the room, and it was absolutely as gruesome as the clerk had said. One single bed, two thin pillows, a dusty, antique night table with a drawer that was stuck and a solitary lamp in the shape of a black falcon (or was it just an owl?). Beneath a cracked mirror (on which I attached the wife's photo in the bottom, left-hand corner) was a dresser containing a torn pair of undies left behind by a former guest. There was also a moldy green rug and a closet with two wire hangers.

The bath was the only bright spot, a strange contrast to the rest of the room. It was spic and span — too clean, in fact — and smelled of a familiar scent which I could not place. There were two large towels on the rack, and the tub was white and spotless, with a bar of French soap in the dish. I took a cool bath, and before I slept I made an effort to sort out the clues. I wrote them down on a 5½ x 8 notepad and folded in the photostats of Marcel and Marie's bridge hands. Then I put the whole bundle under my pillow and fell asleep.

I woke up around noon and felt a lot better. The first thing I did after dressing was try the fire escape. It seemed sturdy and, with my notepad under my shirt, I climbed down to the courtyard. Then I slipped into the back of the Taj Mahal and found myself in the kitchen where a thin little guy with a big knife was chopping cucumbers. I told him I was alone. "Most customers come in by the front entrance," he said with a smile.

I ordered spiced tea and paratha at a dark table with a wooden lamp, took out my notepad and read the clues:

January 23, 1942, 8:35 a.m.

Marcel Moskowitz, racetrack tout, found dead (fully dressed — bridge notes clutched to chest) in room 623 of the Embassy Hotel.

Chambermaid notes nothing stolen, but extra pillows found on bed.

Had reputation as ladies' man.

Hopeless bridge player (Roth).

Police Inspector Gardner reports death as probable heart attack but suffocation by pillow also a possible cause (no autopsy report).

Sends notepad with bridge symbols on it to lab where photos are taken. It is placed in obscure police records and never opened for forty years (then sent to me by whom?).

Inspector goes upstairs to all-night bridge club nicknamed 'The Bucket O' Blood'.

Proprietor (Vic Mitchell) is not in.

At the club that morning are:

Harry (a cop and chess player in debt).

Dr. X. (bridge kibitzer who helped unknown woman named Marie make circles around bridge errors of corpse).

Jinks, a tall skinny kid with stutter (a 'gofer' but high I Q).

Little Lulu, a small, older woman (student of Al Roth).

Other players unidentified, one of whom failed to raise partner with four-card trump support and a singleton in the opponents' suit.

Inspector Gardner never asks key question: "Who is Marie?"

No other records of case until 1983.

Marcel's notes show exclamation points (made by Marcel) and circles (made by Marie and/or Dr. X.) accenting poor bidding and errors from bridge duplicate the night before his death.

Notes also show Marcel and Marie changing directions, which indicates a Howell Movement.

Vulnerability and dealer of first nine hands match Boards 10 through 18 though not in perfect order. Could be groups of three. (Does this mean three boards per round?)

Al Roth remembers Marcel as hopeless player who thought himself quite a wiz, but does not recall any woman named Marie.

Remembers the duplicate of January 22, left early, but confused over who his partner was. (Recalls playing with Jinks and Little Lulu on two separate hands.)

One Ms. Marie Gardner purports to be daughter of the late Inspector Gardner, and warns me of danger in investigating case.

Friends of her father want case closed. Further warnings and threats include fake newspaper article, and clock-bomb.

Have yet to locate Vic Mitchell, who surely has answers.

I added to the list:

Holed up now in unrenovated section of Embassy Hotel—Room G25 — in attempt to:
1) study list of hands in private
2) review case (doing that now), and
3) lure one of Inspector Gardner's friends into the open.

After rereading the list, I was more bewildered than ever. This must be how my students feel after a session of duplicate when I point out too many errors, and say things that seem contradictory. Even the simplest subject matter can become confusing when trying to appreciate every application and nuance to the full. For example, doubles. A double in 1942 was a simple bid. It meant 'I don't think you can make this contract.' Not so today. Besides the old-fashioned penalty double, there are takeout doubles, negative doubles, responsive doubles, support doubles and lead-directing doubles, to name just a few.

Each variety is slightly different, but for the most part they can be sorted into two types:

1) penalty *or* **2) takeout**

Another way of looking at it is to translate the meaning of double into one simple word:

1) stop *or* **2) go**

'Stop' usually occurs late in the auction (and from the doubler's point of view ends the auction). 'Go' usually takes place during the first two rounds of bidding.

These meanings are clear, and do not require judgment from partner. To be effective you must take the double at face value. When partner says 'go' by making a takeout double, and you have no suit to go to, you shouldn't think, 'maybe he's making an optional double'. When partner says 'stop' with a penalty double, and you

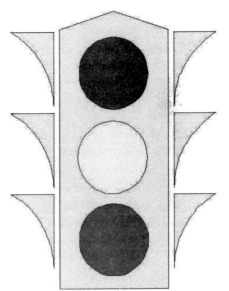

are void in their suit (so it doesn't really look like a good idea to stop), you shouldn't think, 'well maybe he won't mind if I bid.'

A fascinating hand of this type was played on January 22, 1942 in the mysterious duplicate game at the Bucket O' Blood. I found it on Marcel's list that afternoon. Although I had not planned to review hands until safely back in my hotel room, in my quick perusal of the photostats I caught something new on the tenth diagram. It was the name of Roth where Marie had always been, partnered, of course, by Marcel.

Exhibit #10
Board 19

South dealer
East-West vulnerable

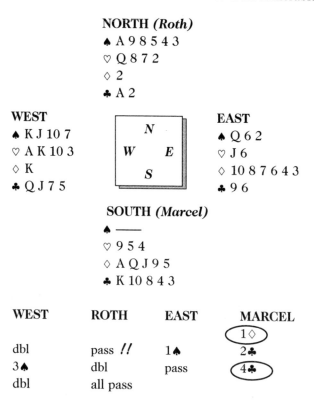

NORTH *(Roth)*
♠ A 9 8 5 4 3
♡ Q 8 7 2
♢ 2
♣ A 2

WEST
♠ K J 10 7
♡ A K 10 3
♢ K
♣ Q J 7 5

EAST
♠ Q 6 2
♡ J 6
♢ 10 8 7 6 4 3
♣ 9 6

SOUTH *(Marcel)*
♠ ——
♡ 9 5 4
♢ A Q J 9 5
♣ K 10 8 4 3

WEST	ROTH	EAST	MARCEL
			1 ◇
dbl	pass *!!*	1 ♠	2 ♣
3 ♠	dbl	pass	4 ♣
dbl	all pass		

Opening lead: ♡ K
Result: down 2

Penalty doubles are warnings to stop partner from bidding

Roth had not mentioned partnering Marcel that evening, and I had half a mind to rush to the pay phone of the Taj Mahal and call the Mayfair Club. But at that moment my paratha arrived toasty warm and my stomach was growling, so business had to wait. Meanwhile, I analyzed the bidding.

Marcel had opened one diamond with only ten points but fine distribution. The bid is circled, perhaps for the lack of high cards. Personally, I would have passed, planning to back in later with the unusual notrump for the minors. West's double was very much for takeout, even in 1942.

It is here where the bidding seems to be out of order. Roth must have bid one spade and East passed. No, wait a second — could the fox have been trapping again? What a grand coup this was! East, with a terrible hand and no suit but opener's, had to make a bid. So he took his best shot with one spade on three to the queen. Marcel next bid two clubs and West jumped to three spades.

Roth, who had yet to make a bid, came from behind the bushes with a penalty double. That meant curtains for East-West. Well, curtains until Marcel rejoined the action. Why, oh why did he pull his partner's double?

Trust your partner occasionally

It was forty years later, and I was only reading a report of the auction, but it made me sick to see Marcel pull three spades doubled. When Roth said double he was yelling 'stop' at the top of his lungs. The only explanation I could see for Marcel's four club bid was that he feared he had overstated his values. He was afraid to leave in the double because he knew he did not have the defensive tricks Roth would expect. Nevertheless, he should not have run. He should have reasoned:

1) Okay, I've overbid. But I have not misdescribed my two suits, and I do have two potential tricks.

2) The void in spades is bad for defending, true, but did I say I had spades? Indeed, maybe the void is a clue that my partner has a fantastic trump stack.

3) My partner came out of the blue with a penalty double. He is saying to me 'stop', so why should I 'go'?

4) It is not my business to bid. Partner told me to do the opposite. His hand is a total mystery. How can I presume to know more about his hand than he does?

5) Partnership is based on trust, so I'll trust him. If he's wrong it's his fault.

6) If I pull the double, and I'm wrong, he'll kill me. (Not meant literally of course.)

Doubling with a singleton in partner's suit

The exclamation points after Roth's first pass indicate that Marcel excused his removal of three spades doubled. "How could Roth have good spades and not bid them at the one level?" he may have argued. The fact that Roth might have been trapping did not enter his mind. Still, even if Roth's double had been made on questionable trumps, where did Marcel think he was going with his four club bid? Surely Roth would have raised one of Marcel's suits with support. Therefore, the double denied support for clubs and diamonds.

Doubles in competitive situations such as this imply shortness in partner's suit(s). I know some players who take a chance and double a contract *only* because they have a singleton in partner's suit. Then they lead the singleton and, because of the double, it becomes clear to their partner that the lead is a singleton. This is an expert strategy, but certainly one that more players could use.

For example, you hold:

♠ A 6 5   ♡ 2   ◇ 10 8 7 6 4   ♣ 5 4 3 2

Your right-hand opponent opens one spade. You pass and the next hand raises to two spades. Partner bids three hearts and the opener bids four spades. This would not be a bad time to speculate with a penalty double. In fact, it will help your partner on defense! The lead of the heart deuce will no longer be misinterpreted as low from three. Because of your double, partner will be confident your lead is a singleton and you will get all the ruffs coming to you.

Sure, it could backfire. But certain risks are worth taking. Like an investigation of murder, competitive bidding can be dangerous. Sometimes you have to watch your step. Sometimes you have to take a chance. In my investigation of Marcel Moskowitz's murder, the auction was over. There was a contract out on me, and I didn't like it.

SIMPLIFY DEFENSE

Too many signals spoil the broth

I ordered some mulligatawny soup to go. From where I sat, I could see a photocopy establishment across Broadway. I gave the waiter Marcel's notes and sent him on a mission. He returned before the soup was ready with a copy of the notes, a manila envelope and some wrapping paper with a skull and crossbones pattern. "What's that?" I asked.

"For my son, Jonny. He is five years old tomorrow. And if I don't hurry and wrap his presents he will have to wait and open them when he comes home from day camp."

"Yes, of course, but—"

"It is very difficult. His mother is visiting in Bombay and missed the flight home. To buy presents is impossible. He wanted the space station; I found only nuclear subs. I did get the machine gun, but I could not find computer war zone..."

"Wait a second," I said, holding my palm up. "How about a deck of cards? I know a really dangerous game he can try."

"Thank you — cards, very funny, ha ha. Good joke. Do you think we allow him to play cards at his age?"

He handed me the envelope, offended at my suggestion, and I addressed it to Zia Mahmood at his Karachi address. I slipped the photocopies inside with a message for him to keep them until he heard from me, and not to mention the hands to anyone. Then I tipped the waiter a fiver and sent him to the post office.

Returning to my room via the kitchen, courtyard, and fire escape, I was surprised to see it had been ransacked. The place was a mess. My shirts were hanging out of the drawers, the pillows were torn open, and feathers fluttered about the bed. The mattress was ripped along the side. However, the door was locked from the inside, and the bathroom was still spic and span. There was that fragrance again, and when I slipped a bit on the tiles I noted some water spots that had not been there when I left. Somebody was using my bath!

I opened the shower curtain expecting who knows what to appear, but found only a warm, wet tub. Sitting down by the open window, I looked out into the courtyard. No one there. The fire escape was dry. I couldn't figure how someone had got in and out of the room. So I gave up, opened the lid to my soup, and found it was still hot (though slightly too spicy). My stomach was jumping nervously. For once I would have preferred chicken soup.

Give attitude at trick one

Opening to Exhibit 11 of Marcel's notes, I tried to concentrate on the hand. Marie was back in the saddle as Marcel's partner, but there was a new twist — someone (Dr. X.?) had scribbled in the play to the first two tricks.

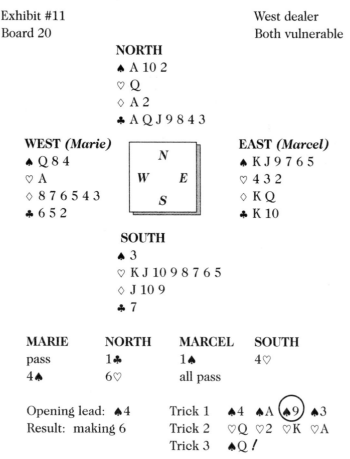

Exhibit #11
Board 20

West dealer
Both vulnerable

NORTH
♠ A 10 2
♡ Q
♢ A 2
♣ A Q J 9 8 4 3

WEST (Marie)
♠ Q 8 4
♡ A
♢ 8 7 6 5 4 3
♣ 6 5 2

EAST (Marcel)
♠ K J 9 7 6 5
♡ 4 3 2
♢ K Q
♣ K 10

SOUTH
♠ 3
♡ K J 10 9 8 7 6 5
♢ J 10 9
♣ 7

MARIE	NORTH	MARCEL	SOUTH
pass	1♣	1♠	4♡
4♠	6♡	all pass	

Opening lead: ♠4
Result: making 6

Trick 1	♠4	♠A ⃝♠9	♠3
Trick 2	♡Q	♡2 ♡K	♡A
Trick 3	♠Q /		

The hand had been overbid to six hearts, and Marie led a low spade. Declarer won the ace in dummy as Marcel followed with the nine. When a trump was played to Marie's ace, she continued spades, but declarer trumped and must have (though it is not reported) drawn trumps, led a club to the ace, ruffed out the club king, and returned to dummy's good clubs via the diamond ace.

NORTH
♠ A 10 2
♡ Q
◇ A 2
♣ A Q J 9 8 4 3

WEST *(Marie)*
♠ Q 8 4
♡ A
◇ 8 7 6 5 4 3
♣ 6 5 2

```
        N
    W       E
        S
```

EAST *(Marcel)*
♠ K J 9 7 6 5
♡ 4 3 2
◇ K Q
♣ K 10

SOUTH
♠ 3
♡ K J 10 9 8 7 6 5
◇ J 10 9
♣ 7

This time the argument was not about the bidding, but the defense. Readers will note the circle around Marcel's spade nine and the exclamation point after the spade queen lead to trick three. A simple analysis of the hand will reveal that a diamond shift at trick three would have knocked out dummy's entry to the club suit. Declarer could return to his hand and draw trumps, but would be forced to finesse clubs through West in the hope of finding her with king doubleton. This would have meant a two-trick set rather than a slam bid and made.

The argument between Marcel and Marie surrounds these two cards: the spade nine at trick one and the spade queen at trick three. Marcel argued against the spade queen play (he was certainly right as the cards lay) and Marie pointed to the spade nine as the card that led her astray. Who was correct?

Marie's attempt to cash the spade queen at trick three seems reasonable. If South had held one more spade, her play would have defeated the slam immediately. Marie had no idea who held the club king and it could easily have been in declarer's hand.

In defense of her play, no argument can be more potent than Marcel's signal at trick one: the spade nine. This was encouraging. If Marcel wanted another suit played, why would he signal so ferociously for spades? Marie must have thought that a shift to any other suit would be equivalent to a slap in partner's face. (Granted, by this time in the evening, with all the errors Marcel had committed, a slap in the face would not be out of line.) Marie's only clue to the hand was Marcel's signal at trick one. The bidding had been abrupt and uninformative. With only one clue to point the way, what could she do but follow its path?

On the other hand, was Marcel at fault for signaling he liked spades with the king sixth? One could argue that Marcel had to play a high spade as an attitude signal to show the king. Or perhaps Marcel was giving count — a high spade to show an even number. Maybe Marcel meant his nine of spades as suit preference — shift to the higher-ranking side suit (diamonds). Marcel might have argued that his spade nine signal was all three combined!

Was Marcel's signal:

> Attitude — the king of spades, *or*
> Count — an even number, *or*
> Suit preference — for diamonds, *or*
> All three?

The complexity of this discussion is enough to drive the average bridge player back to canasta. One card should not have so many meanings. If Marie played bridge in the same way as the majority of good players today, then she used a signal at trick one to deliver a simple message: either "Please continue if you gain the lead" or "Don't continue — shift to something else."

Although the translation of the signal is quite simple ('I like it' or 'I don't like it'), the thought process used by third hand to arrive at one of these two messages is not simple. If you are looking only at the suit led, and send a signal based solely on your holding in that suit, you are not thinking hard enough. Marcel had six spades to the king and, in that isolated context, he liked spades. But if he had examined his holding in accordance with the entire hand he would have concluded that *he did not like spades*!

There are two thoughts that should occur to third hand when signaling, the first being "Does continuing this suit help us?"

If Marcel could count to thirteen he would know he did not want a continuation. He had six spades, dummy three, his partner three, and therefore declarer had one. No spade tricks were cashing for the defense, and he knew it.

The obvious-shift principle

The fact that declarer is going to ruff the next lead of a suit is not necessarily a deterrent to continuing that suit. Very often a good defense is a passive one, in which you break no suits for declarer.

If Marcel had thought before signaling at trick one, he might have concluded that no spades were cashing. However, that would not necessarily mean it would be wrong to continue spades. It was necessary, however, for him to look at the rest of the hand to see whether any other play, in his opinion, would be better than spades.

This brings us to the second thought that should occur to third hand when signaling: "Do I want partner to shift to another suit?"

Had Marcel asked himself this question, he would have answered, "Yes." If partner gained the lead, a diamond shift might be helpful. Upon further reflection, a diamond shift might be necessary to destroy the entry to dummy's club suit. In either case, since a diamond play might be helpful, and since spade tricks could not be cashed, Marcel should have asked partner to switch. He should have done this by playing a low spade, saying in effect, "I don't like spades, make a switch."

This simple message, 'don't play spades', and therefore, 'play something else', would have forced Marie to think about which suit to shift to. It would not have been difficult for her to see that a diamond switch was better than a club switch. You might say that the diamond suit was 'obviously' the better play since dummy's clubs might be established for discards, while dummy's diamonds could not.

In conclusion, the signal at trick one is attitude, telling partner whether you would like a continuation or whether you would like a switch to the 'obvious', or weaker, side suit. For example, had Marcel been dealt two small diamonds instead of the king and queen, he would signal with a high spade at trick one to offer his opinion. Although he would know the next spade would be ruffed, he would want to warn partner off a possibly fatal diamond switch. Again, there is no reason to ask for a club switch, since if declarer has a club loser it will not disappear. This is important to remember, so I'll stress that the request for a shift is always for dummy's *weaker* side suit.

When in doubt

There are times when the so-called obvious shift is not so obvious. For example, change the last hand a bit, and give dummy two equal side suits:

NORTH
♠ A 10 5 2
♡ Q
◇ K Q J 9
♣ K Q J 9

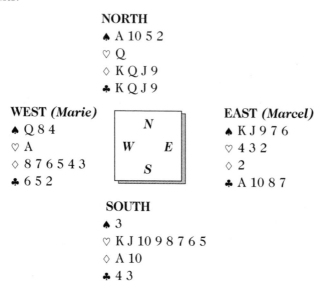

WEST (Marie)
♠ Q 8 4
♡ A
◇ 8 7 6 5 4 3
♣ 6 5 2

EAST (Marcel)
♠ K J 9 7 6
♡ 4 3 2
◇ 2
♣ A 10 8 7

SOUTH
♠ 3
♡ K J 10 9 8 7 6 5
◇ A 10
♣ 4 3

West leads a low spade and Marcel, counting the suit, realizes that the spade king will not cash. If he discourages in spades by playing his lowest card, Marie, upon gaining the lead, will shift to dummy's obvious weakness. Uh oh. There is nothing obvious here.

But Marcel can help Marie find the club shift anyway. This is how. When you want partner to shift, and there are two relatively equal suits to shift to, you can agree to make the obvious-shift suit the lower of the two side suits. Now the play of an unusual honor card, such as the jack in this example, would ask for a shift to the higher of the two side suits. And, of course, a simple 'come on' with a high spot card, such as the nine, would ask partner just to continue spades.

Even if the two side suits in dummy are not exactly equal, yet it is nevertheless difficult to say which one is obviously the better shift for the defense, your partnership should arbitrarily deem the lower of the two suits as the 'obvious-shift suit'.

Returning to the actual dummy but changing the other hands slightly we find a new scenario:

NORTH
♠ A 10 2
♡ Q
♢ A 2
♣ A Q J 9 8 4 3

WEST *(Marie)*
♠ Q 8 4
♡ A
♢ 8 7 6 5 4 3
♣ 6 5 2

```
      N
  W       E
      S
```

EAST *(Marcel)*
♠ K J 9 7 6 5
♡ 4 3 2
♢ K Q J 10
♣ ——

SOUTH
♠ 3
♡ K J 10 9 8 7 6 5
♢ 9
♣ K 10 7

Marie leads a low spade and Marcel desperately wants to tell her that he is void in clubs. If he plays a low spade he will be asking her to shift to dummy's obvious weakness: diamonds. A club shift would be most unusual but could be obtained, in this case, by signaling with an unusual card. For example, if Marcel drops the jack at trick one (or even the king!), he would be playing an unusual card which asks partner to shift to an unusual suit.

The fact that logic is called for at the bridge table often distresses the player who attends the duplicate merely for a night out on the town. Logic, not high-level arithmetic, is the bridge player's most critical tool. If the same card always meant the same thing, the game would be far less interesting. What affects these different meanings is how the card relates to the other cards of the same suit in a player's hand, and how it fits into the scenario of the play.

The same thing happens during the auction, but perhaps it is more obvious. For example, the bid of two clubs is strong when it is the opening bid, natural when it is in response to a suit, and Stayman when partner has opened one notrump. The same changes in meaning occur when you signal on defense. The seven-spot is high when you hold 7-6-5 but low when you've got 9-8-7. Likewise, the play of a jack could mean 'shift to an unusual suit' or simply 'shift to a high-ranking suit'.

Let's review these important signals one more time:

> Scenario A: Partner leads against a suit contract. Dummy wins the trick. Third hand, if possible, sends a message to the opening leader via a signal.

Case 1: *Dummy's two side suits are unequal, one much more tempting to shift to than the other.*

high spot card	encouraging
low card	discouraging, please make the obvious shift
unusual honor card	discouraging, please make an unusual shift

Case 2: *Dummy's two side suits are relatively equal; at first glance there is no clear advantage in playing one or the other.*

high spot card	encouraging
low card	discouraging, please shift to the lower-ranking side suit
unusual honor card	discouraging, please shift to the higher-ranking side suit
high card	continue

> Scenario B: Partner leads an ace or king against a suit contract. Dummy has a singleton in the suit led. Third hand, if possible, sends a message to the opening leader via a signal in the same manner.

low card	switch to the weaker side suit (or lower-ranking if relatively equal)
honor card	switch to stronger side suit (or the higher-ranking side suit)

Give count only when important

The count signal can be a lovely tool for the defense, enabling both defenders to gauge the shape of declarer's hand. Unfortunately, it can backfire when declarer makes more use of your signal than your partner. The next debacle from Marcel's list illustrates this point:

Exhibit #12   Dealer North
Board 21   North-South vulnerable

NORTH
♠ K J 10 7
♡ K 10 6 5
♢ A 5 2
♣ Q 4

WEST *(Marcel)*		EAST *(Marie)*
♠ 8 2		♠ Q 4
♡ J 4 3 2	N	♡ 9 7
♢ K Q J 10 6	W E	♢ 8 4 3
♣ 10 2	S	♣ K 9 7 6 5 3

SOUTH
♠ A 9 6 5 3
♡ A Q 8
♢ 9 7
♣ A J 8

WEST	NORTH	EAST	SOUTH
	1♢	pass	3NT
all pass			

Opening lead: ♢K	Trick 1	♢K	♢A	♢3	♢7
Result: making 7	Trick 2	♠J	♠4	♠A	♠8
	Trick 3	♠3	♠2	♠K	♠Q
	Trick 4	♣Q	♣K	♣A	♣10
	Trick 5	♡A	♡3	♡5	♡7
	Trick 6	♡Q	♡2	♡6	♡9
	Trick 7	♡8	♡4	♡10	♣3
	Trick 8	♡K	♢4	♢9	♡J
	Trick 9	♣4	♣5	♣8	♣2

Declarer claims (♣A and three spades)

This hand must have driven Marie crazy. The opponents
arrived in three notrump when they obviously belonged in spades.
After the diamond king was taken in dummy with the ace, declarer
called for dummy's spade jack. Marie did not make the error of
covering with the queen, and declarer went up ace, possibly with
the intention of finessing the other way around.

Meanwhile in the West seat, Marcel was busy giving count. His high-low in spades was duly noted by declarer who went up with the king on the second round. The spades were all good, so declarer tried an early club finesse. On dummy's club queen, Marie played her king (a correct cover), and South won the ace. Marcel, however, apparently too bored with the hand to play his cards up the line, got into the act again with an early echo in clubs. This play of the club ten set up a finesse later against Marie's nine.

Declarer next attacked the heart suit. Consistent to the end, Marcel high-lowed in hearts, and declarer took full advantage by finessing on the third round.

This is a shocking hand, and must have caused not a little commotion at the table. Giving count in every suit, Marcel was playing the part of a busy bee who feels he must have something to do on every deal, had a bet against himself, or simply didn't know any better and thought he was helping his partner count the hand. Whichever reason, it certainly exhibits the weakness of automatically giving count.

When to give count

The time to give count occurs when partner needs specific distributional information. These situations are usually obvious. For example, declarer is knocking out partner's ace of dummy's long suit, dummy is lacking entries, and partner needs to know how long to hold up. The next exhibit illustrates that even when dummy *has* a long suit, the count signal is not always the best signal.

Exhibit 13   North dealer
Board 1   Neither vulnerable

NORTH
♠ 10 5
♡ 10
◇ K Q J 9 8 6 3
♣ A K Q

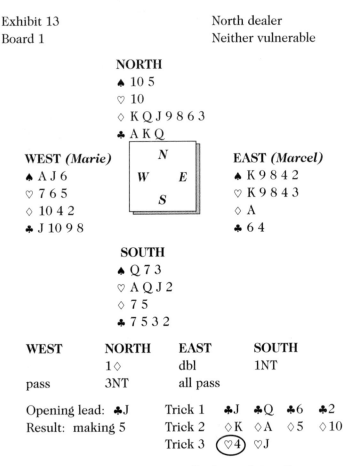

WEST *(Marie)*
♠ A J 6
♡ 7 6 5
◇ 10 4 2
♣ J 10 9 8

EAST *(Marcel)*
♠ K 9 8 4 2
♡ K 9 8 4 3
◇ A
♣ 6 4

SOUTH
♠ Q 7 3
♡ A Q J 2
◇ 7 5
♣ 7 5 3 2

WEST	NORTH	EAST	SOUTH
	1◇	dbl	1NT
pass	3NT	all pass	

Opening lead: ♣J   Trick 1   ♣J   ♣Q   ♣6   ♣2
Result: making 5   Trick 2   ◇K   ◇A   ◇5   ◇10
                            Trick 3   (♡4)   ♡J

Declarer claims 5

The bidding was questionable — Marcel's double with two five-card majors is doubly wrong. Granted, in 1942 the Michaels cue bid had not been invented. Still, double should show support for all the unbid suits. South was clever with his one notrump call, and three notrump became the final contract.

The club lead went to dummy's queen (Marcel relentlessly giving count). Next the diamond king was played. Under normal circumstances, Marie would have played the deuce of diamonds to show an odd number. But it was illogical to give count in this case for two reasons:

1) Marcel had already won the ace before the count could be given; and

2) holding up could not help the defense since dummy had plenty of entries.

Respect partner's signal

When I cross the street I wait for the green light and then go. If I see a truck suddenly passing through the red light, I wait. The truck is bigger than me. The same theory works at bridge. When I see a long suit in dummy and declarer tries to knock out partner's ace, I give count. But if dummy has lots of entries (or if partner wins the ace before I have had the chance to give count), I stop. What is the point of telling partner the count when it can't do any good?

Marie must have understood this. When Marcel won the diamond ace, she played the ten in an effort to show where her strength was. This was a suit-preference signal that should have led to a two-trick set. It was an excellent idea, and many players would not have thought of it. Yet upon reflection, no other meaning for the signal made any sense.

There can be few explanations for Marcel's actual heart return. Perhaps he thought Marie was giving count in diamonds, and therefore her play had no bearing on the hand. Left to his own astute judgment, Marcel tried to guess which major suit to shift to. He might have chosen the heart return because dummy had a singleton. There can be little doubt that he either thought Marie's diamond ten was a count signal or he hadn't even bothered to look at it. The former case is a sign of ignorance, the latter, motive for murder.

At trick one against a slam

Despite the overwhelming virtue of the attitude signal, there are times when count must be given at trick one in order to clear up the distribution for partner. The most obvious instance occurs against a suit contract: partner leads from an ace-king and you play high-low to show a doubleton. Coincidentally, this high-low may also be construed as an attitude signal, 'come on, give me a ruff'.

Two less frequent uses of count are just as automatic. In fact, you must be quite strict about it. The first case occurs against three notrump when partner leads an ace. This unusual lead shows a semi-solid suit such as: A-K-J-10-7-2 or A-K-Q-10-3. Partner is demanding that you drop an honor if you have one (so he will know if his suit is running). Otherwise, you must signal count. Then partner will continue with the king or will try to find an entry in your hand for a lead through declarer's honor (if he now knows it won't drop under his king).

A second case for count at trick one occurs when the defense must cash out immediately, and the location of the high cards is already known. This happens most often against five- or six-level contracts. A typical example occurs when partner is lucky enough to hold an ace-king on lead against a slam. When the first trick holds, he needs the count to decide whether or not to try cashing the second honor.

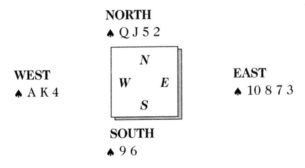

NORTH
♠ Q J 5 2

WEST
♠ A K 4

EAST
♠ 10 8 7 3

SOUTH
♠ 9 6

You are East. Assume the contract is six hearts and partner leads the spade king. If you give count you can tell partner whether or not declarer holds a second spade. In this case you play the eight to show an even number. Partner sees seven spades between his hand and dummy. There are six remaining between East and declarer. Since you show an even number, declarer cannot have a singleton.

Your play is automatic. Even if you desperately want a shift, your job here is to give count. That is the only message your partner cares about.

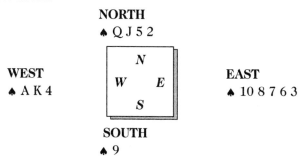

NORTH
♠ Q J 5 2

WEST
♠ A K 4

EAST
♠ 10 8 7 6 3

SOUTH
♠ 9

This time you play the three to show an odd number. Partner will read you for three or five spades, declarer for one or three. Partner won't know for sure if the ace is cashing, but he will probably assume it will not. (If indeed you held three spades and declarer three spades, partner's failure to cash the ace may not cost since declarer must find two discards for his remaining spades. Also, the bidding can sometimes help the opening leader determine if declarer has one or three cards in a suit.)

It is important in these cases to give count clearly; that is, to play your absolute lowest from odd or absolute highest from even (or second highest if the highest is an important honor). Third hand should not offer some middle card that partner will find difficult to read. For example:

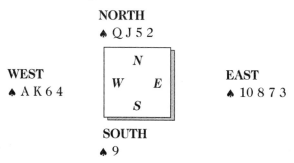

NORTH
♠ Q J 5 2

WEST
♠ A K 6 4

EAST
♠ 10 8 7 3

SOUTH
♠ 9

If on the lead of the king you drop the seven, how does partner know if you have 10-8-7-3 or 10-8-7?

Don't finesse for declarer

Exhibit #14
Board 12

West dealer
North-South vulnerable

NORTH
- ♠ 2
- ♡ 9 5 4 3 2
- ◇ Q 9 8 3
- ♣ Q 10 6

WEST *(Marcel)*
- ♠ 7 5 4
- ♡ A K J 6
- ◇ J 10 2
- ♣ J 9 2

EAST *(Marie)*
- ♠ K 6
- ♡ 10 8 7
- ◇ K 7 4
- ♣ K 8 5 4 3

SOUTH
- ♠ A Q J 10 9 8 3
- ♡ Q
- ◇ A 6 5
- ♣ A 7

MARCEL	NORTH	MARIE	SOUTH
pass	pass	pass	2♠
pass	2NT	pass	4♠
all pass			

Opening lead: ♡K
Result: making 5

Trick 1	♡K	♡2	♡7	♡Q
Trick 2	◇J	◇Q	◇K	◇A
Trick 3	◇5	◇10	◇3	◇7
Trick 4	♣2	♣10	♣K	♣A
Trick 5	♣7	♣9	♣Q	♣3
Trick 6	♠2	♠6	♠Q	♠5
Trick 7	♠A	♠4	...	♠K

Declarer claims

Marcel and Marie found themselves on defense a third consecutive time. (Were they switching positions on every hand to change their luck?) After a 1942 strong two-bid, South ended in four spades, and Marcel led the heart king. The heart position was clear as Marie played the seven and South the queen. At trick two Marcel got busy by shifting to the diamond jack. Hoping to find partner with the king (to set up a trick), Marcel accomplished his goal. His partner had the king. He got his trick. Unfortunately, he set up two tricks for declarer in the process, and also provided an entry to dummy for the spade finesse.

Passive defenses are often best

There are two types of defenses: active and passive. Active defense is necessary when the failure to cash tricks or set up tricks early will provide declarer with time to establish discards for his losers. Passive defense works when declarer cannot do anything with his losers but lose them. More often than not, this is the case. Yet bridge players love to attack suits, find 'killing' shifts and, in the process, give aid to the enemy.

The most recognizable time to remain passive is when dummy is weak. If you can put declarer back in his hand, he must lose the obvious tricks. But if you attack suits, you help declarer develop tricks. As we discussed earlier, this is because — unlike in chess and other war games — the first person to lead a suit is at a disadvantage.

When Marcel shifted to the jack of diamonds, declarer covered with dummy's queen, forced out Marie's king, and captured the most valuable trick possible with his ace:

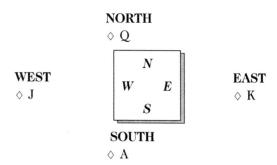

Compare this to what the trick would look like if declarer had to lead the suit from his hand:

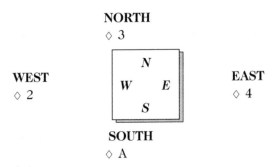

NORTH
◊ 3

WEST
◊ 2

EAST
◊ 4

SOUTH
◊ A

Leading to trick two is like making an opening lead with more information

NORTH *(dummy)*
♠ 2
♡ 9 5 4 3
◊ Q 9 8 3
♣ Q 10 6

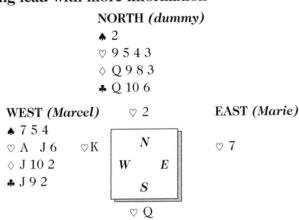

WEST *(Marcel)*   ♡ 2
♠ 7 5 4
♡ A J 6   ♡K
◊ J 10 2
♣ J 9 2

EAST *(Marie)*

♡ 7

♡ Q

Marcel, upon viewing dummy, should have realized that there was no need to attack a new suit. Whatever declarer had to lose could not be ruffed, so there was no reason to switch to trumps. South's losers could not be discarded on dummy's strong side suit since dummy didn't have one (unless declarer held ace-king third of diamonds, making the fourth diamond in dummy a winner).

A club shift looked worse than a diamond shift, and indeed contained the dreaded combination of queen-ten opposite the ace. A shift from the jack through the queen-ten is, unfortunately, a common, dreadful blunder perpetrated by only the very worst players. This is the only way declarer can make two tricks while losing none.

Thus, a club shift was a poor bet, a spade or diamond shift unnecessary. Like a good opening lead that gives nothing away, the lead to trick two, after leading from a safe ace-king combination, does not have to be an attack. Continuing hearts, knowing declarer held no more, would have been smart thinking. Let declarer do his own dirty work, so to speak.

When an army attacks a fortified position, casualties tend to be much greater among the attackers' troops than the defenders'. The same goes in bridge. Except for emergencies, keep the defense on the defense. Unless you see that a suit must be played, don't play it. When you are on opening lead you see only your own thirteen cards, so you must be careful. When dummy comes down, you see much more. It really shows great ineptitude to attack declarer's strength at trick two.

Count hands by distributional patterns

After Marcel's diamond shift, declarer played the suit right back. Marcel won his ten and, in what must have been a state of panic, shifted next to the forbidden club suit (giving declarer a finesse of his club jack and killing partner's king). Did he think declarer had:

♠ A K Q J 10 9 8 3 ♡ Q ◇ A 6 5 ♣ 7

No, declarer would have drawn trumps. More than likely Marcel was not thinking at all — a very poor state for a defender at the bridge table. The least he could have done was count declarer's distribution.

This is always easier than it sounds. Many players believe that counting distribution is work and bridge was meant to be fun. Granted, counting can be tedious, even just counting to thirteen. There are four suits to keep track of, and four different hands for each suit. Wouldn't it be easier to play cards intuitively? The answer, of course, is yes. But counting distribution at the bridge table should not be tiresome because you should not be counting in the traditional sense. That is (for example), 'five and one equals six and three is nine and four is thirteen'.

A better way is to 'see' the count. Every set of thirteen cards has distributional patterns which should be memorized by the bridge player before sitting down at the bridge table! There are only ten shapes that occur with any degree of frequency, five balanced and five unbalanced. Then there are a few wild patterns to remember, for practical purposes.

Balanced	Unbalanced	Wild
4 - 3 - 3 - 3	4 - 4 - 4 - 1	7 - 3 - 2 - 1
4 - 4 - 3 - 2	5 - 4 - 3 - 1	7 - 2 - 2 - 2
5 - 3 - 3 - 2	6 - 3 - 3 - 1	5 - 4 - 4 - 0
5 - 4 - 2 - 2	5 - 5 - 2 - 1	
6 - 3 - 2 - 2	6 - 4 - 2 - 1	

You should memorize these like a child learns the multiplication table. If someone were to rattle off any three numbers, say 5-2-4, you should be able to answer the last number (2 — the one bringing the count to thirteen) without thinking, and without counting.

Once you can do this, you will never have to count distribution at the bridge table in the traditional, slow fashion. You will intuitively see the shape of a suit. Instead of saying to yourself, 'Five and one equals six and three is nine and four is thirteen,' you will visualize '5-1-3... 4'.

Picture declarer's hand

Stanislavsky invented a memory-recall technique for theatrical training. The actor teaches himself to recall an incident in his life and applies it to the scene he is playing. In bridge, recalling a shape and applying it to a hand is good technique as well — and much simpler since there are only a few common shapes to remember. Choosing one or two which might fit declarer's hand is not difficult.

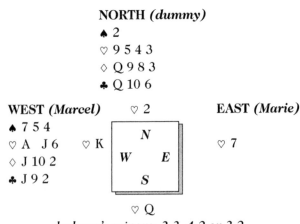

NORTH *(dummy)*
♠ 2
♡ 9 5 4 3
♢ Q 9 8 3
♣ Q 10 6

WEST *(Marcel)*   ♡ 2   EAST *(Marie)*
♠ 7 5 4   ♡ K
♡ A J 6   ♡ 7
♢ J 10 2
♣ J 9 2

♡ Q

declarer's minors: 3-3, 4-2 or 3-2

Returning to the last hand, for example, Marcel knew after trick one that declarer had a singleton heart and at least six spades. Was he 6-3-3-1, 6-4-2-1, or 7-3-2-1? Not a very difficult task, is it? Picturing the three probable distributions of declarer's minor suits, Marcel would have seen the futility of shifting to clubs or diamonds.

The importance of picturing shapes, then editing them like a film director, is paramount (sorry about that) to good defense. You should always return to the original shape when picturing. That way the patterns always add to thirteen. In the middle of the hand or near the end, edit the shape with a flashback to the beginning, then a quick cut to the present moment. The one thing you should never do is count cards!

Remember the bidding

Picturing high cards is not as easy as picturing distribution. You must return to the bidding to paint declarer's high-card palette. If he has opened one notrump you can guess his strength fairly well, but most of the time, you have to count points. This is because bidding is coded with high-card requirements. (Here is another reason why you should not be counting shape: you already have enough burden counting up the high-cards.)

• • •

In summary, the crux of defense is to form a picture of declarer's hand and play accordingly. Think of the shape as the stencil or drawing, lines on a canvas without color. Then the picture cards become the colors painted in. A good painter falls in love with the picture he has created on canvas. A good bridge defender falls in love with the image he has painted in his mind: declarer's closed hand mentally unveiled. Does a good homicide detective fall in love with a solution to the crime before it is proven?

I started to yawn. A hearty Indian lunch will do that to you. I rested my head on one of the torn pillows and tried to picture the night Marcel lay on a similar bed just one door down the corridor. Did the murderer confront him with his bridge crimes? Did Marcel put up a fight beyond the use of exclamation points next to the bids and plays that had done him in at the table? Did he use the pillows, the murder weapon, as a backrest for his own written arguments? When did the writing stop and the real-life murder begin? And who was Marie? Marie... Marie...

TOO MANY CONVENTIONS

Leave your brain some room for thinking

I had been asleep for a short time when I heard the water running. My eyelids were still heavy as I felt about under the pillows for the notes. The first thing that frightened me was seeing them stacked neatly on the desk across the room. The second thing was the realization that the shower was running in my bath. I certainly had not turned it on. The third, and most frightening thing of all, was when I heard the water stop.

Even though I was fully dressed, I climbed (fell) quickly out of bed and put on my trenchcoat. Then I sat down at the desk and pretended to look at my notes.

Bizarre thoughts crossed my mind. Did I dare turn my chair around to face the bathroom door? The mirror above the desk was old, cracked in a hundred places. If I peered into it, I could barely make out the difference between the window to the fire escape and the entrance to the bathroom. I heard a gargling sound followed by a toilet flushing. Then a barely perceptible creak in the door and kaleidoscopic movements in the mirror. There was no question about it. Somebody was standing behind me about ten feet across the room. I was sure that even if I had Emily Post's book handy it would not help. After all, what is the conventional way of greeting a stranger who has been showering in your bath?

"Don't turn around. I'm naked from the waist up."

There was something contradictory about that statement. Still, I did not turn around. But I thought it unfair of her to tell me the reason. My wife would have said, "Don't turn around, I've got my beauty cream on." That is a good reason not to look. When someone is naked from the waist up — well — that is not what most men would call a good reason to keep your back turned.

Taking a deep breath I answered, unable to hide a slight tremor in my voice, "Why are you naked from the waist up?"

"Because you used all of my towels."

Her voice was almost a whisper, deep and doleful. I had heard it before.

"D-do you have a gun?" I asked, rather stupidly.

"I tend not to shower with my gun. It rusts."

Suddenly I smelled that French perfume. Of course, it was Marie Gardner's perfume! Marie Gardner was standing naked from the waist up in my hotel room and the mirror had a hundred cracks in it! I tried to peer through one glossy spot near the bottom left frame. Then I spotted the wife's photograph. Shame engulfed me.

Nevertheless (and against my will), I forced my eyes to focus on that glossy spot. There was a reflection of a long golden leg. Was there any natural reason for me to be sitting there staring at a cracked image in a mirror while a beautiful, flesh and blood woman stood naked from the waist up on the other side? Why is it that a man's instincts control so much of his bodily functions? Must life be played out to the end, restricted by a million artificial conventions?

"I won't turn around," I said, "but I want to know why you are in my room taking a shower. Have you been following me? Are you trying to stop me from uncovering the mystery of Marcel Moskowitz?"

I heard her move a few steps closer to my chair. "You are really tempting me, you know," I threatened. "I'm a married man. If you move any closer I'm going to think about turning around my wife's photo." Then I felt it.

Sharp pain shot through my neck, my head spinning and spinning. After a few seconds of resistance I found myself face to face with her. Alas, my vision was blurring into oblivion. I stood up and fell right down again onto the moldy rug where I resumed my afternoon nap the unconventional way.

Don't play certain conventions

It felt like I had been asleep for years. You know how you start dreaming, you wake up a little and you want to go back to the dream? I turned over on my side and tried to remember what had happened. Either I was out of town at a bridge tournament, or in a room with a man lying dead on a bed. The dream was like a three-ring circus. There was some fellow dressed in a playing card in the fashion of Alice in Wonderland. His name was Mr. Two Clubs. And people were shoveling dirt onto him. Then they started pounding him with the shovel. He was hopping around singing like a lunatic. He didn't seem to know who he was. Suddenly he got up and started to run away. Everyone ran after him, chanting and screaming: "Hey Check Back, come back." "Arty, Arty Ficial." "Go Bro Zel go!" "Steady Cap A Letty!" "Stay man, stay!" He tripped at some point and fell on his head. "Inverted minor... puppet... landy... Michael, Michael... upper two." He rose and began to dance like a jester. He was mad, crazy, nuts. I wanted to do something. Anything to stop him. They had driven him to the point of insanity. "Stop," I yelled. "Stop!" A door slammed. Voices argued. I clutched a gun and ran after Mr. Two Clubs. My gun crumpled in my hand and spurted water. Something or someone was holding me back. I began to shake. Then I woke up for the second time, and I knew exactly where I was, though I had never been there before.

Rarely is reality more scary than a nightmare. For some reason my upper lip felt big and funny. As I opened my eyes I realized that this was not the room I had gone to sleep in. Then it occurred to me, I had not gone to sleep. I had been looking into a cracked mirror. There were pillows all around me. My head turned towards what was supposed to be the bathroom door, but there was no bathroom door. Nor was there a window on the right side of the bed. This had to be Room 623.

My left hand relaxed and out fell some scribbled notes. I could just make out the diagrams on the paper, bridge diagrams. These must have been the original photos. My legs were pinned to the bed. I felt like a corpse must feel if a corpse could feel. Desperately I longed for a human voice to let me know I was alive.

"Wake up Matthew. They're gone now."

Wrong human voice. It was her again. I looked down the bed and saw a woman resembling Marie Gardner, untying the rope that was around my ankles. But it was not the Marie Gardner I had come to love. My Marie was a honey-blonde. This Marie had jet-black hair.

My legs were stiff, but I could move them now. With the blood flowing in them again, I was able to pull myself up into a sitting position. Marie was fully dressed in a flaming-red pants suit, a white scarf around the collar of her jacket. She looked ready to go someplace special.

"It's boiling in here," she said. She was right. I was a puddle of sweat inside my trenchcoat. I pulled off the covers and raised my knees.

"Where is here?" I asked, knowing the answer.

"Where do you think you are?" she snapped back. "Room 623 of course."

I was sorry I had asked. But what was I doing here? Was I playing the part of the corpse, Marcel Moskowitz, forty years after his murder? The whole thing was gruesome. Was she playing the part of Marie? Is that why she was wearing a wig? When was I to be murdered? She looked at her watch. Then she leaned over and spoke to me in a softer manner.

"Listen Matthew. There is no time for explanations. I'm going to ask you to do something for me that you won't want to do. C'mon, you have to get out of those clothes."

With that she stood up again, reached down to her pants and unclasped the snap. Then she moved swiftly past my locked-tight knees to the closet. Taking out two pairs of blue jeans and old sneakers, she tossed one pair to me.

"Get into these on the double," she ordered, a sergeant talking to a private. I looked down at the patched jeans. They were too small.

"Can I at least know what the occasion is?"

She slipped her hand into her pocketbook and pulled something out. I ducked under a pillow.

"Here," she said, "fill this out."

It was a convention card.

The conventions I hate

I looked at it in disbelief, if not in horror.

General Approach ___**Modified K-S**___ Pair # _____

"It's already filled out," I quipped. "And it's not very pretty either."

She turned on me with murder in her eyes.

"Look. I have no time for your criticisms. You will play the conventions I'm familiar with and like it. If you want to add anything else you've got seven minutes to redo the card." Reaching into her pocket she pulled out a small, black rectangle. It was not a pocket mirror, however, because it unfolded before my eyes and reflected a yellowish light.

Good God! I had been acting like an idiot. Marie Gardner, like her father before her, was a detective on the Homicide Squad of the New York City Police Department!

I rose and quickly dressed, squeezing into the jeans. We left the room through the fire escape only to crawl through another window a few feet away. We were back home in Room 625.

"Here, put this on." She handed me a wig of blond hair tied in a pony tail. "There's no bath in Room 623. That's why I was using your shower."

"It seems to me you also used the bath."

"It's a hot August day and I'm a clean cop. Go ahead, fix yourself in the mirror."

I received a shock when I saw my face. My mustache was missing. The wig was even worse. Was I supposed to be a woman or a 1970s hippie?

Out the fire escape she led me, into the courtyard and through the back entrance to the kitchen of the Taj Mahal. "Do we have time for a bite?" I inquired, though I was not really hungry.

She gave me a nasty look and marched straight through the dining area. I passed the waiter and grabbed him by the shoulders.

"Remember me? Earlier today, without the wig. I had a mustache... here."

"No, sorry; please be seated."

"Listen to me. You have a little boy you were buying gifts for. I gave you some papers to mail to Karachi. Remember? Did you mail them okay?"

"Ahh, Mister Matthew. Yes. What is wrong with your hair? Here, come here. I keep the papers here behind the menus." He took the envelope off the counter and handed it to me.

"*What are you talking about?*" I screamed. "You were supposed to mail these!"

"Ahh. Now I see. But your wife, she took the papers and gave to me these to keep here."

"My wife? What wife?"

"That wife, Mister Matthew." He pointed to Marie who was halfway out the front door.

"That's no wife, that's a cop." I snatched the envelope and looked inside. There were only blank sheets where the photostats had been. Rushing out to the street I overtook Marie.

"What did you do with my copy of Marcel's notes?"

"Forget your stupid copy. I threw them in the hotel incinerator."

"What! Which side are you on? The only other copy I have is inside... inside..." I wasn't wearing my trenchcoat.

"Inside my pants," she said, patting her rear. "These notes are your death warrant, so you're better off without them."

I shook my head in dismay as she led me to the front of the

Embassy Hotel. Those notes were the only evidence that Marcel spent his last night at the Bucket O' Blood Bridge Club.

"Listen," she insisted, "you'll have to trust me. You're the bridge teacher, I'm the detective. Those notes must not be seen by anyone else. This case is being closed by dawn tomorrow one way or the other. Either we solve the murder or the murderer gets rid of us... permanently."

"I strongly prefer the former."

"Then do what I say. There will be two men at the duplicate tonight who were associates of my father. I've been staked out in Room 623 since last Tuesday. I spotted them in the hotel today. Why do you think we had that little dress rehearsal this afternoon? After the game they will be coming back to the room."

"In that case, I think I'd better check out now."

She grabbed my arm. "I already checked you out. They're coming back to Room 623, not 625. When they see you disguised as the reincarnated Marcel Moskowitz, they will be so scared, they'll confess everything."

We entered the elevator with a few other people who were discussing bidding. 'Penthouse' was pushed. Somebody turned and thought he recognized me. Then he shook his head.

"Why are they coming to Room 623?" I whispered into the detective's ear.

"To kill you," she whispered back.

"That's a lousy reason," I insisted.

We got off the elevator and sat down as soon as we found table thirteen, East-West. "I prefer North-South," I said.

"Shut up and finish the card," she answered. "We sit East-West for mobility."

"Good thinking." All the better to dodge bullets. Then I glanced back at the convention card, took a pencil from the table and crossed out weak notrump. In its place I scribbled, '15+ to 18-' and with one stroke of the pencil I felt much better.

As I went down the card I could see Marie had been brought up on all the wrong systems. She had gone to get some coffee and our first-round opponents, two lovely, elderly ladies sat down North and South. In the time it took Marie to stir in some cream and grab two pieces of sponge cake before it was all gone, I had drawn a line through the more detestable conventions on the front of the card:

NOTRUMP OPENING BIDS

15+ to 18-

1NT _12 to 14_   3NT

2♣ Non-Forc. ■ ~~Stayman~~   Solid Suit ■   *Gambling*

2◇ Forc. ■ ~~Stayman~~   ~~No ace or king outside~~

　　　　　　　~~Lebensohl~~

MAJOR OPENINGS	MINOR OPENINGS
RESPONSES	RESPONSES
Double raise forcing ☐ ~~Limit~~ ■	Single ~~raise forcing~~ ■
Conv. raise: 2NT ■ *Jacoby*	
1NT forcing ■	

2◇　WK. ☐
　　　INT. ■　　　　~~Flannery~~
　　　STR. ☐

OTHER CONVENTIONAL CALLS

~~New minor forcing~~

I turned to the back of the card and also crossed out:

~~Brozel over one notrump~~

Michaels cuebid in the majors (other major
　~~and unknown minor)~~
~~Lebensohl over takeout doubles~~
Leads: vs. notrump ~~10 or 9 promises 0 or 2 higher~~

"Young woman, er, young man, whatever you are," said the lady sitting North. "You had better fix that convention card before we start. There is no way I can read this sloppy writing."

"I'm not finished," I told her. (Isn't it irritating how your first-round opponents study your convention card as if they're going to play a hundred boards against you?) "Besides," I said indignantly, "we're only playing two lousy hands."

"Well! I say! Impertinent... (examining me out of the corner of one eye) something or other."

I unbuttoned my jeans and straightened my wig. Where the heck was my partner? There she was winding about the tables carefully juggling two cups of hot coffee. I was pleased to see her. I suppose it takes only one common enemy to inaugurate a new ally. Marie sat down and handed me a cup. "Drink this," she ordered.

I brought the Styrofoam to my lips, then noticed some peculiar white bubbles. "I take my coffee black," I said, pushing it across the table.

"Drink it. It has Benzedrine. It will keep you alert."

"You drugged my coffee?"

The white-haired North looked aghast. "Youth and drugs!"

"And the alert system!" her partner added.

I grabbed the cup and drank up spitefully. Meanwhile Marie was surveying my changes to the card. "But these are all my favorite conventions," she protested.

"Look, I left you five-card majors and forcing notrump. What more can I do?" Suddenly I spotted something. "Damn, I forgot to cross out Jacoby Two Notrump." She seized my wrist.

"Stop it," she pleaded. "That's the only forcing raise I know."

The woman sitting North pushed a board over to my side of the table. I took out the cards and shuffled.

"One spade-three spades is now our forcing raise," I explained.

"One spade-three spades is limit," insisted Marie.

"I crossed out limit raises. Nobody ever knows what a limit raise looks like and nobody ever knows when to bid on after a limit raise. So I play all jumps are forcing."

Did I actually note a tear in her eye? "Look," I continued, "you're the detective and I'm the bridge teacher."

"But I was taught to play limit raises. That's all I know."

The director's voice was loud and raucous. "Begin play please. Two boards per round, twelve rounds, average is 132. Any pair who gets a seventy-five percent game will win the running jackpot. Tonight it's... uh... twenty-three dollars. Good luck."

"There is no time to argue over this," she said. "We can fix up the card as we go along. For now we'll play it as I know it. Besides, your wife just walked into the room and is heading for table three, so keep your voice down."

My wife! What the **** was she doing here? Talk about wanting to crawl under a table. I quickly covered my face with my cards and peeked out between the hearts and clubs. Good God, there she was sitting North at table three! We were table thirteen and there were only sixteen tables in the section. We had no chance of skipping her. As my cards touched my upper lip I remembered my mustache was gone. I leaned over to Marie. "Is my wig on straight?"

"Don't worry. She'll never know it's you."

"I dare say you people chat a great deal and never make a bid." North looked at the board and realized she was the dealer. She passed. Marie opened one notrump, weak I'm afraid. The next hand passed. My hand was:

♠ A K 6 4   ♡ 4 3 2   ◇ 6 5   ♣ Q 9 8 3

I started to bid two clubs. Then I realized a weak notrump is twelve to fourteen points. With nine points in my hand there was no chance for game, so I passed. North grabbed the convention card and took out a magnifying glass.

"Well, which is it, strong or weak?"

Before I could answer her partner had a card out on the table, ready to lead.

"Your partner hasn't passed yet," cried Marie.

"Pardon me," she answered. Back went the card, North passed, and out came the lead again. I tabled the dummy. They took the first five heart tricks, followed by the ace-king of diamonds. Down one. Here were our two hands:

ME		MARIE
♠ A K 6 4	N	♠ Q J 9 8
♡ 4 3 2	W E	♡ 6 5
◇ 6 5	S	◇ Q J 10 9
♣ Q 9 8 3		♣ A K 6

The illustrious auction

ME	NORTH	MARIE	SOUTH
	pass	1NT	all pass

Marie shook her head in irritation. Three spades was cold our way. The weak notrump had got us a bottom on the very first board.

"Unlucky," she said. "Usually I get good scores with the weak notrump."

"Usually I get good scores by playing the best contract," I remarked, trying not to sound too sarcastic. She groaned. Yes, that's the word for it. It was a mean groan if I ever heard one.

Then she pulled out the cards to the next hand, mumbling just loud enough for me to hear, "The weak notrump is a gambling bid I admit, but it puts the opponents at a distinct disadvantage."

I looked at our opponents. They didn't seem to need our help to be at a distinct disadvantage. "We play strong from now on," I said firmly.

Marie studied her cards, groaned again, looked around, and finally, with torture written all over her face, opened one notrump. North grabbed the card again, this time, out of turn. Suddenly I heard a bang and a shriek! Marie had come down on the old lady's hand with one of her famous karate chops. The woman was screaming in pain. I was afraid the whole room would rush over to the table (including my wife), but then I should know bridge players better. There was only a momentary pause, and soon everyone went back to their cards. The director meandered over.

Marie eyed the wounded woman with a wicked stare. "Well it serves her right; it's the only way to stop this sort of thing."

The director, a young man twenty pounds or so underweight, asked if anything was wrong. North was now holding her wrist in a sling of handkerchiefs, her hand dangling like a flag on a calm day. "No," I answered. "What could be wrong? North tried to look at our convention card out of turn and my partner broke her wrist." The director took out his rule book, thumbed through it for a minute, then asked us to continue play.

Drying her tears, North sorted her cards again with her five remaining fingers and held her head erect. "It's all right, Mabel. Just bid." Mabel overcalled two spades. With partner opening one strong notrump, and a two spade overcall to my right, I examined my hand:

♠ A 2   ♡ K 9 5 2   ◇ A 4 2   ♣ 8 7 6 3

I started to say three spades, Stayman, when I realized we were playing Lebensohl. A fast (immediate) cuebid would deny a stopper and and a slow one (bidding 2NT first) would show a stopper. So I bid two notrump, forcing Marie to bid three clubs, and planning to come back with three spades on the next round. Before my partner could alert, my left-hand opponent raised to three spades. The bidding came back to me:

ME	NORTH	MARIE	MABEL
		1NT	2♠
2NT	3♠	pass	pass
?			

I could no longer use Stayman to locate a 4-4 heart fit, so I took my best shot by bidding three notrump. Unfortunately, partner did have four hearts; and though Marie played the hand nicely (aided somewhat by two revokes from her wounded opponent), we scored only 600 when 620 would have been easy in the correct four heart game.

As we moved to table fourteen I found a red pen on the floor with the word 'Bellevue' on it. I took our convention card and put a steady line through Lebensohl. Marie was ticked. "Just because the convention doesn't work doesn't mean it's a bad convention."

"True," I answered, "but it's a good indication."

The pair ahead of us was still playing. Marie was annoyed. She glanced back at table thirteen where two mild-mannered men sat down. One was quite elderly and wore a seersucker suit with a blue bow tie. The other, middle-aged, had on a fashionable white summer suit. "Hurry up," she whispered to me.

"Hurry up what?" I asked.

"Those two. The ones following us East-West." I looked again. The man in the seersucker eyed me inquisitively and said something in a German accent to his partner. The younger man glanced in my direction and put his hand in his inside jacket pocket.

"They are the men," she said. "Father's cronies. The ones who are trying to cover up Marcel's murder."

I started to hit the deck, but the man in white pulled out a pen, not a gun, and gave it to his partner. "Are they the ones who are trying to kill me?"

"Don't worry," she said patting my hand, "they won't try anything here."

I spotted my wife at the refreshment table. Quickly I pushed

Marie's arm away. What the hell was I doing here playing bridge with this woman detective? If my wife recognized me, it would mean *sayonara*. "Why don't we leave now?" I suggested. "I mean, why are we risking life, limb, and marriage?"

"Shut up, they'll hear you. Nobody can recognize us. Trust me, these guys are more nervous than you are. They think we have evidence against them, but we have nothing conclusive. Tonight, after the game, when we reenact the crime — that's when we trap them."

"You don't really think I'm going to play the corpse?" She pushed me against the wall. Lord, she was strong.

"Be quiet. You will do what I say or I'll tell your wife things that she will not take kindly."

I sat down and sorted the next hand. How had I got myself mixed up in a murder case? Two killers following me and one over-zealous female detective blackmailing me. I looked at my sixteen high-card points and made a silent prayer. Get me out of this mess, Lord, and I'll never investigate another murder.

I was dealer and I opened one notrump. North passed and Marie responded two diamonds, forcing Stayman, which I alerted. South, a serious looking young man, thought for a few seconds and passed. We proceeded to our 4-4 spade fit. However, the suit broke 5-0 and I went down two tricks. When the score slip was opened we noticed the other score was plus 500 our way. The hand had been declared by South in two spades, doubled.

Marie grabbed South's cards:

♠ Q J 10 9 4   ♡ —   ◊ 8 7 3   ♣ A J 9 8 2

After Marie's forcing Stayman, South had made a wise decision not to enter the auction. The young man smiled and said, "They were probably using simple two clubs Stayman at the other table. But your two diamonds game force warned me against overcalling."

His partner, who looked like his mother, added her two cents. "Good pass, Herbert. I've always taught my children to stay out of auctions that don't belong to them."

I thought Marie was going to hit her. Even I had to hold back the urge to strangle her. On the next board we finally got something back when the mother opened the bidding with three notrump. This ended the auction and Marie led the heart queen. Here was the full deal:

NORTH *(Mother)*
♠ 9 2
♡ 5
◇ 10 8 7
♣ A K Q J 7 4 2

WEST *(Me)*
♠ 10 8 7 4
♡ A 7 6 2
◇ K 5 3 2
♣ 10

```
      N
  W       E
      S
```

EAST *(Marie)*
♠ K J 3
♡ Q J 10 9 8
◇ J 9 4
♣ 5 3

SOUTH *(Herbert)*
♠ A Q 6 5
♡ K 4 3
◇ A Q 6
♣ 9 8 6

We took the first five heart tricks. Obviously three notrump should have been declared by South, who held all the tenaces. Herbert was quick to criticize. "I told you the gambling three notrump is an inferior convention." His partner looked hurt and reached for his hand like a lover, not a mother. "Don't touch me," he continued, "and don't bid notrump unless you have some stoppers." She retracted her arm and took out a pillbox.

"I don't know why I put up with you," she sniffled. Then she smiled at him. "Yes, I do."

Meanwhile Marie had taken my red pen and crossed out Two-way Stayman and the Gambling Three Notrump from our convention card. I was pleased to see that she was willing to change her ways, unlike the majority of stubborn duplicate players.

At table fifteen we started off with another good score. South opened one spade and North raised to three, limit. South held:

♠ A 8 6 5 2   ♡ K 10 8   ◇ Q J 6   ♣ K 2

Should South pass or go on to game?

With only thirteen points and a balanced hand, South intelligently elected to pass. Partner held:

♠ K Q 7 3   ♡ 4 2   ◇ K 10 7 3 2   ♣ Q 5

Game wasn't cold, but it was pretty good. In fact, the heart ace was right and declarer made ten tricks.

On the next board our run of good luck ran out. I opened one heart and Marie bid two notrump (forcing raise). I held:

♠ 9 8 7　♡ K Q J 9 2　♢ 2　♣ A Q 5 4

Although I had a minimum opening bid, the convention forced me to rebid three diamonds (which showed a singleton). Marie held:

♠ 10 4 2　♡ A 10 8 7　♢ A 10 5 4　♣ K J

We stopped safely in four hearts, but unfortunately gave the opening leader too much information. He had Q-J-6-3 of spades and Q-J-9-8 of diamonds. Since he knew I had a singleton diamond he led a spade and held me to ten tricks, +420. The pairs who bid a straightforward four hearts without revealing the singleton received a diamond lead, and made two overtricks (by discarding two spades on two club winners) for +480.

Marie took me aside. "It doesn't make sense to show your singleton if you're not interested in slam." What could I say? I had been teaching this for years. "Then why," she continued, "do good players use this convention?"

"Players get a thrill from reaching twenty-six-point slams with perfectly-fitting hands. They don't realize that bridge is a percentage game, and the chance of finding the rare perfecta is remote. Most of the time they just tip their hands to the defenders."

Out came the red pen as she crossed off two more items on our card. This was going to be a constructive evening after all, at least for Marie's bridge game.

At the next three tables more conventions came up and were just as quickly discarded by Marie. Sometimes we suffered the disaster, sometimes the opponents took a turn. Here are some of the lessons she learned:

OPENER		RESPONDER
♠ A K J 2	N	♠ Q 9 8
♡ K 2	W　　E	♡ 5 4
♢ A 3 2	S	♢ K 10 9
♣ A 9 8 7		♣ K 10 6 3 2

OPENER	RESPONDER
1♣	1NT
3NT	all pass

Three notrump went one down when a heart was led through the king. East should have have responded two clubs. However, inverted minor-suit raises got in the way of normal bidding. Since two clubs would have shown a ten-point hand, and three clubs would have been preemptive, East was forced to respond one notrump. The most fundamental bidding objective is to declare from the right side of the table whenever possible. Obviously, West should declare here, and would declare if the bidding went normally, beginning with a simple one club-two club raise.

Then:

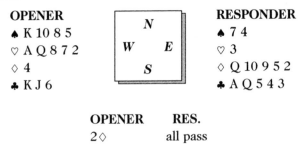

OPENER		RESPONDER
♠ K 10 8 5		♠ 7 4
♡ A Q 8 7 2		♡ 3
◊ 4		◊ Q 10 9 5 2
♣ K J 6		♣ A Q 5 4 3

OPENER	RES.
2◊	all pass

A fine auction. Two diamonds, 'Flannery', showing five hearts and four spades, was a contract to remember. Some pairs played in the optimum two club contract after opening one heart and rebidding two clubs over a forcing notrump. Other pairs passed the one notrump response to one heart and made seven tricks. The pair playing Flannery got a zero and had only their convention to thank.

Next:

OPENER		RESPONDER
♠ 3 2		♠ A J 7 5 4
♡ A K 4 2		♡ 9 8
◊ Q 8 7 4		◊ 3
♣ K Q 7		♣ J 9 8 6 4

OPENER	NORTH	RESP	SOUTH
1◊	pass	1♠	pass
1NT	pass	2♠	all pass

Over the one notrump rebid North was stuck. North-South were playing two clubs (new minor) as a checkback for spade support or four hearts. If North-South were in the habit of raising immediately with three-card support they would have no need for a check-back. Then North could bid both his suits naturally and land in a reasonable contract. A few pairs made one notrump. Two spades went down after diamond plays tapped the north hand. Two clubs, however, was laydown and usually produced an overtrick.

WEST			EAST
♠ K 9 8 7 5 2			♠ Q 4 3
♡ 2			♡ A 9 8 5 4 3
◇ K 10 2			◇ Q 6
♣ A 8 5			♣ 10 9

WEST	NORTH	EAST	SOUTH
			1NT
dbl	3◇	all pass	

On this hand, West's double of one notrump was 'Brozel', show-ing a one-suiter, with the suit unknown. Two pairs were playing 'Cappelletti' in which the bid of two clubs similarly shows a one-suiter, unknown. None of the East players facing this descriptive call uncovered the unknown suit. Needless to say, it was difficult for East to support West's unknown suit. (Marie was quick to cross this one out.)

Many supporters of these electrifying conventions claim they work well when the partner of the one notrump bidder remains silent. If one could gag one's opponent, I suppose almost any convention requiring two rounds of bidding could work well.

Proponents of the natural overcall, in which (going against all modern trends) the bidder actually has length in the suit mentioned, believe they have a better chance of finding a fit.

Conventions which leave partner guessing do little to improve one's score. The following example was instrumental to my losing a major team championship a few years ago:

South dealer   Both vulnerable

NORTH
♠ Q J 5
♡ K 9 7 5 4
◇ 10 9 8 7 6
♣ —

WEST		**EAST**
♠ A 8 6 4 3	N	♠ 9
♡ —	W E	♡ 10 8 6
◇ Q J 5	S	◇ K 4 2
♣ A Q 10 8 7		♣ K J 9 5 4 3

SOUTH
♠ K 10 7 2
♡ A Q J 3 2
◇ A 3
♣ 6 2

WEST	NORTH	EAST	SOUTH
			1♡
2♡	4♡	pass	pass
dbl	all pass		

Opening lead: ◇ Q
Result: making 5

My teammates, East-West, were playing 'Michaels Cuebids'
(showing the other major and an unknown minor). West cuebid
two hearts, planning to show his clubs over partner's two notrump
response.

North, however, rudely jammed the auction. West could not
venture five clubs with any degree of safety, so he tried a delayed
takeout double. East guessed that West's second suit was diamonds
and took a sure profit in four hearts doubled. The sure profit turned
out to be minus 790 instead of six clubs making, plus 1370, a mere
swing of 2160 points.

Getting back to the evening's duplicate, the following set-up
caused no small amount of grief:

WEST		EAST
♠ 5	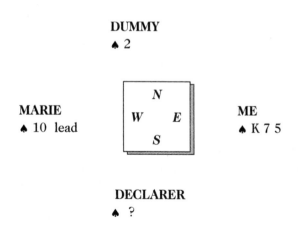	♠ Q J 6 4
♡ A 10 7 4		♡ 6 3 2
◇ A J 6 4 3		◇ K Q 7
♣ A 9 8		♣ J 3 2

WEST	NORTH	EAST	SOUTH
			2♠
dbl	pass	2NT	pass
3♣	pass	3NT	all pass

Here, Lebensohl, dressed up in another dreaded form, forced East to choose between passing two spades doubled (disaster), bidding a three-card suit (defined as a constructive action at the three level), or bidding two notrump (which forces three clubs from partner in order to sign off somewhere... but where?).

East did his best by bidding two notrump, no doubt hoping his partner would forget the convention and pass. Unfortunately, West remembered and bid three clubs. East, his back to the wall, tried three notrump. West alerted but couldn't recall what this intricate sequence meant, and passed. Three notrump was only down one, which these days really *is* 'good bridge'!

On the next deal my partner led the ten of spades against three notrump. This was the spade layout from my point of view:

DUMMY
♠ 2

MARIE		ME
♠ 10 lead		♠ K 7 5

DECLARER
♠ ?

We were playing that the lead of the ten or nine shows zero or two higher honors. I'm sure this is a fine convention for psychics or players with X-ray vision. Unfortunately I, a mere mortal, had to guess whether my partner was leading from A-J-10, in which case I should play the king and return the suit, or 10-9-8, in which case I should not put up the king into declarer's A-Q-J.

I won't go into the whole hand because it is irrelevant. I sat there for two minutes or so and finally guessed wrong. This convention must have been invented by the same contortionist who has half the world bidding unknown suits. After the hand, we switched our lead signals to 'jack denies and ten implies'. That means the jack lead is always from J-10-9-8, and the ten is led from an interior sequence such as K-J-10-9 or Q-10-9-8.

The conventions I like

We rose from the table and reviewed our convention card. It was a sea of red crossings-out. However, most of the harmful conventions had been eliminated, and a few good ones added. Here were some of our subtractions and additions:

~~12-14 notrump~~	**15+ to 18-**
~~Two-way Stayman~~	**4-suit Jacoby Transfers**
~~Lebensohl~~	
Gambling 3NT	
~~with nothing outside~~	**2 outside stoppers**
~~Limit raises in the majors~~	**Forcing jump raises**
~~Jacoby 2NT~~	**Forcing jump raises**
~~Inverted minors~~	
~~Flannery~~	
~~New minor forcing~~	
Over one notrump:	
~~Brozel~~	**Landy (2 clubs for majors)**
Cuebid in major shows	**Color cues (other major**
~~other major and~~	**and a minor of**
~~unknown minor~~	**the same color)**
~~Lebensohl over takeout doubles~~	
Leads vs. notrump:	
~~10 or 9 = 0 or 2 higher~~	**Jack denies, 10 implies**

There are other good conventions, but I was unwilling to play them in a casual partnership. Had I been playing with my wife, I would have added these:

The Granovetters

Over 1 notrump:
>   4-suit Jacoby (3♣ transfers to 3◊)
>   1NT - 3◊ forcing with both minors
>   1NT - 3♡ or 3♠ — natural and forcing
>   Transfers at 3 level after interference over our 1NT

One of a major opening:
>   May be a 4-card suit
>   1NT response not forcing
>   1 M - 3NT — a splinter somewhere
>   1 M - 4♣ — raise, 1G or better
>   1 M - 4◊ — good preemptive raise to game
>   Drury

1NT response to 1♣ shows 8-10
Weak jump shifts by an unpassed hand
All second-round jumps by responder are forcing
Responder's second-round bid of 2NT is forcing

Negative doubles
Responsive doubles (only after we overcall)
4♣ response to a preempt is a slam try in opener's suit
Key Card Blackwood (only when suit is bid and raised)
Dopi, Depo when they interfere over Blackwood
Leads:
>   Fourth best leads
>   Ace from A-K
>   MUD (Middle from three small)

These conventions and stylistic bids were chosen over a period of three years. In order to play them with a new partner, I would have had to sit down and go over each bid in detail, then bid some randomly dealt hands to practice each convention. But I was playing with Marie, not my wife... MY WIFE! Talk about escapism at the bridge table! I had become so wrapped up in the bridge game, I had forgotten that Pamela was at table three! The round was about to be called when I rushed over to the director to remind him of the skip in our section.

"No skip until the next round," he informed me nonchalantly, not realizing the consequences it had for my marriage. I searched my pockets for my wallet. Dammit, I was wearing those stupid

jeans. The jeans! I could barely get myself into them let alone
a wallet. I offered him a hundred
dollars on credit to call the skip
immediately. He laughed, and
told me it wasn't fair to the other
players who also had to play
against Mrs. Granovetter. As I
raised my offer to a thousand, he
stubbornly called the change.
Marie grabbed me by the collar.

"We better go to the next table
now. Otherwise we'll be conspicuous." Conspicuous! Look at me! I
glanced around for a paper bag to put
on my head. "Trust me," she said,
(how many times could I trust this woman who had broken into my
room, knocked me out cold, dragged me into a bed, shaved off my
mustache, and blackmailed me?) "nobody will recognize you."

"What about my voice? Can we order some bidding boxes
quickly?"

I let my voice fall and rise in vastly unauthentic modulations as
I staggered over to table three resisting the temptation to jump out
the nearest window. When I sat down, I quickly took out the first
hand and put my head under the table, pretending to count my
cards. The button to my pants was still open, and I sucked in my
stomach to close it. The wife was wearing her new alligator shoes.
Then I noticed my own partner was wearing two different-colored
socks. The guy on my right was very chicly dressed in Guccis,
dark-blue Italian trousers with cuffs... The guy on my right! I
looked up at him for the first time. Wait a second. While the cat's
away! Who the hell was he? So far as I knew, my wife didn't have
any bridge students who looked like movie stars. He sported a well-
manicured, Clark Gable mustache which gave him quite a debonair
look (the bastard).

The wife loves mustaches, I thought, as my cards brushed up
against the bare white skin above my lip.

THE SLAM ZONE

Slam tries are made at the four-level in long suits, not short suits

Yes, I was upset at finding my wife out on the town with a bridge partner who looked like Clark Gable, but what could I do? There I was, looking like Phyllis Diller, trying to conceal my identity from that very same wife for two full boards. I adjusted my ponytail and threw Gable a mean stare. He ignored me, and promptly began the proceedings with a resonant, "No bid".

My hand was:

♠ A K 8 6 4 2   ♡ K 2   ◊ A 9 8 5 3   ♣ —

I decided to go with a Yiddish accent and bid, "Vun spade." The wife rolled her eyes and passed. She was obviously fooled by my accent and thought I was one of the typical weirdos who often show up at the local West Side duplicate.

Marie thought for a second, then jumped to three spades. "No bid," on my right. I contemplated slam, perhaps a grand slam. Of course my next call should be four diamonds. It's best to begin a slam try with a second suit so that partner can judge whether she has good or bad values. If she has a good-fitting hand she will go past game or insist on slam. If she has only a fair-fitting hand, she can cuebid, but not go beyond game. If she has a poor-fitting hand, she must sign off in game.

The auction having gone:

ME	THE WIFE	MARIE	GABLE
			no bid
1♠	pass	3♠	no bid
?			

I checked my hand again:

♠ A K 8 6 4 2   ♡ K 2   ◇ A 9 8 5 3   ♣ —

It was time to introduce the diamond suit and initiate a slam try. However, peering through my club void, I could see the wife studying our convention card, then examining my face a little too closely. She must have realized that something was afoot, since very few duplicate players use forcing major-suit raises nowadays, one of those very few being her husband. Add to that the fact that the wife is not somebody who tends to make a habit of staring at opponents at the bridge table, and I could smell suspicion growing in her mind. In order to squelch that suspicion I would have to do something to convince her I was not her husband.

Since she knew me like a book, I decided to start out with a four club cuebid. Her husband would never do that. He would rather give up the game. She knew it, and when she eventually saw my thirteen cards she would know it couldn't be me.

Stop all those cuebids

Over my four club bid, the wife passed and Marie bid four diamonds! Gable gave it another no bid, and I wondered how the heck my partner could cuebid diamonds when I had the ace. Perhaps she was one of those mad-scientist bidders who likes to cuebid every second-round control in sight. Well, playing my part, I duly rebid four hearts on my king doubleton. The wife frowned (she must have been thinking, 'Matthew would never make so many cuebids') and passed. Marie sung out five clubs, Gable no bid it again, and not missing a trick, I tried five diamonds. When this got to my partner, she called five hearts (ace? singleton? who knows?) and when it got back to me I threw in a six club call that should have been good enough to detonate most partnerships.

Marie hesitated. Was she thinking of passing? She finally called six diamonds and, assuming she was cuebidding third-round diamond control, I cuebid my third-round heart control with six hearts. I think at this point the change of round was called and we hadn't even completed the auction to the first board. Marie bid seven clubs. I corrected to seven spades which finally ended what was sure to become a candidate for auction of the year. Here it is one last, excruciating time (explanations submitted by various scientific experts), both hands unabashedly revealed:

M.G.
(disguised as mad cuebidder)
♠ A K 8 6 4 2
♡ K 2
◇ A 9 8 5 3
♣ —

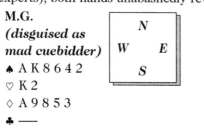

MARIE
(a real mad cuebidder)
♠ Q J 7 5
♡ A J 5 4
◇ K 4 2
♣ K 3

1♠ (normal)

4♣ (first in a series of cuebids in the modern style)

4♡ (cuebid, first- or second-round control)

5◇ (first-round control, though how anyone could distinguish it from second-round is a mystery)

6♣ (third-round control since first and second rounds have already been called)

6♡ (3rd third-round control in a row — setting a record that good bridge players hope will never be broken)

7♠ (failure to cuebid fourth-round control of hearts shows lack of knowledge in modern style)

3♠ (forcing)

4◇ (lowest indiscriminate first- or second-round control)

5♣ (control; spurning old-fashioned Blackwood)

5♡ (another in a series of first-round controls finally popping out of the woodwork here at the five level)

6◇ (trump-asking bid for a grand slam, but interpreted as third-round control)

7♣ (back on track, lovely bid to show fourth-round club control in case fourteen tricks are available)

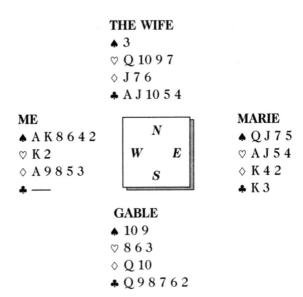

THE WIFE
♠ 3
♡ Q 10 9 7
◇ J 7 6
♣ A J 10 5 4

ME
♠ A K 8 6 4 2
♡ K 2
◇ A 9 8 5 3
♣ —

MARIE
♠ Q J 7 5
♡ A J 5 4
◇ K 4 2
♣ K 3

GABLE
♠ 10 9
♡ 8 6 3
◇ Q 10
♣ Q 9 8 7 6 2

The wife led a trump and Marie was ticked when I didn't claim seven. "I figured you for the king-queen of hearts when you bid six hearts," she complained. I ignored her. Running the trumps I came down to seven red cards in my hand. On the last trump the wife could not hold four hearts, three diamonds, and the club ace.

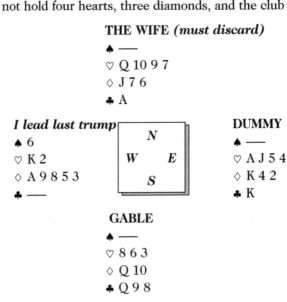

THE WIFE *(must discard)*
♠ —
♡ Q 10 9 7
◇ J 7 6
♣ A

I lead last trump
♠ 6
♡ K 2
◇ A 9 8 5 3
♣ —

DUMMY
♠ —
♡ A J 5 4
◇ K 4 2
♣ K

GABLE
♠ —
♡ 8 6 3
◇ Q 10
♣ Q 9 8

She did her best by discarding her ace. I cashed the heart king, took the heart finesse and played the club king squeezing her again. Not one of her four kibitzers understood what had happened: a triple squeeze.

Marie cocked her head and bragged to the kibitzers about her bidding. "My seven club bid was best. It not only showed fourth-round control, but gave partner a choice of spades or notrump."

The wife pursed her lips. Obviously she had been fixed. Cuebidding like this is tantamount to murdering the art of bidding. No one really knew what they were doing, least of all me. We had landed in a hopeless grand slam that required a miracle to make. It just went to prove that bridge is not a perfect sport; bad bidding is sometimes successful (especially when you know how to execute a triple squeeze).

Before the next deal was started, the director came over to tell us we had to take a late play. Marie's head shook violently. "No way, no way. I've got an appointment after the game. We'll take average minus, anything, but no late plays." She glanced up nervously at the two 'suspects' waiting to sit down in our seats. They seemed calm and patient enough, and gave away no clues to their true, criminal nature. Even though Marie had told me there was nothing to fear from them while we were in the bridge club, it was plain to me that she herself was afraid. Were these two gentlemen merely cohorts of her detective father? Or were they accomplices in the murder of Marcel Moskowitz? Or, worst of all, were they high-tech hit men, hired to put a permanent lid on my investigation?

Don't tell them what to lead

I didn't want to speak up. I didn't want to play the second board. I didn't want to show up for a late play. But I could see that Marie was desperate for us to finish the game on time and get on with her entrapment of the two suspects. When I noticed the middle-aged couple at table four still playing, I finally did speak up. "The next table ees not finished yet. I'm sure ve can finish quickly."

"Quickly?" said the wife. "Why this... person is even slower than my husband!" Now that was a mean thing to say. The director laughed and allowed us to play the next hand so long as we did it rapidly. This was our rapid auction:

M. G.	MARIE	
1♣	1♠	(The Wife and Gable
2♠	3♡	remain silent...
3♠	4♣	but listen.)
4♡	4♠	
5♣	5♡	
5♠	pass	

An incredibly delicate sequence. It would take a master bridge detective at least five years to distribute twenty-six cards in a manner that could make such an auction plausible. These eleven bids remain a valuable source for how not to bid a bridge hand. Without looking at the actual cards (mere catalysts, and not the culprits), even the most elementary student can detect flagrant inconsistencies at all levels. To be precise:

1) Clubs, a maligned minor suit that nobody at any time had any intention of suggesting as trumps, was bid three times. Introduced at the one-level, then dragged back into the picture at the four and five level, it served only as a springboard in two desperate attempts to hear a diamond cuebid.

2) Hearts, suddenly making their way into the auction at the three, four, and five level, seem to be mentioned for no other reason than repeatedly to admit to everyone at the table that "No, I can't cuebid diamonds, but I can cuebid hearts — you want to hear me cuebid hearts again?"

3) Spades, the trump suit, was mentioned at all five levels of conversation in one repeated message "minimum, minimum, stop, stop," while no one stopped.

4) Diamonds, the missing link, became ever more prominent as bids were made around it, through it, before it, and after it. You could almost hear the wife's kibitzers thinking, "Where the heck are the diamonds?"

Needless to say, Gable, the opening leader, with a perfectly good lead in three other suits, led from his A-Q-10 of diamonds to defeat five spades.

Here was the full hand:

THE WIFE
♠ Q
♡ 7 6 2
◇ K 6 5 4 3
♣ 6 4 3 2

ME
♠ A 6 4 3
♡ K 5 4
◇ J 2
♣ K Q 7 5

MARIE
♠ K 8 7 5 2
♡ A Q J 3
◇ 9 8
♣ A J

	N	
W		E
	S	

GABLE
♠ J 10 9
♡ 10 9 8
◇ A Q 10 7
♣ 10 9 8

Perhaps Marie was unlucky to go down in five spades (the spades splitting 3-1). But even so, five pairs in our direction were plus 680 (four spades making six), and one pair was plus 1430 when South failed to lead his diamond ace against the slam.

Don't look for slams — never bid grands

♠ K 8 7 5 2   ♡ A Q J 3   ◇ 9 8   ♣ A J

M.G.	MARIE
1♣	1♠
2♠	?

Marie's slam investigation on this hand after my raise of her spade response was predicated on the chance of finding the perfect fit. This chance is approximately equal to that of finding a shop selling fresh bagels in the upper Yukon. Millions of bridge players all over the world, every day, go down one at the five-level or in slam because they have been searching for the elusive perfect fit.

It would have been better for Marie to leap to six spades than to investigate the perfect fit with her series of cuebids. At least she would not have revealed our diamond weakness. Alternatively, and preferably, she should have simply jumped to game over two spades. South would have led a heart, and we would have scored average-plus for making a game with two overtricks.

Many readers will ask, then when do you look for a slam? The odds necessary to make slam a good contract are fifty percent plus. Thus, it's best to look for a slam only when you have more than a fifty percent chance of finding partner with a hand that produces one. Once you mentally start placing precise cards in partner's hand in order to have a chance for slam, you're probably below fifty percent.

The point is, it's not free to look for a slam. You pay a price even when you stop safely in game, that price being the information you pass to the opponents. When you help them to make a better lead than others are making with the same cards, you do not score well.

There have been many times in my career when my partner and I patted each other on the back for stopping at the five-level, knowing we were off the first two tricks in a suit. At duplicate, we received little else but aesthetic satisfaction. "Well bid partner, good stop... (we open up the score slip)... unlucky, half the field made seven." Successful bridge is not the result of precise, scientific bidding. On the contrary, good scores usually result from contracts that have been reached in less than three rounds of bidding.

The fewer bids you take to reach a contract, the higher your score will be. The failure to realize this concept is a major stumbling block to most duplicate players, who were taught erroneously that scientific bidding is the key to success. When pairs try to bid scientifically they tend to investigate contracts which have a low percentage of making. Great slam bidders come from this brilliant group. They often brag at the end of the evening about the slam they bid and made. But the pairs that don't bid any slams are the ones that usually come in the money.

The reason for this is quite simple, and is based on the fact that fifty percent slams are bid by less than half the field (and often require good dummy play to make). If you reach a difficult slam that makes, you receive a top score, while the winner of the duplicate gets next to top anyway for bidding only game and making the two difficult overtricks. If you bid a difficult slam that goes down you receive a bottom, while the winner of the duplicate is still scoring average-plus, again, for stopping wisely in game. It follows that fifty percent is really not a good enough percentage for a slam at duplicate. If you are scoring nicely on most of the game and part-score hands, why risk a bottom by bidding a slam that most other pairs will not reach?

When you talk about grand slams, this reasoning becomes even more potent. During the second half of the evening Marie and I bid three more slams, one small and two grands:

ME		MARIE
♠ K Q 9 7 5 4	N	♠ A 3
♡ 10 8 3	W E	♡ A 2
◇ A 7 4	S	◇ K Q J 10 5
♣ 2		♣ K 5 4 3

ME	MARIE
2♠	2NT
3◇	5♠
6♠	6NT

On this deal, I opened a weak two-bid and she bid two notrump. I showed a diamond feature and she jumped to five spades to ask how good my spades were. There was a good deal of risk in this bid, but luckily I had good trumps and was able to bid six. Counting twelve tricks (six spades, one heart, and five diamonds) she converted to six notrump to protect her club king, and also to score the extra ten points for being in notrump.

The slam was quite reasonable, requiring only a three-two spade division (68%). A club was led to the ace, and another club returned. Marie won her king, cashed her red winners, but alas, the spades divided four-one and she could take only ten tricks.

Down two was worth half a matchpoint. There was only one other pair in slam. Two pairs had stopped in a partscore! Most others bid four spades. It was interesting to note that three notrump making the same ten tricks was worth a top. This was all very unlucky when you consider that the slam was a fine contract.

Or was it so unlucky?

Later:

ME		MARIE
♠ A K 5 3		♠ Q J
♡ A 9 2	N	♡ J 10 6 4
◇ A Q 4 3	W E	◇ ——
♣ A 2	S	♣ K J 10 7 5 4 3

ME	MARIE
2NT	3♣
3♠	4♣
4◇	5◇
5NT	7♣

Not satisfied with bidding to the six-level, we reached for the Milky Way on this deal.

After Stayman, Marie introduced her club suit, and I bid four diamonds to show some interest in slam. Marie now risked a terrible misunderstanding by cuebidding five diamonds. I was careful to say five notrump, which would allow her to pick the best slam. Here her optimism got the best of her. She convinced herself that my five notrump bid was a grand slam try. Since I had previously shown interest in a club slam and now failed to cuebid either major, she deduced I must have both major-suit aces. Her interpretation of five notrump was, 'go to seven with two of the top three honors'. If I had A-x-x of clubs, her seventh club would be enough to bring in the suit. So she leaped to seven.

She actually caught me with quite a good hand and had reasonable play for the contract. However, clubs were three-one, the queen not dropping, and she had to concede down one. Too bad. Had we bid only six clubs we would have tied for a top score. Many pairs stopped in five clubs for average. Interestingly enough, three notrump making five or six was an average-plus.

Then:

ME		MARIE
♠ A 7 5		♠ K 9 8
♡ A 6 4		♡ K Q 8 7 5
◇ Q 8 7 4		◇ A K 5 2
♣ 8 7 2		♣ A

ME	MARIE
	1♡
2♡	3◇
4◇	5NT
5♡	7◇

This time Marie really went off the deep end. After I made a simple raise she tried for slam with a three diamond bid. This was reasonable, and my raise to four diamonds encouraged her. Blackwood revealed we had all the aces, and at this point my partner should have settled for a small slam. To find me with ten points after my simple raise was very lucky. To bid the slam in diamonds showed tremendous knowledge of the game, since the 4-4 fit would produce an extra trick. Her heart suit could be used to pitch a spade and club from my hand, and one club could be trumped in her hand. If the hearts and diamonds split she would make thirteen tricks.

Trumps divided all right, but the hearts were four-one. This translated to down one in our seven diamond contract, and surprisingly we received just under average. A number of pairs were in six hearts down two. The one pair that managed to get to six diamonds had misplayed it and was down one. Three pairs stopped in four hearts for +450, tied for next to top. Then there was one lone pair in three notrump of all places! They must have received a spade lead because they made +460 for a complete top! Three notrump is often right

The most popular contract in bridge is three notrump.

At duplicate, three notrump usually scores best, even when there are other, safer places to play the hand, and sometimes even when you can make a slam. This doesn't mean you should rush into three notrump on every hand. What it does mean is that every time you pick up a new deal you should consider the possibility of playing in three notrump (from the right side), and bid with that possibility in mind.

More often than not, the opponents' busy bidding in your game auction will help you determine whether three notrump is a better contract than four of a major. For example, we had this deal come up at table six:

South dealer   Neither vulnerable

NORTH
♠ 10 9
♡ A K 9 6
♢ 8 7 6 3
♣ K 9 3

ME
♠ Q 7 6 5
♡ Q J 10 8
♢ Q 9
♣ A Q J

MARIE
♠ A K J 8 2
♡ 7 3 2
♢ K J 10 5
♣ 2

N
W   E
S

SOUTH
♠ 4 3
♡ 5 4
♢ A 4 2
♣ 10 8 7 6 5 4

ME	NORTH	MARIE	SOUTH
			pass
1♣	1♡	1♠	pass
2♠	pass	3♢	pass
3NT	all pass		

Opening lead: ♡6
Result: making 4 (top score)

I dutifully raised spades, but when my partner showed her diamond suit, I could see three notrump as a fine alternative contract. Without the overcall, my partner would have leaped to four spades over my raise (why tell the opponents what to lead?). But the one heart bid forced Marie to be concerned about her three small hearts. Her three diamond probe was an excellent bid, and gave me the chance to judge my values. In short, North's clever, lead-directing overcall helped our side, not his partner.

When does a cuebid ask for a stopper and when does it show one?

Before we sat down at table seven Marie took me aside. "These people are in on it," she whispered.

"In on what?" I asked.

"The conspiracy. What's the matter with you? Have you forgotten why we're here?"

"You mean the conspiracy to stop our investigation of Marcel's murder?"

She gave me one of those cat-like stares that told me to keep quiet and observe. That's exactly what I did.

Our opponents seemed like the nicest young couple I had ever seen at a bridge table. Presumably they were husband and wife (their convention card read 'Jan and Leslie Barkowsky'). Leslie (or was it Jan?), South, had blonde hair, and I had a faint recollection of having seen her some place before. The young man sitting North was also blonde, though a shade darker, and had the pleasant air of a healthy Midwesterner rather than a New York games player. The two of them were so nice they didn't even argue after two back-to-back disasters, both of them involving cuebids, this time below the level of three notrump.

On the first hand the young man got so confused he thought his partner was cuebidding at the two-level for slam purposes! The two-level is about as far from the six level as you can get. The three-level is not much closer. Cuebids at these low levels should be for the purpose of reaching three notrump, not for reaching slam.

On the second hand, there was confusion as to when a cuebid shows a stopper for notrump and when it asks for one. Let's have a look. Here was the first hand:

West dealer   North-South vulnerable

YOUNG MAN
♠ K 6
♡ K 8 6 5
◇ A K J 8
♣ A 6 2

ME   **MARIE**
♠ 10 3 2   ♠ A J 9 8 4
♡ 10 4 3   ♡ A J 7
◇ 9 4 2   ◇ 6 3
♣ 10 9 7 4   ♣ 8 5 3

	N	
W		E
	S	

YOUNG WOMAN
♠ Q 7 5
♡ Q 9 2
◇ Q 10 7 5
♣ K Q J

ME	YOUNG M.	MARIE	YOUNG W.
pass	1◇	1♠	2♠
pass	3♡	pass	3NT
pass	4NT	all pass	

Opening lead: ♠2
Result: down 2

North opened one diamond on his eighteen points (he must
have been using a strict 15-17 one notrump range). Marie overcalled one spade and South cuebid two spades. This was a thought-
ful bid. Players tend to jump to two notrump on a square hand like
this without realizing the possible advantage of declaring notrump
from partner's side. Two notrump is certainly not a wrong bid with
the South cards, and without the overcall it would be the automatic choice. But East had overcalled and West was about to lead a
spade. If dummy came down with king doubleton of spades, the
lead coming through the king would be devastating. In that case,
the right side of the table (for declaring) would be North.

Readers will note that a spade lead from my side through the king doubleton defeats three notrump (we set up four spade tricks and the heart ace, while declarer can cash only eight tricks). However, imagine North as declarer. The spade lead comes away from the ace and up to the doubleton king. South's spade queen still stops the suit, and declarer has time to set up a heart trick as well as a second spade trick. The pairs that declared three notrump from the North seat made ten tricks. Most of the field, however, declared from the South side and went down one. The young couple at table seven did worse. North interpreted the spade cuebid as a slam try. He showed his heart suit (a silly thing to do, since his partner would have made a negative double with a four-card heart suit). Then, when South did her best by retreating to three notrump, he bid four notrump intending it as Blackwood. South passed this in desperation, ending up with only eight tricks and a bottom score.

The two of them were quite contrite, and took the bottom with as much good sportsmanship as I had ever seen a married couple demonstrate. (It suddenly occurred to me that they must be brother and sister.) While each was apologizing to the other, I desperately wanted to point out where North had gone wrong. To think that a two-level bid is a slam try when partner never subsequently raises your suit is downright silly. Granted, North had a big hand for his opening bid, but he could have shown it by rebidding two notrump over two spades, then four notrump on the next round.

Of course I did not speak up. Not only would it have been impolite, but if these two were criminally involved with the other two men following us from table to table, I did not dare reveal my true identity by entering into a discussion on the aesthetics of low-level cuebids. Instead, I picked up the cards for the next deal:

When they've bid and when they haven't

South dealer   Both vulnerable

BROTHER?
♠ A Q 2
♡ 10 7
◊ K Q J 9 8 3
♣ 6 4

ME
♠ J 8 7 6
♡ A K 8 6 5 2
◊ 6
♣ Q 7

MARIE
♠ 5 4 3
♡ Q 9
◊ 7 5 4 2
♣ K 10 3 2

SISTER?
♠ K 10 9
♡ J 4 3
◊ A 10
♣ A J 9 8 5

ME	BROTHER	MARIE	SISTER
			1♣
2♡	3◊	pass	3♡
pass	3♠	pass	3NT
all pass			

Opening lead: ♡6
Result: down 2

Here was one occasion where three notrump was wrong, although a few pairs managed to make it after the heart-king lead. Confusion occurred after my powerful 'weak jump overcall', a tactical call that tends to hurt the opponents more than the very weak variety. South was poorly placed over three diamonds. Should she bid three hearts or three spades? Does three spades show spades or merely a stopper? Does three hearts show or ask for a stopper? All these questions are confusing to most players. Actually they can be cleared up with two short rules:

1) When one suit has been bid by the opponents, the cuebid asks for a stopper; and

2) When two suits have been bid by the opponents (or no suits), a cuebid shows a stopper.

Therefore, South's three hearts asked for a heart stopper, whereas three spades by South would have merely shown spades without a heart stopper. This makes common sense because if South held a heart stopper she would simply bid three notrump.

When North now tried three spades he might have been thinking, "I have already denied four spades by failing to make a negative double over two hearts." Or maybe he was unsure of the meaning of the three heart cuebid. If his sister meant it as showing a stopper, he wanted her to bid three notrump. If it had been asking, he wanted her to bid something else.

South, however, thought her bid had been understood as asking for a stopper. Since her hand could hardly have changed from one round of bidding to the next, she rebid three notrump to show that she had half a stopper! This brilliant call would have worked if North held one more heart (the hearts would block if Marie held the singleton queen) or if North held a half a stopper as well, such as the Q-x. When this was not the case, and I relentlessly led my fourth best, the contract went down two tricks for a very poor score.

In short, the young woman had bid excellently on both hands, only to have her brother misinterpret her cuebids. Suddenly, a thought occurred to me that I had never really considered before: "Perhaps good bids are not necessarily good bids when made with a partner who is likely to get confused by them." Perhaps the young woman should have realized from the previous hand that her partner would not understand the second cuebid either. The cuebid might be technically correct but it is of no use if partner is not on the same wavelength.

This thought frightened me as I realized how it applied to my own situation that evening. I was not only playing bridge with a partner who had no understanding of the style I played, but I was risking my life investigating a murder in partnership with a person I had not known for more than a few hours, a person who had some crazy scheme in mind that was more mysterious than the mystery I had started out to solve.

10

AS DECLARER, DON'T PLAY TO TRICK ONE UNTIL YOU HAVE A PLAN

When attention is called to an irregularity — CALL THE DIRECTOR.

BD # PAIRS	DLR AND VUL	BD # TEAMS	VS	CONTRACT & DECLARER	PLUS	MINUS	PTS EST.	PTS.
1	N NONE							
2	E N-S			GRANOVETTA -13				
3	S E-W							
4	W BOTH							
5	N N-S							
6	E E-W							
7	S BOTH							
8	W NONE							
9	N E-W							
10	E BOTH							
11	S NONE							
12	W N-S							
13	N BOTH							

BD # PAIRS	DLR AND VUL	BD # TEAMS	VS	CONTRACT & DECLARER	PLUS	MINUS	PTS EST.	PTS.
17	N NONE							
18	E N-S							
19	S E-W							
20	W BOTH							
21	N N-S							
22	E E-W							
23	S BOTH							
24	W NONE							
25	N E-W							
26	E BOTH							
27	S NONE							
28	W N-S							
29	N BOTH							

Any plan is better than no plan

On the last deal of the night I passed out a hand in fourth chair with nineteen points. This is not ordinarily good practice. But as I began thinking about the two hit men following us East-West, the brother-sister conspirators at table seven (obviously too sweet to be anything other than covert crime figures), and Marie's crazy plan (for me to pose as the late Marcel Moskowitz as live bait), I came to the sane conclusion that the faster I bolted out of that bridge club, the better.

Unfortunately, as often happens with a passed-out hand, the other three players recounted their points. One opponent claimed five points and the other four, whereupon Marie lunged for my cards, spread them faceup on the table, and almost cried. She had passed a twelve-point hand, which meant we had thirty-one points between us.

To say that it surprised me how important the bridge game was to a trained detective in the midst of a murder investigation is putting it mildly. I swear her ears and nose flushed red; she grabbed the convention card and pointed it at me like a knife.

"Fixed again," said the fellow sitting North. The unfolded score slip revealed twelve East-West pairs in slam contracts or five of a major, all minus. Marie quickly wiped away a teardrop and began to blush. "You really are a brilliant player, aren't you?" she said as she drew the convention card back from my throat.

I suggested that we depart immediately, if not for fear of the hit men, then for fear of seeing our score. She insisted on waiting for her matchpoints, and I told her I was going to the bathroom.

The woman was mad.

I came to that conclusion when I realized her so-called plan was no plan at all. It was like tossing cards without thinking. And I was one of the cards! Maybe she claimed to have a plan in order to seduce me into an evening's duplicate. If this was an example of the New York City Homicide Squad, the city was in deeper trouble than most people thought. Meanwhile, I wasn't sticking around while hit men and conspirators got the upper hand.

Hustling towards the door, I ran straight into the middle-aged East-West couple we had been following all night. The two of them were huddled by the soda machine comparing scores with the brother and sister from table seven. The man's card fell to the floor as I jostled over his leg. I retrieved it and handed it up to him (he was a tall fellow with thick glasses), but I was shocked when I saw what was written on the inside. There were no bridge scores. There was only a handwritten name running across the card, with a number next to it. It read, 'GRANOVETTA — 13'.

"Excuse me," I said, and escaped through the door.

As I ran down the twelve flights of stairs marked 'Fire Exit Only', I tried to think of what to do. Why did that couple have my name misspelled on their convention card? What kind of notes were they comparing with the brother and sister? Where was I to go now? Maybe I had underestimated Marie. Maybe the idea to steer them all into Room 623 wasn't such a crazy plan after all. I felt like a complete dummy. I had no idea what I would do and where I would go, and my only protection was the person I was flee-ing. I rushed on without organizing my thoughts, like the typical declarer playing a bridge hand.

The fire exit ended in the courtyard. It must have been past 11:00 p.m., and the only light I could see was a bulb burning over the back door of the Taj Mahal. I ran through the kitchen and straight into the maître d'.

"How many, please?"

Since I had no idea of how to continue at this point, I decided to sit down and reconstruct the whole situation. I had deserted my so-called partner on the penthouse level of the Embassy Hotel. I was on my own. If I could sort out this mystery in the serenity of a Pakistani restaurant, I could form my own plan. If I could have a bowl of extra-hot lamb curry while I was thinking, all the better. My friend, the waiter, came over to the table, fresh raita and condiments in hand. He bent down to my ear.

"Mister Matthew. I have spoken to our friend."

"What friend?" I asked, no more puzzled than usual.

"Mister Zia, from Karachi."

I grabbed him by the collar, a plate of peppers and onions spilling to the floor. "What are you talking about?" I tried to whisper. "I never gave you his phone number. I told you to mail a copy of bridge hands to him this afternoon. There's no way he could have got them yet." He began to wave his arms as I continued spouting, "Besides, you told me you didn't mail them. That the woman stopped you—" His arm was pointing.

"Mister Matthew, please. Mister Zia."

Then I saw where he was pointing. It was Zia Mahmood in the flesh, sitting at a table by the front window, with five or six plates of food in front of him, a half-empty bottle of Beaujolais next to his wine glass, and several beautiful redheads hanging to his right arm, left leg, and upper thigh. I rushed over, ecstatic to see my debonair friend.

"There you are," he said, swallowing a hot pickle. "Jaggi, bring another plate." There was no place to sit, and Zia told one of the girls to go home, call him later at the bridge club, and perhaps meet him in his hotel room at 4:00 a.m. the following week.

I was delighted, overjoyed and elated to see, half-hidden under his plate of onion kulcha, another copy of Marcel's hands, which the trusty waiter must have photocopied this afternoon and not handed over to Marie. "The waiter is my second cousin, you idiot," said Zia, swirling his wine. "I just flew in with his wife this evening and couldn't get a hotel room. So I rang the Cavendish Club, told them I'd be there at midnight for a few rubbers, and brought my bags here to my cousin's restaurant."

"But where are you going to stay?" I asked.

"Jaggi here got me a room at the Embassat Hotel—"

"Embassy," I corrected.

"Embassy, Embasso, no matter. I'm in room... room...(the two remaining redheads held up keys)... Room 625."

"Room 625! It's one hell of a room." He ignored me.

"Then my cousin here gives me these bridge notes of all things. He can't even play parcheesi, but when he described you I knew they must be yours. To tell you the truth, they are the worst display of bridge I have ever seen." He pulled out the curry-stained sheets, then looked up at me for the first time. "Good God, man! What have you done to yourself?"

I reached for my wig and pulled it off. One redhead offered me a comb and helped straighten my hair as I tried to bring my friend up to date on the case.

"You're always involved in something weird," he scolded. "Where is your wife all this time?"

"She's safe at home, I hope." I didn't tell him about Pamela's Gable lookalike or he'd thrash me. Instead I tried to make Zia understand the importance of the bridge notes before him. They were the only clues I had to Marcel Moskowitz's murder. The waiter, Jaggi, appeared with another wine glass and my keema curry, which Zia immediately began to eat.

"Quite frankly," he said pointing to the papers, "these early bidding disasters do not interest me. The declarer play on some of these later deals, however, is somewhat challenging. Let me see."

Declarer play is Zia's favorite part of the game. At the rubber bridge table Zia is frequently declarer more than he is entitled. Over the years he has somehow learned things about declaring that few duplicate players have ever even thought about. However, all his ideas — no matter how complex they seem — are usually based on the elementary concept of forming a plan before playing to trick one.

"Here," Zia said, "this six spade contract. The criticism of this man Marcel is incorrect. Granted, his line was pitiful and demonstrates a player in his bottom heat—"

"Heat? What do you mean, 'his bottom heat'?"

"Every player has four heats. The first heat is the worst. You have those days all the time I'm sure. You know, when you can't do anything right. Your bottom heat at bridge is the session where you misguess every queen, go down in every slam, confuse your partner with every bid. Like your man Marcel here."

"What are the other heats?" I asked.

"Second heat is just a mediocre night. Your judgment is slightly off, and though you make a few technically correct plays, they don't work well at the table. It happens to me sometimes, for example, when I play bridge the same night I get off a plane.

"Now the third heat is the most interesting because it's the most frustrating." Zia took a single pea from his plate, and held it between his thumb and index finger. "You are this close to the top of your game. Your bidding is disciplined and your analysis is accurate. But when a truly great opportunity comes along, you misread the table and blow it." He popped the pea into his mouth. "Mind you, most of the time this is a decent heat to be in. But it can't come close to the top heat."

"You mean the fourth heat?" I asked the guru.

"No, I mean the ninth heat! Of course the fourth heat, shmigeggie. It almost never happens." Did I detect a strange glow in Zia's eyes, or was it just the wine? "In the fourth heat, every bid, every card is not only perfect, it's as if you were playing in Shangri-La, a beautiful dream."

The glow faded. "Don't worry my friend," he continued, "you'll never see that day. Now cover the East-West cards, and tell me what your plan is on this hand. Here, wait, don't peek, you bastard."

Zia broke a piece of nan bread into two halves and placed them over the East-West cards. I studied the hand. But if today was any indication, I had the feeling my mind was floating somewhere between heat one and two.

Exhibit #15   South dealer
Board 3   East-West vulnerable

NORTH *(Marie)*
♠ K J 4 2
♡ A 2
◇ K 8 4
♣ A K 7 5

SOUTH *(Marcel)*
♠ A Q 10 7 3
♡ J 4 3
◇ A 10 7 2
♣ 6

Contract: 6♠
Opening lead: ◇ Q
Result: down 1

It seemed like a good lead. My plan was to win the ace, draw trumps, and lead the diamond ten. This would force West to cover with the jack, dummy's king would win, and a third diamond would drive out the nine. On the good diamond seven, I would discard dummy's heart loser. Even if West started with Q-J-9-x of diamonds, I would make the slam.

Zia listened to my plan and waved his crusty bread in disgust. "You simpleton. That's the plan proposed in these bloody notes." I removed the pieces of nan from the East-West cards.

NORTH *(Marie)*
♠ K J 4 2
♡ A 2
◇ K 8 4
♣ A K 7 5

WEST
♠ 9 5
♡ Q 10 8
◇ Q J 9 3
♣ J 9 8 2

```
       N
   W       E
       S
```

EAST
♠ 8 6
♡ K 9 7 6 5
◇ 6 5
♣ Q 10 4 3

SOUTH *(Marcel)*
♠ A Q 10 7 3
♡ J 4 3
◇ A 10 7 2
♣ 6

Indeed, the Q-J-9-3 of diamonds were with West. Underneath the diagram was the line of play taken by Marcel. He had won the king in dummy, drawn trumps, then finessed the diamond eight to West's nine, eventually losing a heart as well. After this description of the play was a handwritten analysis:

Win diamond ace.
Draw trumps
Lead ten of diamonds towards king

This was the same line I had proposed.

"Your line is successful on this layout," said Zia, "but you would have failed if the queen lead was a singleton or from Q-x. This is a simple hand that should be solved at trick one, as so many hands can be.

"My first thought is that I want to succeed no matter where the jack of diamonds is. Granted, the lead is probably from the queen-jack against a slam, but why take the chance? Personally, I duck smoothly from both hands, falsecarding with my seven spot along the way. When the queen holds, West will think his partner has the ace. There is no human being on earth who could resist continuing the suit."

He took a sip of wine and summed up. "The world tries to make the seven spot high, but I throw it away at trick one, receive a second diamond lead and spread my cards. Not only do I make my slam, but my left-hand opponent trembles for the rest of the night. Over. Finito. Next hand." With that, he delved back into the notes on his lap, redhead number one offered a congratulatory pat on the thigh.

He then showed me a very difficult three notrump contract. Again Marcel had declared:

Exhibit #16   West dealer
Board 4   Both vulnerable

NORTH (*Marie*)
♠ K 8 4
♡ 10 5 4 2
♢ 6
♣ A J 8 5 2

```
        N
    W       E
        S
```

SOUTH (*Marcel*)
♠ A 10 7 2
♡ J 9
♢ A Q
♣ K Q 10 7 3

Contract: 3NT
Opening lead: ♠Q
Result: down 1

"I will tell you what actually happened," Zia said as redhead number two shifted anxiously in her seat. "This fellow Marcel won the spade ace and led the ten just as he might have done on the previous slam hand you both played so wretchedly. This time, however, West won the third round of the suit, saw his partner's deuce of diamonds signal, and shifted to hearts."

I examined the whole deal:

NORTH *(Marie)*
♠ K 8 4
♡ 10 5 4 2
◇ 6
♣ A J 8 5 2

WEST
♠ Q J 9 5
♡ K Q 6
◇ K 8 7 3
♣ 9 6

```
        N
    W       E
        S
```

EAST
♠ 6 3
♡ A 8 7 3
◇ J 10 9 5 4 2
♣ 4

SOUTH *(Marcel)*
♠ A 10 7 2
♡ J 9
◇ A Q
♣ K Q 10 7 3

"Even looking at all four hands, shmigeggie, won't help you if you lack imagination. As you can see, the defense took their spade trick and four rounds of hearts to defeat three notrump. The suggested plan was to win the spade king in dummy, dropping the seven spot, and take an immediate diamond finesse. If the finesse wins, voila. If it loses, there is an excellent chance West will continue spades into your ace-ten. Good idea not to attack clubs first and allow them to signal each other, and at least it is a plan that has a chance.

"But can you imagine how naive West would be to continue spades? East can simply play his jack when declarer leads dummy's diamond, and West will know to return the suit."

"Yes of course," I smiled, "I see your plan. On the spade queen declarer simply ducks from both hands. West continues spades at trick two and South claims nine tricks."

Zia gave me a look as though I had insulted him. "Do you think I would be so stupid as to make the same coup two hands in a row? And then give it to you as a problem?"

"O-k-kay," I stuttered, "I win the spade lead with my ace and lead a small spade, sneaking it through West's jack-nine to dummy's eight spot."

Zia took his napkin and tried to hit me. "You do no such thing."

"Yes, I see it," I said in desperation. "I win the spade lead in my hand and go to dummy with a club; then I finesse the diamond. West will never suspect I have won the opening lead in my hand with a good tenace like the ace-ten, and he will surely return a spade away from his jack."

Zia was exasperated. "No wonder your wife has left you."

"My wife hasn't left me," I said.

"Well, if she hasn't she should." Pouring the last of the wine into his glass, he continued, "If you want to teach your readers how to plan a hand correctly, let them listen to me, please. Look at the diagram again."

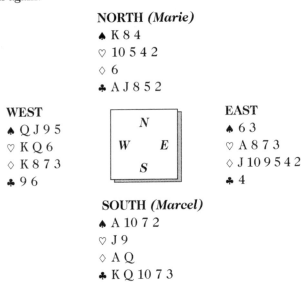

NORTH *(Marie)*
♠ K 8 4
♡ 10 5 4 2
◇ 6
♣ A J 8 5 2

WEST
♠ Q J 9 5
♡ K Q 6
◇ K 8 7 3
♣ 9 6

EAST
♠ 6 3
♡ A 8 7 3
◇ J 10 9 5 4 2
♣ 4

SOUTH *(Marcel)*
♠ A 10 7 2
♡ J 9
◇ A Q
♣ K Q 10 7 3

"You are correct about one thing, which is a surprise. When West leads the queen of spades, you must win in your hand on the off chance East holds the nine singleton or doubleton. But to go to dummy and attack your tenace in diamonds is shocking. What has gone wrong with your game, eh? Is it so hard to win the spade in hand and lead the club queen?"

"The club queen?"

"Yes, as if you are about to finesse. Then you go up with dummy's ace, just to confuse matters. What do you think would be the effect on West?"

I looked at Zia and shook my head. "To be honest, I think West would see right through the ruse. Anyone who leads the club queen to the ace, then attacks another suit must hold the club king and be trying to fool his opponent into thinking he is missing that card. West will still win the diamond king and return a diamond."

"Who said anything about diamonds? I lead the club queen to the ace and play a heart to my jack."

"What?"

"It is a simple plan," Zia went on. "As anyone can see, hearts is the only safe suit to play, since it is the only suit where you can give up the lead and not go set. Also, it is the one suit you do not want West to return. And even if he does, you will end up squeezing him in the endgame, but that is another matter.

"The simple approach is always the best plan. I win the spade-queen lead in my hand, play the club queen to the ace, and lead a heart to my jack. If East goes up he has blocked the suit. Needless to say, West will win this trick and not even consider returning a heart. He will say to himself, 'This declarer is trying to trick me into thinking my partner has the club king.' He will refuse to be tricked into a club return and will choose either another spade or a diamond, presenting me with a trick.

"This time I do not claim until trick three, voila, kaput, end of hand, next deal." (With that, redhead number two gave Zia a congratulatory pat.)

I marveled at Zia's thinking. But was his plan really so simple? Maybe. After all, there are two suits he doesn't want played, so he attacks them first. This was planning beyond the average player's capabilities. This was that fourth heat business. Or was it? Many times in notrump, when you have no strong suit to set up, it's best to attack your weak suit. The opponents often win and lead back something to your advantage.

Once dummy hits, it's your problem

Jaggi cleared the table and took dessert orders. Glancing out of the window, I could see Marie looking for me down the street. I ducked under the table and suggested that we move to a booth in the darkest corner. Zia squawked, "I like to sit by the window to look at the girls outside." With that, his two redheads, who had been giving each other unearthly stares, considered the unknown enemies outside and moved closer to their man. "Here," Zia continued, hand-

ing me a paper napkin under the table, "a hand I played last week in London."

I asked Zia for a match, redhead number one passed a pack down to me, and I lit one above the napkin. To tell you the truth, there were lots of interesting legs to look at down there, but I kept my eyes glued to the paper:

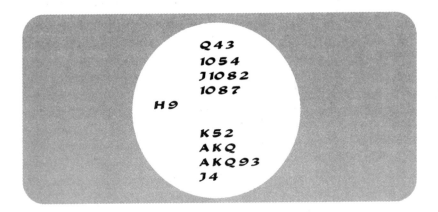

Q43
1054
J1082
1087

H9

K52
AKQ
AKQ93
J4

"The contract is three notrump," said Zia.

"Wait a second," I mumbled. "How did you reach this contract?"

"Don't ask how I got there. That is not your problem. All you Americans ever care about is the bloody bidding. When dummy comes down you should not concern yourself with what went wrong in the auction. You must concentrate all your attention on the play."

Well, I thought about it. They hadn't cashed the first five tricks. That was in my favor. But my choices were few. I could win the heart with some deceptive honor and run diamonds, hoping somebody pitches away his club tricks. Or I could utilize Zia's ploy of attacking the club suit myself. No, no, not the same ruse twice in a row. Well, what about sneaking a spade trick past whoever has the ace? Since West is behind me and will have a harder time switching to clubs after winning the spade ace, I'll travel to dummy's diamond jack and lead a spade through East. If East has the spade ace, he may duck, and if West has it, he'll have to find the club shift to beat me.

I called up my plan from under the table. Zia choked on his wine. "You think anyone is dumb enough not to rise spade ace and switch to clubs after you expose the strength of your diamond suit? Why do you continue to spoil my supper?"

His face suddenly appeared upside-down beneath the chair. "Simple plan, simple plan. With eight top tricks, I needed only one more without letting them on play. Therefore I had to make a spade trick. When I want someone to duck his ace, I simply make it look like I want him to win it. So I cashed the diamond king, then banged down my spade king, daring anybody to let me get to that hopeless dummy for a diamond finesse."

"Where was the spade ace?" I asked.

"How do I know?" cried Zia. "What do I care? Nobody in their right mind would win it. I simply claimed my nine and went on to the next deal. Kaput, finito Benito."

With that, he rose back up to his seat, for I could smell the spice tea being served. I decided to stay put, however, at least until the tea had fully brewed. Suddenly redhead number one shoved another napkin into my hand.

Don't squawk about partner's bad bidding

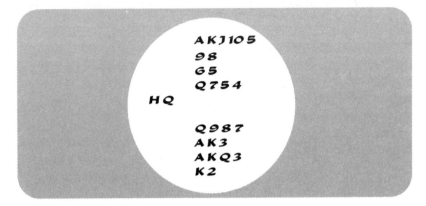

"Six spades I presume?" I called up.

"Six spades my eye!" Zia cursed. "Anybody can make six spades. This was a beautiful duplicate contract of six notrump."

"Who bid six notrump? You must have opened two notrump and partner would bid spades, or transfer to spades, or something."

"Partner raised directly to six notrump. Now you have to play it."

"Wait a second," I objected, "before I play a card, I give partner a balling out. How dare he not show his spades? Why should I have to play this in notrump?"

Zia's head popped down. He was furious. "You give your partner a thrashing at the table, you bloody fool? Why, the first thing everyone will realize is that you belong in six spades and have losing red cards to trump in dummy! Just keep your mouth shut and don't complain about partner's misbids.

"Besides, I took it as a compliment that he went directly to an inferior contract which would allow me to show off my skill as declarer."

The bluff by declarer

Okay. I shouldn't say a word at the table. Typical bad habit I picked up early in life from late-night New York bridge circles. Zia was right. The minute you scream at partner, you give away something about the hand. The best approach when dummy comes down is to say nothing and concentrate on your play. Even the slightest frown can give aid, comfort, and information to the opponents. But how was I to come up with twelve tricks? I looked again at the napkin.

Perhaps there was some squeeze that would materialize, though I doubted it because squeezes usually require entries back and forth, and once I run dummy's spades I also run out of entries. Then I remembered Zia's philosophy: simple planning. All right then. What if the clubs are divided 5-2 with a doubleton ace on my right? I go to dummy in spades and lead a club through East's ace doubleton. Upon winning my king, I lead a low one and duck it around to the stiff ace, setting up dummy's queen. A lot to hope for, mind you, but what else is there? Then I got a brighter idea. I popped my head up on Zia's lap.

"Okay, I got it. I win the lead with the heart ace, cash the ace and king of diamonds to make it look like my diamonds are solid, go to dummy's spade ace and lead a low club. Say East ducks his ace. I win my king, return to dummy's spade king, and lead another low club! If East has the ace without the jack he might go up, thinking I'm sneaking through the thirteenth trick."

Zia lifted his teacup and I retreated back under the table. "You are really off tonight, aren't you?" he said. "Granted, technically your play is best, but the 5-2 club split is too much to hope for, and no bridge player is going to fly up with the ace of clubs when you lead low off the board. Can't you see the best play is the simplest plan? Run your spades and make them suffer before they know what suit to hold."

A basic technique, running your long suit early. I wanted to kick myself, but that was physically impossible. "Okay," I called up. "I run my spades. What do they pitch?"

"How do you run them?"

I stuck my head up again. "What do you mean, how do I run them? They're solid, aren't they?" I took another peek to make sure: A-K-J-10-5 opposite Q-9-8-7.

Zia frowned. "Just tell me in what order you play your spades."

I shook my head. It was getting late. What difference did it make how I ran the suit? "I lead to dummy's jack, cash the ace dropping my queen, and then cash dummy's king—"

"Down one," said Zia. "Here's the whole hand." He wrote it neatly on the side of the tablecloth:

```
                    A K J 10 5
                    9 8
                    6 5
                    Q 7 5 4
    4 3                                 6 2
    Q J 10                              7 6 5 4 2
    J 10 7 4                            9 8 2
    J 10 8 6                            A 9 3
                    Q 9 8 7
                    A K 3
                    A K Q 3
                    K 2
```

"When I played the hand," Zia continued, "I said to myself, Zia, if you're going to run your spades, who are you going to put pressure on first, East or West? The queen of hearts lead indicated that East would have low hearts to discard, while West, the hand with the Q-J-10 of hearts might be first to have a problem. Therefore it was best—and rather simple planning—to run the spades in such a manner as to force West to make an early discard before he could see his partner's signal.

"I cashed two high spades ending in my hand, then led a third spade through West towards dummy. He had to make a choice of discards, and reasonably enough he let go a diamond rather than a heart honor or a club, staring at dummy's four-card club suit."

I examined the hand in awe. Why don't I think of such simple things?

"Obviously," Zia went on, "most players would run all five spades without planning; half would fall into my plan by luck while the other half would allow East to throw his diamond deuce before West had to decide what to pitch. So many players run off all their winners and never squeeze anybody. I prefer a simpler approach of running a minimum number of winners, squeezing my opponent early on, then claiming the balance. *Voilà*, the end, *finito* Benito, *au revoir*."

Decide your play before you call a card

I sat under the table feeling quite gloomy. Here I was the bridge teacher, the writer, the so-called expert, yet I was the one receiving the bridge lesson.

"Are you coming up for tea tonight?" Zia called down.

"I can't," I said. "There is a beautiful woman detective looking for me out on Broadway."

"You must be hallucinating. Beautiful women do not look for you," Zia said, trying to comfort me. "Besides, if you mean the lovely lady who has been up and down the street three times, she is gone."

I rose up to the table, embarrassed, and poured my cream. I was determined to get the next problem right. The check arrived and Zia began to write on the back of it. "You love to hide under tables and sneak tricks here and there, so try this hand."

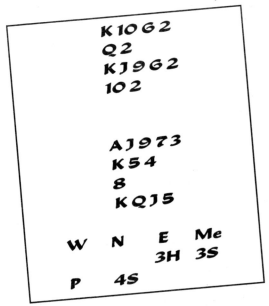

"This occurred the last time I was in New York. It was at duplicate against one of your modern young preempters sitting East. West led his partner's suit, and continued hearts at trick two as East signaled with the jack. What is your plan?"

"I'd like to sneak that diamond through to the king, if that's what you mean by sneaking," I said. "However I'm in dummy after the queen of hearts wins. Wait, I see a neat deception. I win the second trick in dummy and lead a trump to my ace. Then I triumphantly plunk down my heart king. If West ruffs, he solves the trump situation for me. If he doesn't ruff, I'll assume he started with the queen third of spades, and finesse him to make my contract."

Feeling rather proud of myself, I signaled Jaggi for another pot of tea. Zia nodded in complimentary fashion. "Not bad," he said, "for a beginner. However when I play duplicate, I prefer to make overtricks. So without a second thought, I overtook the queen of hearts with my king — as if I had only a doubleton king — and led my diamond up to the king-jack. I am not likely to hold both a doubleton and a singleton, West observed, and so he ducked his ace of diamonds smoothly. Here was the whole hand:

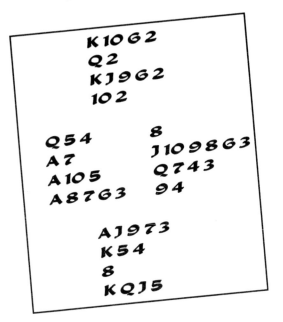

"East gave diamond count, so I led a club to get the count from him in that suit also. Then, adding it all up, played East for a singleton trump. Making five, top score, finito Benito shmigeggie and all that jazz."

Nice play, I thought. But real fast thinking. How could he expect most players to make a move like that trick-two overtake so quickly? I questioned him on this.

"This is a perfect lesson for you and your students," he said graciously. "Make a habit of not calling a card when dummy comes down until you have realized some sort of plan. Even if it is a terrible plan, or no plan at all, at least give yourself a few seconds to think."

Zia was right again of course. Even if you don't make plays as great as his (who does?), the habit of thinking at trick one can help immeasurably in your dummy play. It doesn't matter whether you're thinking about the whole hand or merely the suit led. Here Zia gave himself time to work out the importance of sneaking through a diamond to the king. The simplest way to do that was to overtake the second trick. At the same time this would give West the impression that declarer held only two hearts.

Thus, having paused to analyze the hand, Zia called low from dummy. By the time West continued a heart at trick two, Zia was ready for his unique overtake, without having to think about it at the crucial moment.

Pulling trumps

I poured some more spiced tea through my strainer and asked Zia what he thought I should do about the Marcel Moskowitz affair.

"Is there any way you could go off to a bridge tournament for a couple of weeks?" he suggested.

I shook my head. The investigation had gone too far. There were hit men involved, and conspirators of the most unlikely sort. If I didn't find out who killed Marcel, they would soon find me, and that would be that.

"As long as you're about to be rubbed out any moment," said Zia, "why not come to the Cavendish and play in the all-night fifty-cent game? I'm sure a cheapskate like you carries no life insurance; at least if you have a big rubber or two, your wife will be taken care of for a week."

Since I had no intention of returning to the Embassy that night, I decided to accept Zia's suggestion. At least I would have some sanctuary until morning and a chance to recoup my thoughts and plan some sort of action.

I took a quick last sip, forced Zia to pay the check (after all I didn't have a wallet), and told him to hail a cab while I waited inside. When a taxi stopped, Zia and the redheads got in the back and opened the front door for me. I ran quickly from the restaurant, hopped in, and squeezed myself under the dashboard.

"Where to?" asked the cabbie, "Bellevue?"

"Close," answered Zia, "the Cavendish Bridge Club, 73rd and Park."

After a few blocks I sat upright on the seat and looked out. We were moving up Broadway to Central Park at what would normally feel like a horrific pace. In New York City, however, tailgating and jumping lanes are necessary ingredients of successful driving. We entered the park at 59th Street, almost running down a horse and buggy, two hoodlums in red leather jackets, a gang of prostitutes, and five or six groups of couples returning home at 1:00 a.m. from foreign films.

Staring at the shadowed trails around the lake, I was thankful to be inside the cab, and wondered what it would be like stranded in the park at this time of night. I asked myself why I had postponed the investigation of Marcel's murder just when it was coming to a climax? Fear of the hit men? Fear of the mad woman detective? Or because posing as a corpse to trap killers was a fantastic scheme with no sound reason to it. There must be a way to find out what happened that night forty years ago without risking my own life in the process.

We came out of the park, turned up Madison from 72nd Street and whizzed over to Park Avenue. The four of us left the cab at the corner of 73rd and walked down the street until we came to a renovated brownstone. The lobby was dark with black paneling and hundred-year-old etchings on the ceiling. Zia pushed a bell next to 'Cavendish Club' and while we waited to be buzzed in, he told the redheads to have a drink down the block and come back in a couple of hours. Then the two of us entered the foyer and squeezed into a tiny elevator.

When the door opened on the fourth floor, I wanted to die. There was Marie, in a flaming red dress, her blonde hair back to normal, flowing down her back. She was sitting calmly at a card table chatting with an older gentleman who was wearing sunglasses. I quickly tried to push the down button, but the ancient lift was too slow and she had just enough time to stride across the room and get in while Zia got out. I noticed her purse and saw the impression of a gun's barrel forcing the alligator skin in my direction. When we started down again, I took the offensive.

"Have you found the killer yet?"

"Shut your face you creep. We missed topping our section by two match-points."

"As long as we're on the topic, I have a date for a late-night bridge game with my friend Zia."

"You have a date at the Embassy Hotel, Room 623 as the corpse of Marcel Moskowitz."

"Don't worry, I found you another body. Zia's booked in Room 625 and is looking forward to a little action around four a.m."

"No good," she said, sticking her purse into my ribs. "I left word with our suspects to meet at Room 623 to see the body. They expect to congregate around three."

"Do they think Marcel is coming back from the grave?"

"Shut up. They know it's you disguised as the corpse. They're coming to kill you."

"All the more reason for someone else to stand in for me," I explained.

The elevator door opened, but I managed to push the 'Close' button. Back up we went.

"Don't worry," she said, hitting button '1'. "We'll have the entire police force ready to move in the minute they enter the room."

Somehow I couldn't quite imagine the entire New York City Police Force surrounding Room 623 at the Embassy Hotel to solve a forty-year-old murder.

Suddenly we stopped, and the door opened on the first floor. Zia and the older gentleman were standing in front of the elevator with two decks of cards. Both of them were out of breath. Obviously they had run down the stairs. Was it to rescue me?

"There you are," said Zia, panting. "We're ready to start. Hurry up, old Pigeon Smidgeon here has to leave by two-thirty. Can your blondy friend fill in?"

The gun barrel moved deeper into my stomach. Then there was a pause. She was obviously tempted. "One or two rubbers," she said. "Then we go."

We sat down in the card room and Zia took out a scorepad and placed it next to Marie. "We're playing for fifty dollars a hundred," he told her. "Do you want to be carried?"

"So you're the great Zia Mahmood," answered the charming Marie. "I'll play for my own stakes." With that she shuffled the deck seven different ways inside and out. Then with a flourish Houdini never had, said "After all, I'd like to see how great you really are."

Zia's eyes began to shine. "One game at a time," he countered, and cut the deck.

I edged Zia aside. "This is the one, you idiot. Don't mess with her."

"I know how to take care of myself you bloody fool."

With that, the older gentlemen, Zia, Marie, and I cut to see who would be partners the for the first set of Chicago. Zia picked a deuce, the older gent a three spot, and once again I was stuck with Marie across the table. Zia ordered champagne, and Marie asked if anyone minded if she bet extras. Zia and the old gent each took twenty more cents and I dealt the cards, my hands shaking. To play serious money bridge under these conditions was insane, and the first deal demonstrated how nervous I was.

MARIE
- ♠ Q J
- ♡ A K 8 7
- ◊ A 7 5 2
- ♣ A Q 7

ZIA
- ♠ 6 5
- ♡ Q J 4 3
- ◊ K Q J 9 4
- ♣ K J

OLD GENT
- ♠ 10 9 8 7
- ♡ 9 6 5
- ◊ 10 8 6
- ♣ 10 5 2

ME
- ♠ A K 4 3 2
- ♡ 10 2
- ◊ 3
- ♣ 9 8 6 4 3

ZIA	MARIE	O.G.	ME
			pass
1◊	dbl	pass	4♠
pass	6♠	all pass	

Zia led the diamond king. "There," said Marie laying down the dummy. "I didn't cuebid, like you said."

I tried to study the hand carefully before playing to trick one, but my mind wasn't working. Yes, I could see twelve tricks if the clubs divided three-two with the king onside. But then there was the matter of drawing trumps. A three-three trump split would make it simple for me to draw them, then set up the clubs. How about the more likely four-two split?

Suppose I cash the queen and jack, then come to my hand with a diamond ruff. No good, since after drawing trumps I'll have none left, and no way to get back to the clubs even if I could establish them. My head was pounding.

She's liable to unload that pistol if I don't make this, I thought. Maybe it was safer to return to the Embassy. I looked towards the window. Should I make a dash for it? I could jump out one flight down and scramble home. Scramble... scramble. Too complicated a plan, I thought. Zia wouldn't like it. Is this that sort of hand where I reverse the dummy? With only two trumps over there?

Yes, perhaps I could trump all of dummy's red suit losers in my hand, and lose a club at the end. That's three diamond ruffs and two heart ruffs. I'll need to be in dummy five times. That's simple: the ace of diamonds, the ace-king of hearts, and the ace-queen of clubs are five entries. So I embarked on my plan.

I won the lead with the diamond ace, ruffed a diamond in my hand, and led to the heart king. I ruffed another diamond in hand, and led back to the heart ace. Next I led the last diamond and East trumped in with the spade ten. I cursed. Maybe I should have ruffed a heart first. This was the position with me to play after the ten of spades:

MARIE
♠ Q J
♡ 8 7
◇ 7
♣ A Q 7

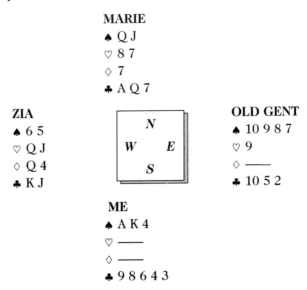

ZIA
♠ 6 5
♡ Q J
◇ Q 4
♣ K J

OLD GENT
♠ 10 9 8 7
♡ 9
◇ ——
♣ 10 5 2

ME
♠ A K 4
♡ ——
◇ ——
♣ 9 8 6 4 3

I over-ruffed the ten with the king, took a club finesse, and ruffed a heart in my hand with the spade four. A club to the ace and the last heart ruffed in hand with the trump ace left everyone with three cards. But dummy's queen-jack of spades had to win two tricks, and the slam was secure.

I heard Zia's teeth grind. He muttered something under his breath about 'lucky bastard' as Marie merrily wrote down 980 on our side. Headache and all, I had planned the hand nicely. I had counted to twelve, and scrambled home the tricks I needed, strangely enough without drawing a single trump. "Is there anything I must do before pulling trumps?"

I suppose I was a bit lucky, and maybe I should have played for three-three trumps, drawing them immediately. The simplest plan often involves just managing the trump suit properly. I can't tell you how many times I've gone down in contracts by fooling around in other suits before pulling trumps. However, there are many deals where trumps must wait until more important matters, like ruffing losers or establishing a side suit, are taken care of. The question of how to distinguish the hands where the postponement of the trump suit is vital must be addressed every time you declare in a suit contract. The simplest way is to ask yourself 'Is there anything I must do before pulling trumps?' I got a chance to ask myself this question on the second deal:

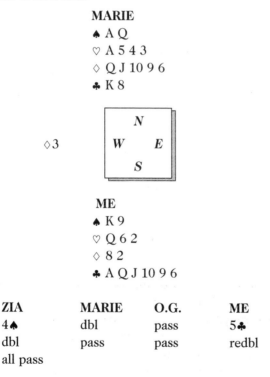

MARIE
♠ A Q
♡ A 5 4 3
◊ Q J 10 9 6
♣ K 8

◊ 3

ME
♠ K 9
♡ Q 6 2
◊ 8 2
♣ A Q J 10 9 6

ZIA	MARIE	O.G.	ME
4♠	dbl	pass	5♣
dbl	pass	pass	redbl
all pass			

Quite cocky from the hand before, I redoubled with my extra strength, then made the mistake of underestimating my opponents by a lot.

TO DRAW TRUMPS OR NOT TO DRAW TRUMPS?

There was little to plan upon examination of dummy. I needed to set up dummy's diamonds, and Zia had obligingly led one. Hopefully his partner would win and continue. I played quickly from dummy and the old gent, who up until now had never said a word, turned to me. "You trying to fast-card me?"

I was a bit taken aback. I mean, well, I guess I should have paused before playing to trick one. Now the old gent paused on defense, I suppose, to make up for my speedy play. Finally he produced the diamond king and returned the ten of hearts. That return was not good for me. The play of the queen was my best shot. After all, there was a 50% chance the old gent held the king of hearts. Alas, on the queen of hearts Zia produced the king, and I won in dummy with the ace.

It was at this point I should have asked myself the key question:

"Is there anything I must do before pulling trumps?"

On this hand there really wasn't much to do besides pull trumps and hope for a miracle (that the hand with the ace of diamonds had no more hearts).

I did not pull trumps, however. Instead I looked for an immediate way to make the contract. And I found it. I would sneak through a diamond before East knew what was happening. I led dummy's smallest diamond toward my singleton eight in the hope of getting it by the old gent. Ha, ha, the old gent fell for it! He followed low, I played the diamond eight holding back a grin, but Zia won the ace! I forgot he was capable of underleading that card. Suddenly Zia put a spade on the table and the old gent ruffed! This was the whole layout:

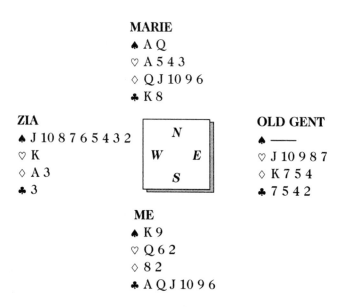

MARIE
♠ A Q
♡ A 5 4 3
◊ Q J 10 9 6
♣ K 8

ZIA
♠ J 10 8 7 6 5 4 3 2
♡ K
◊ A 3
♣ 3

OLD GENT
♠ ——
♡ J 10 9 8 7
◊ K 7 5 4
♣ 7 5 4 2

ME
♠ K 9
♡ Q 6 2
◊ 8 2
♣ A Q J 10 9 6

Next Old Gent tried to cash his two good heart winners, but Zia trumped the second one to give his partner another spade ruff.

My head was spinning as I held it in both hands and when I looked up I was down four tricks! At Cavendish vulnerability, that meant 2200 points to the opponents.

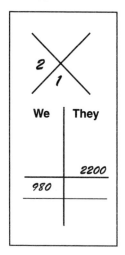

This time it was Zia who merrily wrote down the score. Marie was hopping up and down in her seat in a frenzy and I was really scared of what she might do. I quickly explained, "No way to imagine that this madman (pointing to Zia) underled an ace against a redoubled contract."

"Why didn't you draw trumps?" Marie asked, trying her best to hold back hysterics.

Yes, why didn't I? Zia cut the deck, and added his two cents. "Naturally I could have beaten you a couple tricks off the top by leading spades, but I had no idea my partner was void. Really, you should have worked out the diamond position. If my partner had the ace-king he might not have paused at trick one. As it was, he made a fine play covering the queen with the king. After all, he was playing with the one player in the world who would underlead the ace.

"There again we could have beaten you one trick with a diamond return and a spade ruff, but how was he to know I had underled a doubleton ace? His ten of hearts return cleverly deceived you. Granted it was hard for you to resist covering the ten, but after winning in dummy it was child's play to draw trumps before continuing on. I'm sure even your students know this much. Had you drawn trumps and then knocked out my diamond ace, you would have been pleasantly surprised to learn I had no more hearts to return, and you would have made your redoubled game."

"He would have made it?" screamed Marie.

"Yes," said Zia, "but what's a mere swing of three thousand points between friends? Eh?"

Marie sprang up and, thankful for the earlier practice, I bolted right down under the table. I swear I saw her go for her purse, but then I heard Zia say some words of appeasement, and I got back into my chair.

"I never rush my debtors," Zia said to Marie, a Casanova smile on his lips.

"Uh, are we breaking up?" said Old Gent suddenly.

"No, no," said Zia.

"Then nobody owes anybody anything yet. Right?"

Counting winners or losers

The third deal put the old gent on play in a precarious three-diamond contract:

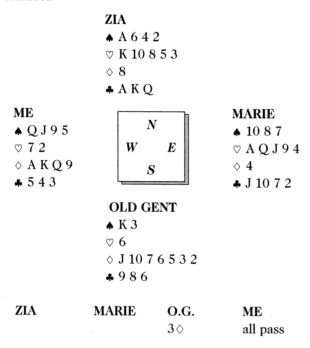

ZIA
♠ A 6 4 2
♡ K 10 8 5 3
♢ 8
♣ A K Q

ME
♠ Q J 9 5
♡ 7 2
♢ A K Q 9
♣ 5 4 3

MARIE
♠ 10 8 7
♡ A Q J 9 4
♢ 4
♣ J 10 7 2

OLD GENT
♠ K 3
♡ 6
♢ J 10 7 6 5 3 2
♣ 9 8 6

ZIA	MARIE	O.G.	ME
		3♢	all pass

Old Gent opened three diamonds and I passed happily with my trump stack. I was hoping, of course, that my partner would reopen with a takeout double, which I would convert to penalties. Zia made a good pass without pausing (which would have given away his strength). Marie, who was really too weak to balance, thought about it for a few seconds because of her singleton diamond, but in the final analysis she had to pass.

Defending a partscore at money bridge can be more vital than defending a partscore at duplicate. However, my four sure trump tricks gave me a sense of security, and I relaxed. This was a mistake.

I led the spade queen, dummy hit, and Old Gent studied the hand briefly. He played low from both hands, and I continued the suit without thinking. After all, I now had a sure set.

As the reader will already have noted, Old Gent was no ordinary old gent. He won the king of spades at trick two and led a club to dummy. Then he discarded his singleton heart on the spade ace, and ruffed a heart. Another club to dummy and another heart ruff in hand followed. Finally a third club to dummy and a spade ruff in hand left everyone with only four cards:

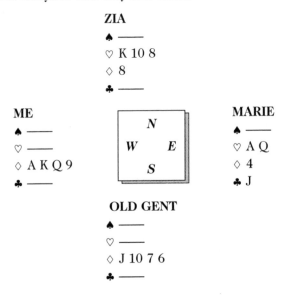

ZIA

♠ ——
♡ K 10 8
◊ 8
♣ ——

ME

♠ ——
♡ ——
◊ A K Q 9
♣ ——

MARIE

♠ ——
♡ A Q
◊ 4
♣ J

OLD GENT

♠ ——
♡ ——
◊ J 10 7 6
♣ ——

Old Gent was in his hand, with a choice of leading a low diamond or the jack. If Marie had held a diamond honor she would have ruffed in on the fourth spade, so he now tabled the diamond jack. I won and had to concede the last trick and the contract.

This was a brilliantly played hand. Any ordinary declarer would have counted his losers: one heart and three trump tricks if the diamonds divided three-two. Personally, I would have won the opening lead in dummy and led a trump. Then, whatever they returned, I would have played another trump hoping for a normal split. This is a simple plan which would work most of the time. On this occasion, however, the four-one trump division would have done me in. Yet not only had this old geezer played for a four-one trump split, but he also did it by making an incredible deceptive duck at trick one, followed by a dummy-reversal strip and an endplay in trumps!

"Well done," said Zia, honestly impressed. "But how did you know about the 4-1 split?"

"Wasn't I doubled?" said Old Gent.

"I didn't double," said Marie.

"Well," said Old Gent, "it sure sounded like I was doubled. And it sounded like somebody on my left made a loud penalty pass."

Was he putting us on, or what? Did he mishear the bidding or had he deduced the bad trump split by the split second hesitations in the bidding? If he knew what he was doing, he was the best bridge player I ever saw.

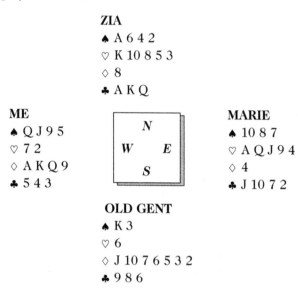

ZIA
♠ A 6 4 2
♡ K 10 8 5 3
♢ 8
♣ A K Q

ME
♠ Q J 9 5
♡ 7 2
♢ A K Q 9
♣ 5 4 3

MARIE
♠ 10 8 7
♡ A Q J 9 4
♢ 4
♣ J 10 7 2

OLD GENT
♠ K 3
♡ 6
♢ J 10 7 6 5 3 2
♣ 9 8 6

Even with his sensational table presence, if he had counted his losers, he would never have seen the successful line of play. Contrary to everything we've learned about declarer play in a suit contract, he must have counted winners. Two spade tricks, three club tricks, and four diamond tricks were needed. By ducking the lead he could pitch his heart later and use three entries to dummy to trump three cards. Finally he would get his fourth trump trick by leading the suit and making the defenders play to him. When I thought about this afterwards, his plan did not seem so complex. Yet how did he know to count winners rather than losers? In notrump you count winners; in suit contracts you count losers, or do you?

On the fourth hand Zia graciously allowed Marie to take her

deal. I ended up back in the declarer's seat, and even though it was a trump contract, I was determined to count my winners.

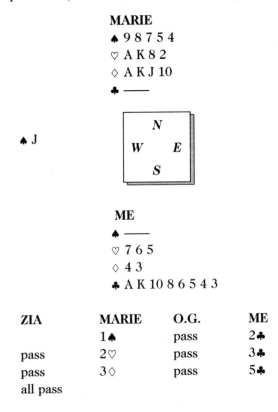

MARIE
♠ 9 8 7 5 4
♡ A K 8 2
◇ A K J 10
♣ ———

♠ J

N
W   E
S

ME
♠ ———
♡ 7 6 5
◇ 4 3
♣ A K 10 8 6 5 4 3

ZIA	MARIE	O.G.	ME
	1♠	pass	2♣
pass	2♡	pass	3♣
pass	3◇	pass	5♣
all pass			

To suggest that Marie put down her dummy in a bad frame of mind would be to put it mildly. She stared at me and said "Make it." Somewhere in my imagination I heard two more words: "...or die."

As I said, I was determined to count my winners, and I did just that. Zia led the spade jack and I tallied up: two sure heart tricks, two sure diamond tricks, and seven sure club tricks if they divided 3-2. That came to eleven sure tricks on a good trump split, otherwise ten, in which case I would still need another trick, presumably from the diamond suit.

To be honest, I couldn't resist counting losers too, just for old times' sake. So I looked at my hand, the master hand, and added them up — one possible heart loser and one or two club losers. To heck with this counting winners business! No wonder counting losers was recommended by every bridge teacher in the country — it's so much easier than counting all those winners.

I trumped the spade lead and led out the ace and king of clubs hoping to claim if the trumps split. They didn't, however, and with two sure trump losers I was forced to locate the queen of diamonds to keep from losing another trick. I could either take a straight finesse through Zia on my left, or play off the ace and king, then ride the jack through East.

As I tried to find a sound reason for guessing the diamond queen, the importance of locating that card began to seem ridiculous. There I was at two in the morning playing a game that had little to do with real life. Yet, if I failed to locate a stupid picture card, I ran the risk of being murdered by my partner. I looked up at her. A madwoman for sure. I supposed she had to be a bit mad to become a homicide detective in a jungle like New York City. Yet she too, somewhere very early in life, had succumbed to the magic of contract bridge. The fact that locating the queen of diamonds might mean more to her than solving the murder of Marcel Moskowitz scared me, and created a fog about my brain that wouldn't let me think clearly. Yes, Zia had only one club, so was likely to hold more length in diamonds. But he had made that strange jack of spades lead. Could that be from A-K-Q-J? Did that mean he held the spade length and that Old Gent had the diamonds?

Suddenly Marie made another move for her purse and I almost dropped my cards. She came around behind me to kibitz (just what I needed). How could I count a hand that had so few clues? I felt the bulge of her purse against my neck. Maybe I could sit there all morning and never play a card. Maybe I would have a heart attack before the next trick. Counting my losers might have been easy, but it didn't help, did it? Was it too late to replan the hand? Old Gent counted winners. Why? Winners are harder to count, but I guess sometimes it's necessary. All right, one more time.

Two sure heart tricks, two sure diamond tricks, seven sure club tricks if the suit divides three-two. It hadn't. Only six sure club tricks, since I must lose two of them... no... stop it now... don't count losers, count winners. Four red tricks I can cash. How many trump tricks can I make? I ruffed the opening lead, that's one. I cashed the ace and king; we're up to three. I have five more trumps left... and four entries to dummy! Four more trump tricks and I make seven trumps in all!

I led a heart to dummy and trumped a spade in my hand. Another heart to dummy and another spade ruff. Next a diamond to dummy and another spade ruff while Old Gent pitched a diamond. Finally, a second diamond to dummy leaving this position:

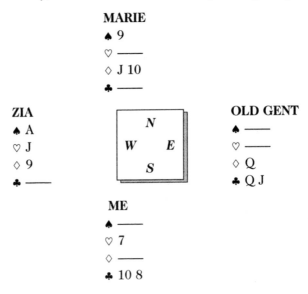

MARIE
♠ 9
♡ ——
◊ J 10
♣ ——

ZIA
♠ A
♡ J
◊ 9
♣ ——

OLD GENT
♠ ——
♡ ——
◊ Q
♣ Q J

ME
♠ ——
♡ 7
◊ ——
♣ 10 8

I led dummy's last spade and Old Gent tossed his cards in. He could not stop me from making my seventh trump trick for eleven tricks in all. Two realizations came over me. First, counting winners may be harder than counting losers but it certainly works better. Second, when your original plan fails, you can often replan and find you still have time to recover.

With that second thought in mind I slowly slipped my hand behind my neck and caressed Marie's arm. Then I turned and grabbed her purse. I ran to the window and jumped. Sick and tired of playing patsy to a mad bridge addict, I decided to regroup and plan a new course of action, with myself as declarer, myself in charge.

11 SPORTS PSYCHOLOGY

Bridge is a mental sport

I headed west towards Fifth Avenue clutching the purse, a woman's footsteps clicking on the pavement a block or so behind me. Then I saw a police car parked near the Metropolitan Museum. I slowed down to a brisk walk and entered Central Park at 79th Street. This time I was on foot, but it was my only safe haven.

Once inside the park, I started to run again. I ran and ran and ran. It was too bad I was only a bridge player. Had I been a professional in any physical sport I would have been able to keep going.

When I stopped, my heart was beating rapidly. Looking up at the skyline, I could see checkerboard squares, dark and light windows of high-rise apartments across the West Side. West would take me out of the park, so I started again, at a slower pace, turning right about fifty yards where I paused by a statue of a man and his dog. I thought I heard a sound. Behind me Central Park South loomed higher, rooftops pasted together of Pierre and Plaza look-alikes, their 19th-century arches concealing hotel rooms still designed for romantic interludes. Somewhere further back must be the Embassy, and I shivered in the August stillness.

There was a giggle to my right. It was a horse-drawn buggy carrying two lovers eastward. The Cavendish was in that direction, and I knew it was a mistake to stop.

Crossing the road, I jogged past the skating rink, then up a horse-riding path, northbound. If only I could be dummy for one hand, then I could rest. I needed time to think, to concentrate, to get in my shell.

A lake came into view on my left, reflecting lampposts and moonlit stars. Bodies were strewn across a line of benches, covered by blankets of newspaper and food cartons, and magazine pillows. I hurried on, climbing across a series of rocks near the water. There was a broken rowboat floating on the edge of the boathouse. Why shouldn't I rest? What was there to be scared of? Wasn't I the one holding the gun? I clambered in, and the boat began to drift slowly across the lake.

There was a sharp pain in my abdomen. I had run too fast. Out of shape, like most bridge players, I considered how my physical condition was affecting my mind. If there is such a thing as a mental sport, bridge is it. Yet training the bridge player's brain to think clearly without strain or headache was not part of any teaching method I knew. The strain of hours at the table with little relief from problems and anxieties must be worse than the strain of a long-distance runner. There should be practices, exercises, psychological techniques for this mental sport. The enormous potential for great thinking still remains untapped in even the best players. We all know to varying degrees how to bid, how to declare, how to defend. What we lack universally is the most important ingredient: how to prepare.

Concentration

Few of us have much time to sit down and think. Our lives are too hectic — work, money, families and all our other responsibilities take their toll. Perhaps this is why most of us enjoy escaping to the bridge table and its aesthetic cardboard world. There we can relax. There also we have designated time for thought. "Fifteen minutes a round." "Stay in your seats." "Please pause ten seconds." "I'm not thinking about this trick, I'm thinking about the whole hand." At the bridge table we use time periods to deliberate, but the level of our success often depends on the degree of concentration we can muster.

Get in your shell

Many of us go to the evening's duplicate after a long day of work. Our brain and body are both tired. The advantage of the person who sleeps late and wanders into the club fresh and relaxed is obvious. Even a short nap before coming to the bridge club can improve your score.

A good remedy for a tired mind is acting exercises. These can be done a few minutes before you begin play. Roll your neck around, close your eyes and concentrate on distributions. Repeat: 4-3-3-3, 4-4-3-2, 5-3-3-2, etc. Forget about the other activities of the day. Shake your arms and legs and head. Reach for the ceiling, as if a top score hung down from the roof, and try to grab it. Chant silently to yourself, "I am in my shell, I am in my shell, I am a great bridge player, I am a great bridge player." These types of exercises can help a player refresh his brain for the three hours of mental strain to come. You can try different methods, or make up your own chants until you find something that works for you. It doesn't matter what techniques you use as long as three things are accomplished in this preparatory stage:

1) You empty your brain of the day's activities,

2) You start working on picturing cards, and

3) You convince yourself that you are a competent player about to reach a new peak.

The concept of getting (and remaining) 'in your shell' is important to these preparations. The fact that most bridge experts play at a level far below their potential is frightening. This is mainly because they do not concentrate well. They allow opponents, partner and kibitzers to distract them. Getting in your shell can increase your score because your thinking process will expand. If I recollect the tournaments I've won, I can barely remember anything but the hands — not the location, not the players, and often not my partner!

When you sit down at the table for the start of a duplicate, take a few seconds to imagine a shell around you. Pretend you cannot see your partner or your opponents. You can only see the table directions and cards. Now you are into the game. The second someone speaks (for example, partner asks you what you did today or how the kids are), you may come out of this 'shell'. But each time you take your cards out of the duplicate board, return to your shell. As you sort your cards, don't listen to the chatter at the table about what might have been on the hand before. Time marches on. Each deal must represent a new challenge, and the sorting of cards is the trigger mechanism you can use to return to your shell.

Now the bids are made around the table, the bids enter your shell, but not the people who are making them. When the play begins, you allow the cards to join in the circle of your shell, and so forth. No matter what craziness, ineptitudes, or hopeless plays are being made around you, you stay cool inside your shell.

Enjoy yourself like a ballplayer

Just thinking about these matters made me forget where I was, and the danger I was in. Unfortunately, when you are sitting in a broken rowboat in the middle of Central Park Lake at two-thirty in the morning, being hunted by a mad detective, two hit men, and other assorted conspirators, it may not be to your advantage to forget where you are.

Indeed, the boat I was in had drifted away from the shoreline. Looking in that direction, I could make out a young woman struggling with the oar of another rowboat. Three men surrounded her as she pointed towards the water. I glanced behind me like an idiot. Of course she was pointing at me.

I scurried about for an oar and found one on the bottom of the rowboat. It was a mixed blessing, however, for when I lifted it up a spout of water opened up where the oar handle had been. I tried to stick my shoe over the hole while rowing only on the right side. It was a struggle, but even when it was successful I kept turning the boat in circles instead of heading in any direction. I heard quacking as a family of ducks swam by me on the left. Behind me I saw the woman coming, the three men close behind in rowboats of their own. Time was running out, so I took the plunge and felt the cool water flow through my clothes.

The way to do this is not to panic, I thought. Like a good bridge

player, I must concentrate on what I am doing, not on the end result. I took a deep breath and went under water, swimming in sound strokes, reviewing my breath patterns. Suddenly I remembered the purse, lifted my head up and like a mirage saw it floating on top of my deserted, sinking rowboat. I swam back and grabbed it, hearing voices in the distance. Then, without looking south again, I put it around my wrist and headed north.

I had to think of swimming and only swimming, yet there was little time to prepare my brain for this. So I concentrated on the swimming lessons I had as a boy in school. I made it a game. I made it fun! That's what professional ballplayers do, don't they? By taking the attitude of going out and enjoying themselves, they end up playing their best. It's losing strategy to keep looking up at the scoreboard, or down into your convention card.

Pressing onward,

almost enjoying it, I soon reached the embankment. I pulled myself up and pretending I was in a triathlon, started to run the half mile, into the woods, deeper and deeper into the woods.

Coping with disaster

I must have put ten city blocks behind me before I fell. Grass and pebbles filled my mouth, and when I got up I saw what had happened. A rope tied to a tree along a jogging path had been set up as a trap to stop anyone running across the grass. Three men and a woman dressed in leather and chains appeared from behind the trees. I looked down at the ground and saw Marie's purse. Reaching for it, I also saw the gun had fallen out and lay partially hidden next to a rock.

"Lose your purse, Sweetie Pie?"

"Aw, poor girl lost his purse."

"I wonder what he's got in that nice purse?" The woman reached down and took it out of my hands, then pushed me over the rock where I hit the ground a second time. The gun was now under my left ankle.

The woman saw there was nothing inside, cursed, and bent down to see if the contents had been knocked out.

It occurred to me that I always handled disaster well at the bridge table (having an inordinate amount of practice). The closest I'd ever come to being mugged, however, was the time some clever teenager stole my vulnerable game with an 8-10 notrump opening. My philosophy has generally been to fight back on the next deal, and if I could get that gun into my hand, I was going to even this score pretty quickly.

"Twenty-six lousy dollars, and it's soaking wet. Mirror. Lipstick. Hair dye."

"Oooooh, Sweetie's gonna dye her hair tonight."

"A key, Room 623."

"Whoa, baby, Room 623."

"A list."

"Here, let's see."

"What the hell is this? A-K-9-7-3. Q-10-9-4."

"Gimme that. Those are playing cards, you jerk."

"How do you know?"

"My folks are always fighting over some crazy game called bridge. There, see, spades, hearts, diamonds, clubs."

"Holy shit! Look at this — a detective badge!"

"Lemme see."

"New York City Homicide."

"Hey, let's get outta here."

"Don't tell me Sweetie Pie is a cop."

"That's no detective badge."

"What are you talkin' about?"

"I've seen detective badges, this one's a phony."

"How do you know?"

"Look, there's no number."

"You mean Sweetie Pie's a cop impersonator?"

"He's a transvestite, and I hate transvestites."

The three men took out some chain thing and I knew I'd better make my move. I had edged the gun up near my wrist. There was a strange thumping sound in the distance. It was driving me crazy.

"Stand where you are!" I jumped up on the rock and spun the gun in all four directions. Unfortunately I spun too fast. Trying to get it all back on the next board has its drawbacks too, and this time I tried too hard. My wet shoes went out from under me, and four bodies converged on my stomach at once. The woman took out her chain and lifted it high above my cheek. I gritted my teeth, unable to move. The thumping sound was louder now. Suddenly a giant white thing flew up and snapped its teeth into the woman's forearm. She let out a scream, the chain dropping across my neck. More loud thumping, now barking, now other screams, obscenities, chaos.

I lifted my head and saw four Siberian Huskies and one beautiful mutt jumping up and down, pulling chains from the mob. The mutt was the only one barking, and he came over to me, sniffed my ear, and growled. Then one of the men pointed the gun at a husky. But it didn't go off, thank God. It just clicked and clicked, so he dropped it and ran with the rest of them. The dogs chased for a short distance, then returned to a whistle from a man in sunglasses who emerged from behind the treeline.

"Get over here! Sash! Imp! Little Imp! Bambi! Shut up, Tag!" Tag, the mutt, wouldn't stop barking. The huskies all came back, happy to see their master. I got up and went to retrieve the gun, the purse, and whatever else was left behind. Marcel's notes were missing. I took a closer look at the man in sun glasses. It was Old Gent from the Cavendish!

"All right, hush now." He dipped in his pocket and pulled out some small biscuits. Each dog except Tag sat down politely and took one from his hand. Tag jumped around until Old Gent gave him one too.

Finally, after all the dogs were content and settled, he addressed me. "Are you all right now?"

"Yeah, thanks. Thanks for saving my life."

"Don't thank me, thank the dogs."

"Yeah," I said, "well, uh..." I looked at the dogs. It was hard to find the right words to say to them.

"C'mon, let's go," he said. "Here, help me with these." He gave me two leashes, and I asked him where we were going.

"Where do you think we're going?" he barked back at me. So I shut my mouth and followed the herd as we headed north, then east through the park exit at 97th Street. Halfway down the block we entered an apartment house.

The doorman looked at me. "Picked up a stray, Vic?" Vic, I thought, my mind still dazed, how do I know that name? We crowded into a small elevator, all seven of us, and rode up to the tenth floor. On the apartment door I saw the names, Jacqui and Victor Mitchell. Then I remembered who he was.

Don't criticize partner's play of the hand

We entered a small foyer where we hung up the leashes, and the dogs quickly disappeared under various pieces of furniture in the living room. It was a small place, and I looked around for a place to wash my wounds. One husky was let into the bedroom by Mitchell. Was his wife sleeping inside? Then I found the bathroom and was as quiet as I could be, but almost died of shock when I saw myself in the full-length mirror. My hair was flying in all directions, and dried blood was everywhere. I was still wet, and when I saw a terry-cloth bathrobe hanging on the door I called into the living room to ask if I could use it.

"No, it's for the dogs," Mitchell said.

It took me a few seconds to realize he was being facetious. Then I stripped and put on the robe. Mitchell had made two cups of tea, one cup sitting by the sofa where I sat. The hot liquid went quickly to my head, contrasting sharply with the aches and pains that swarmed my exhausted body. I noticed some slippers on the floor and slipped my feet inside. There was a growl. Were they the dogs' slippers?

Meanwhile, Mitchell had said not another word. He sat on a

chair opposite the sofa, watching a television screen without sound. Some mystery movie was on. A corpse with multiple stab wounds was discovered on a train in Europe. Completely ignoring me, he proceeded to open up a racing form for the next day's betting at Saratoga.

I had never met Victor Mitchell, but I had heard of him. He had retired from bridge circles fifteen years ago, but his legend lived on. For nearly four decades he had been the greatest of the top New York bridge players. More importantly, this was the man who knew better than anybody else what happened on January 23, 1942, at the Embassy Hotel, Room 623. Victor Mitchell had been the owner and manager of the Bucket O' Blood, the bridge and chess club where Marcel Moskowitz spent his last evening playing duplicate with a woman named Marie.

Ten minutes went by and not a word. It must have been after 3:00 a.m. and I wondered whether I should break the silence. Suddenly from behind the racing form I heard, "You want a cookie?"

A husky popped its head out from under a chair. I wondered if Mitchell was talking to me. Another minute of silence. On the television, a French detective with a mustache was taking charge of the investigation. I took courage and spoke up. "What kind of cookie?"

Mitchell rose and went into the kitchen. He came out with a huge plate of homemade chocolate chip cookies. Furniture moved and the huskies reappeared. We all consumed our cookies, and I decided to attempt some conversation before I spent the rest of the night on the couch.

"You're the same Victor Mitchell from the Bucket O' Blood, aren't you?" No answer. "You know I've been investigating the murder of Marcel Moskowitz. Apparently a set of bridge notes was found on the body which prove he played duplicate the night before at your club, right?" Still no answer. "There was a woman named Marie who was his partner, and a Dr. X. who helped her analyze the hands. It's all on some photocopies from police records that were sent to me in the mail. Unfortunately the last copy was taken by those hoodlums in Central Park. Well, I mean, don't you have anything to say about all this?"

He put the racing form down and looked at me. "You're a com-

plete fool. Is that what you want to hear?"

I almost choked on a chocolate chip. "Uh, no, I just want to find out what you know."

"You want me to criticize the job you've done so far? Let's see, as a detective I'll give you a D-minus. What do you think Tag?" He was addressing one of the dogs.

The mutt scratched his neck, then whimpered. "Tag says I'm too lenient. So — you flunk."

"Gee, I mean, no I don't want you to criticize me; what I want is for you to help me analyze the case."

Mitchell adjusted his sunglasses. "I notice you like to criticize your partners. Do you think that helps them when they try to analyze the next hand?"

I looked down at the rug. What could I say? Yes, I did have a reputation for criticizing my partners. But no more so than the next guy. Everybody criticizes their partner. It's natural. But it's not so smart. Take any other sport. Can you imagine a tennis player turning to his partner who misses a shot, and bawling him out? How about a shortstop in the Major Leagues who makes an error? What would happen to his performance on the next play if one of his teammates ran over to tell him where he went wrong? It's absurd of course. Then why is it acceptable practice in duplicate bridge? When you think about it rationally, it must be worth tons of matchpoints simply to keep your mouth shut after partner makes a blunder.

The same could be said for my antics as an amateur sleuth. The last thing I needed to hear at this stage was criticism. I was exhausted and desperate to close the case. I needed help from Mitchell, not a verbal thrashing.

Don't even watch

"Sorry," I said. "I really have bungled this. You were the person I searched for at the beginning of the case, but I just couldn't find you."

"Are you aware of the fact that I go to the races every day?" asked Mitchell.

"Yes, I heard you were a horse player."

"Did you ever once think of coming out to the track?"

"Yes, I went once, but you weren't there. No one was there. All the local tracks are closed in August. Do you travel two hundred miles to Saratoga every day?"

"I go to Monmouth Park, New Jersey."

"Oh. I forgot about New Jersey."

"Well, if you had found me," continued Mitchell, "I wouldn't have talked to you. I do my best these days to stay away from incompetents."

I wiped my runny nose on a napkin. Mitchell didn't let up. "I've had years of practice trying not to notice my partners' incompetent declarer play. You can get ulcers sitting there as dummy watching partner bungle a hand. My wife reads catalogs or needlepoints while she's dummy. Some people think that's rude. I think it's self-preservation. There was a student of mine who never let me sit down at the bridge table until he had given me a copy of the next day's racing sheets. That was a considerate fellow. He knew what would happen if I had to sit there and watch him declare. Then one night he declared nineteen hands. There's only so much handicapping you can do in one evening. So I had to watch."

"What happened?" I asked.

"I went to a movie."

"You went to a movie?"

"Yeah. *Gone with the Wind* was playing at the corner. So I went over and bought a ticket. I told the ticket seller I was playing duplicate next door, that I'd be in and out. I had seen the movie already so it was okay. In fact, for the last three rounds I let him play all the hands. But after that night I told him unless a good film was showing next door, I couldn't play."

"He agreed to that?"

"He had no choice," said Mitchell. "But he figured out a way to get more sessions out of me." Mitchell shook his head and laughed.

HOLLYWOOD

Gone With the Wind
Starring Vivien Leigh and Clark Gable

Then he took off his sunglasses and held them up. For the first time I could see the man's eyes. They were the red, tired eyes of someone who has just been dozing. "He got me these. Special sunglasses that you can wear indoors or out."

Mitchell put his glasses back on and looked at the television. Flashbacks to the scene of a kidnapping revealed some of the train passengers as household staff in a huge white country estate. The plot of the movie was familiar. Somehow all the people on the train were connected to this kidnapping years earlier.

"What do your sunglasses have to do with watching partner play the dummy?" I asked.

"I use them to sleep."

Sleep, I thought. No wonder he hadn't talked to me before. He was probably dozing.

"In fact, it was a great idea," he continued. "I no longer had to insult my opponents by handicapping at the table. And when they closed down the theater next door, I still never had to watch partner bungle a hand. It was such a good method that I decided to wear them when I played with better players as well. Why not rest while even a competent partner plays the hand?"

Yes, why not, I thought. It's energy saved. You can't possibly criticize your partner for something you don't see. And on top of that, you're completely fresh for the next board. But to take a snooze behind sunglasses was going too far. Why not simply close your eyes or stare away from the table? "Then how do you reach for a card when partner calls it?" I asked.

"You can pull cards without analyzing can't you? I know every stupid thing you've done this week, and I haven't watched you one damn bit. You know why?"

I looked at the man. What was he talking about? My murder investigation? How could he know every stupid thing I've done this week?

"Spies," he said.

Don't play with him again

"You had me followed?" I asked bluntly.

Mitchell took off his glasses and gave me a look I was not unused to this week. "Follow you? I'd rather follow Tag over there under the TV stand." Indeed, there was the mutt licking the floor under the set. "Did you ever wonder why I quit duplicate bridge?"

I shook my head no.

"Even when I was dozing I dreamed of the mistakes my partner was making. I had to drop my worst students. It was a terrible thing. They took it personally. I don't suppose you'd understand that."

I shook my head no.

"Then my regular partners began to misplay hands. They tried to explain they knew what they were doing. So I dropped 'em all, no mercy."

I shook my head 'yes'.

"What else could I do? I was developing an ulcer. Health comes first, so if I caught anybody drawing trumps too early in the hand I gave 'em the brush off. Soon I stopped playing altogether. Doctor's orders." He looked around the room for a while, as if somebody were listening through the wall, then turned back to me. "It didn't help. Nightmares. The hands came to me in my regular sleep."

He paused for a very long time. Finally I made a suggestion. "Instead of counting sheep maybe you should count high cards."

"What?"

"Well, you could force yourself to begin dreams with the auction. And by the time the opening lead was made, with luck you'd wake up."

"Are you nuts or something?"

Don't lecture partner in front of the opponents

What Mitchell was saying about ending bridge relationships is true. It's much better to break up an unhappy partnership than to risk ulcers. Like a marriage, however, it's not so easy or necessarily wise to break up a bridge partnership over a few mistakes. Okay, if it becomes intolerable, if partner is not going to improve, then find someone else. Certainly that's preferable to lecturing on every other deal. Like having a fight with your spouse, the last thing you want to do is argue in front of other people. The spectators like to put their two cents in, and pow, you're fighting with them as well. Not only can battling with your partner become embarrassing, it gives aid and comfort to the 'enemy'.

On the other hand, if you don't say a word at the table, you risk keeping your anger inside, which can have an adverse effect on your own ability to concentrate. One way to let off steam after a bad bid or play is to put it in writing inside your scorecard. This is not, however, always the best solution. One fellow I know did this during a mixed pairs. After half the game was over, he left to go to the bathroom, but made the mistake of leaving his convention card on the table. His partner reached over to copy a score she had missed. When she opened up the convention card she saw this:

Bd. #	Contract	Plus	Minus	Estimate
1	4H		50	stupid idiot!
2	3S		140	what a jerk!
3	3NT		100	can't take a finesse!
4	6D		50	hopeless moron!!

Her partner came back to the table, and she quickly closed the card in a state of panic. On the next deal she went down in a three club contract. When he opened up the card to record the score, she leaned over and cried, "What are you gonna write this time?"

Don't discuss his errors behind his back either

The idea of letting off steam (without letting partner know about it) is a fine idea, if it can be done discreetly. Many players do this after the session by squealing on partner to other players. This is not such a good idea if you're hoping for a long-term partnership. Bad-mouthing usually gets back to your partner one way or the other, and some of the worst fights occur when one person rushes around the room to ask other 'designated experts' their opinion of partner's hopeless bid.

Surely that's what this Marie woman must have done to Marcel Moskowitz the night before he was murdered. How else could Dr. X. have been involved with the handwritten analyses? Al Roth seemed to recall Marcel's blunders as well. That's certainly cir-cumstantial evidence against Marie. She must have buttonholed the better players to let off steam after the session. Considering the dreadful bridge Marcel played that night, it's hard to blame her. But was it good for their partnership? I doubt it. In a few hours he was found dead, the analyses in his hands, their partnership ended for-ever.

Take the blame and say you're sorry

When I reintroduced the subject of Marcel's death to Mitchell, he was no longer averse to the discussion, at least within the context of partnership harmony.

"You're right in a way," he said. "Moskowitz was a hopeless player who never apologized at the table. Saying you're sorry when things go wrong, even if it's not your fault, can make things square again. But not this guy. He was like you — always thinking noth-ing was his fault. Yes, they ganged up on him afterwards in the post-mortem, but he had it coming because he had no humility."

Personally I didn't mind the insults so long as Mitchell spilled a few more beans my way. True, I rarely apologize at the table, but then I'm not a psychologist, I'm a player. I take care of my side of the table and I expect my partner to take care of her side.

Suddenly Mitchell stopped. He realized he was talking about the case. We both turned to the TV. Now I remembered this movie. It was the film version of the book I had been reading a few days ago. The murder of the man on the Orient Express was solved now.

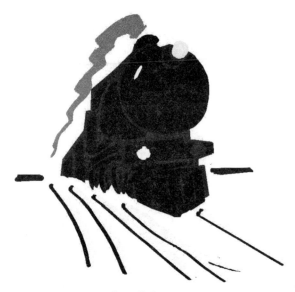

It was a mass revenge by *all* the passengers.

Mitchell clicked the TV off with the remote control. Was Marcel Moskowitz's murder also a mass revenge? It's not easy for a woman alone to smother a man to death. If Marie had accomplices in the analyses, then why not in the murder?

Mitchell went over to his desk and took the phone off the hook. Who was going to call him at three in the morning? However, the apartment buzzer rang a few seconds later. It was the doorman — a woman was looking for me downstairs. I jumped off the couch and shook my head violently. Mitchell spoke into the intercom. "It's all right, Harry. Send her up."

I argued with him. I tried to tell him that this female cop was crazy. Mitchell told me to shut up.

"Please," I said, "you don't know what she's liable to do. In one day she's knocked me unconscious, shaved off my mustache, blackmailed me, and chased me into Central Park Lake. She devised some crazy scheme to catch these hit men, with me disguised as Marcel Moskowitz, a sleeping duck in the same bed where he was killed. Worst of all, she forced me at gunpoint to play a full session of duplicate with her under the pretext of capturing these suspects, and committed sins at the bridge table far more criminal than any murder."

Mitchell stared at me through his dark lenses. "I don't suppose you helped her any."

"Helped her? Didn't you see her? At the Cavendish, she was going to kill me if I went down in six spades! Let's get outta here!"

"I'm talking about the bridge table. You never once said you were sorry, did you? Never once took the blame, just to smooth things out and help her play better. 'I love me, I think I'm grand. My partner can go to hell.' That's what all you young players think." Mitchell stood there, determined not to budge. I could swear I heard the elevator moving up to the tenth floor.

"I'm sorry. Okay. I'm sorry, sorry, sorry. I admit I should have come to you first before investigating this murder. But I'm in trouble now. Look — I should have said 'I'm sorry' to Marie. OK, I'm sorry. I'll be a good partner from here on in. For the rest of my life, all right? I'll take the blame, I'll smooth things out. I'll— " Mitchell handed me a leash, then opened the bedroom door.

A dog came out. "C'mon, Little," he said. The white husky followed orders, and the three of us stepped briskly into the service elevator, down to the basement, out of the side entrance, and once again into the safer haven of the dark August night.

After session discussions

When we reached the park, Mitchell let the dog off the leash and she bounded across the field until she was a white speck in the distance. This left me not a little concerned, since I thought the husky had come along for protection. We moved over to a lamp post about fifty yards inside the park entrance, and Mitchell lit a cigarette. "Mind if I smoke?" he asked. "Or are you one of those players who thinks a little smoke is going to kill you?"

I didn't say a word. I was looking around now, checking for a certain mad detective. There was nobody in sight. Just a bum stretched out on a bench about a city block away. The stillness of the air made the park seem eerie. Smoke curled up to the lamp light, creating an atmosphere that could have come straight out of a spy novel.

If there was a setting that would loosen Mitchell's tongue, this was certainly it. I was sure he knew the answers to the forty year old mystery. It was just a question of getting him to talk. Like at the end of a duplicate session, when two partners reveal the whys and wherefores of the hands they just played, I was hoping Mitchell would become my partner in a Central Park post-mortem.

Privacy helps

"There's no one around," I said. "Please tell me why Marcel was murdered. After all, it's over with, it was years ago. Why do all these people care so much so many years later?"

Mitchell considered my words as he puffed on his cigarette. I knew he wanted to talk. All players, no matter what the game, have a strong desire to speak the truth. I myself have screamed at my partner at the table, only to apologize the next day and admit I was wrong. It's just a matter of settling down, getting away from the other players, confessing your sins, and relieving your soul. Mitchell had saved my life, taken me into his home for shelter, and chastised me for my faulty investigation. Now he was ready to reveal the truth.

"All right," he said, stamping out his cigarette butt, "I suppose after all you've been through you deserve something." He took out some papers from the inside pocket of his jacket. I was surprised to see another copy of Marcel's notes. Did everybody have copies? He took off his sunglasses and thumbed through the sheets. Then he nodded to me to walk with him behind the lamppost. "Here. Look at this hand. It was the next to last round of the evening."

After a bad board, try harder on the next hand

Exhibit #17
Board 6

East dealer
East-West vulnerable

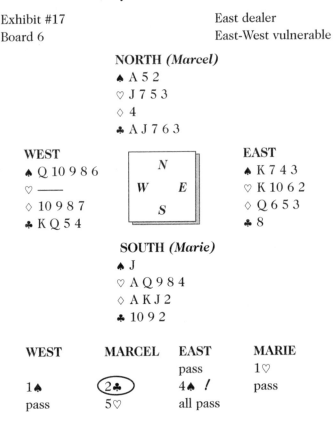

NORTH (Marcel)
♠ A 5 2
♡ J 7 5 3
◇ 4
♣ A J 7 6 3

WEST
♠ Q 10 9 8 6
♡ ——
◇ 10 9 8 7
♣ K Q 5 4

EAST
♠ K 7 4 3
♡ K 10 6 2
◇ Q 6 5 3
♣ 8

SOUTH (Marie)
♠ J
♡ A Q 9 8 4
◇ A K J 2
♣ 10 9 2

WEST	MARCEL	EAST	MARIE
		pass	1♡
1♠	2♣	4♠ /	pass
pass	5♡	all pass	

Opening lead: ♣K
Result: down 1

I noted the criticism of Marcel's two club call. Over four spades he felt compelled to bid five hearts, having yet to support his partner with four trumps.

Five hearts seemed like a reasonable contract, but the 4-0 trump split made things difficult. After winning the ace of clubs, Marie might have attempted to pull trumps quickly. She probably laid down the trump ace. There was the threat of a club ruff, and the heart king might be offside anyway. After the ace of hearts was played, however, it was difficult to recover.

She couldn't play clubs until all the trumps were drawn, and she couldn't ruff two diamonds in dummy because one small trump was needed to finesse against East's heart ten. So her best chance was to lead a trump to the jack. If East won the king of hearts, and returned a spade, destroying dummy's entry to the clubs, she could still make the hand, finessing the diamond queen, ruffing a diamond, and finessing the heart ten.

East must have held up his heart king on the second round of the suit. Now Marie was in trouble. If she continued hearts, East would win the king and make the deadly spade switch. If she finessed the diamond queen next and ruffed one, she would be stuck in dummy while East still had a trump. There would be no way to get back to her hand to draw it except by ruffing a spade, thus shortening her own trumps before a second club trick was established.

What a headache for declarer. Yet Marcel was blamed once again. Had he done anything terribly wrong by bidding two clubs before raising hearts? Wasn't it good practice to bid your second suit to help partner evaluate her cards? I posed these questions to Mitchell.

"You talk like somebody who just learned the game and tries to hit the daily double on every deal. You want to be perfect? Play chess, don't bother me about bridge. You want to be a winner? That's another story." He held up the notes under the lamp. "You see this? Case of a guy who only reads the past performance sheet and never sets foot in the paddock."

"What are you talking about?"

"What are you talking about? Are you talking about coming home a winner or betting every race? You want to bet every race, go ahead. Have a good time. Have a ball. But don't come running to me when you're busted."

I looked at the paper again to make sure we were discussing bridge, not the racetrack. Mitchell looked up at the sky and recollected.

"Morris used to like to have a lot of fun. A different woman every night, which was dangerous, and a new adventure on every bridge hand, which was even more dangerous."

"Morris?" I asked. "Who's Morris?"

"Marcel, Morris, same thing. He was the son of a very religious fellow, believe it or not, a tailor who kept a little racing office in the back of his shop. We all grew up in Brooklyn together. Attended the same local pool hall. Didn't matter, Catholic, Jewish, it was all the same in the bookie business. But Morris, he was always trying to be someone classier than he was. Took the name of Marcel to impress women. I think he actually spoke a little French. Yeah, come to think of it, I heard him once at the track talking in a foreign language." Mitchell rubbed his chin. "But maybe it was Yiddish. Anyway, he was always trying too hard to be something he wasn't."

"What about this hand?" I asked, trying to lead the conversation back to the night in question.

"This hand?" Mitchell said, adjusting the paper to the lamp light. "If you studied these sheets, you would know how many disasters he had."

"If I ever had so many disasters in one evening I'd think of killing *myself*," I said. Suddenly I felt cold. I looked down at myself. I was still wearing Mitchell's robe.

"Naw," said Mitchell. "Nobody ever got depressed at the Bucket O' Blood over disasters. Guys were always losing their shirts or getting wiped out at gin or something. It was my policy to keep 'em all happy. Psychologically, you see, the people who came to my club were pretty tough. They came to play games, win or lose. If somebody in a bridge game had a disaster, he would pick up his cards to the next hand, and say, 'Balls! I'm gonna get it back!' That was the Bucket O' Blood attitude. So when Morris picked up this hand, it was only natural for him to try even harder. He was that kinda guy to begin with, or he wouldn't have been in the club."

"But that doesn't explain why he bid two clubs rather than raise partner's hearts immediately," I interjected. "Was it that he didn't really care — win or lose, it was all the same?"

"Do I have to draw you a map?" snapped Mitchell. "It was just the opposite. *He was trying too hard.* You can't play bridge that way. You've got to relax, let loose, permit your reflexes to work. Yes, you want to get back a bad result from the last board, but you don't want to cause a new disaster by over-trying.

"Actually, the best and simplest way to get a good score is to bid less scientifically. If I held the North cards, and it went one heart, one spade to me, I would simply raise to four hearts. Slam is possible, but it's a long shot. You don't win duplicates by looking for long shots, do you?"

I looked at the diagram again, and imagined Mitchell in Marcel's seat. Would a direct four heart raise have worked better? I think so.

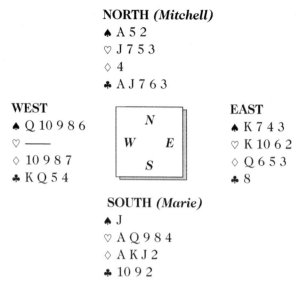

NORTH *(Mitchell)*
♠ A 5 2
♡ J 7 5 3
◇ 4
♣ A J 7 6 3

WEST
♠ Q 10 9 8 6
♡ ——
◇ 10 9 8 7
♣ K Q 5 4

EAST
♠ K 7 4 3
♡ K 10 6 2
◇ Q 6 5 3
♣ 8

SOUTH *(Marie)*
♠ J
♡ A Q 9 8 4
◇ A K J 2
♣ 10 9 2

WEST	MITCHELL	EAST	MARIE
		pass	1♡
1♠	4♡	4♠	pass
pass	dbl	all pass	

Opening lead: ◇4
Result: down 3

Down three doubled would surely have been a top for North-South on favorable vulnerability. And even at unfavorable, plus 500 points is better than minus 100. I could see the practicality of that jump to four hearts.

Nevertheless, if South had a little strength in clubs instead of diamonds, making five or six hearts might be a better result than four spades doubled. This bothered me because I am one of those perfectionists Mitchell was talking about earlier.

He must have been reading my mind as he turned to me and said, "I know what you're thinking. Quick bids like this don't have to work so well. But you can lose just as much on other hands when you start fussing around with side suits before supporting your partner. Believe me, the quick approach to bidding is usually the deadliest to the opponents. They don't know anything, and you don't leave 'em any room to find out anything either."

I looked down at the paper. Was Marcel's death just as quick? Before he knew what was happening? Or had he been threatened first, told what was going to happen, tortured slowly like the accursed auction he had tortured his partner with? I saw Mitchell looking at the next deal, and chuckling!

Don't think about the last hand; it's history

Exhibit #18　　　　　　　　　North Dealer
Board 5　　　　　　　　　　North-South vulnerable

NORTH (Marcel)
♠ —
♡ A K J 7 6 4 3 2
◊ —
♣ Q J 7 3 2

WEST
♠ 9 7 5 4
♡ 8 5
◊ 8 7
♣ 10 9 6 5 4

EAST
♠ A Q J 10 8 3
♡ —
◊ K Q J 10 6 5
♣ 8

SOUTH (Marie)
♠ K 2
♡ Q 10 9
◊ A 9 6 4 3 2
♣ A K

WEST	MARCEL	EAST	MARIE
	1♣	4♠	dbl
pass	4NT	5♠	6◊
pass	pass	dbl	all pass

Opening lead: ♠4
Result: down 4

"Wait a second," I said. "Look at Marcel's heart suit. There's something funny here."

Mitchell laughed again. "Morris's partner didn't think the dummy was funny. Oh, c'mon now! He obviously had some of his hearts in another slot and thought they were diamonds." I looked closer. His bidding actually isn't so bad if you consider what he thought his hand looked like:

♠ —— ♡ A K J 7 ◇ 6 4 3 2 ♣ Q J 7 3 2

If he were really three-suited, his four-notrump bid would have been a nice takeout of four spades doubled. It seems a shame that when Marcel finally made a good bid, it turned out that he had mis-sorted his cards.

"When he put the dummy down his partner gave a scream you could hear from across Broadway. And I should know. I was across Broadway at the time. Two cops at Hector's dropped their coffee cups when they heard it. But I told 'em to forget it. I could detect the type of scream it was — a reaction to one of Morris's dummies. It was later when Dr. X. was going over the hands that I found out why it had happened. Morris was so busy yapping about the last hand, about how unlucky he was, about how his partner didn't know how to take a finesse, etcetera, etcetera, that when he picked up the new hand, he didn't see his cards correctly."

It wasn't anything new, I thought. Lots of players screw up a hand simply because they're moaning over the last one. Only this time, the guy's partner had to play a moronic six diamonds doubled contract down 1100 instead of the partnership scoring a grand slam in hearts.

Mitchell asked if I had ever heard the expression about the straw that broke the camel's back. I nodded. "Well, this was Morris's worst blunder of the night, and the worst bridge disaster of his life. It was the next to last round and you might say he had made just one too many errors that evening. His fatal mistake, however, came in the post-mortem."

All players make mistakes — great players admit it

Mitchell lit up another cigarette. "His worst fault was never his bad bridge. Most of the games at the Bucket O' Blood were money games, and it was obviously to everyone's advantage to have Morris at the table. His worst fault was his stubbornness. He refused to admit his bridge crimes — he had a big ego, of course. After mis-sorting his hand on the next to last round of the duplicate, the entire club ganged up on him. Morris insisted he had been unlucky. He insisted he was a great bridge player whose partners always let him down."

"I don't understand what you mean. Why was the whole club angry with him? It was his partner, Marie, who was his victim. The rest of the club benefited from his mistakes."

"What are you, stupid? It was an Individual."

"*An Individual!* It never occurred to me."

"So what else is new? Morris loved the Thursday night Individual. It was the only time he could get a partner. Always took player number 23. He thought that was his lucky number, but the son-of-a-bitch never won a numbers bet in his whole life."

Twenty-three? Like in Room 623? Wait a second. Didn't Al Roth say he had partnered both Jinks and Little Lulu? Then there was the deal where he faced Marcel. Yet all these other hands — it didn't make sense. What about the positions? Next to last round. Seven rounds. Changing positions every board? Yes, it had to be an Individual — that was the only possible explanation. On every round, each player plays one hand with each of the other three players at the table. One hand. But what about Marie?

"I'm confused," I said. "Marie was my prime suspect. How could Marcel play with her all night when it was an Individual?"

Mitchell gave me another one of those looks, like I wasn't all there or something. "There was no Marie," he said. "She was a cover-up."

Preparation

Many pieces fell into place. The reason Inspector Gardner never discovered who Marie was became self-evident. The reason Al Roth had never heard of Marie was because there had never been a Marie. The reason Marcel was able to finish a duplicate that no partner on earth could ever tolerate was that his partner never last-ed more than one board. The fact that Dr. X., chief kibitzer of the Bucket O' Blood, had the same handwriting as that of the notepad, meant that it was the doctor who had been designated by the play-ers to write up the hands, twenty-one disasters by the worst player ever to play bridge in the weekly Individual.

Every single partner must have had a say in those notes. They were a mass rebuttal by the members of the club, an angry ledger of bridge crimes committed by one Marcel Moskowitz, bookie, tout, and son of a Brooklyn tailor! Yet not one member of the club signed his name to that ledger. Instead, a fictitious character by the name of Marie was entered in each diagram as the unlucky partner of Marcel. This was the cover-up. Here were the motives for the murder that followed.

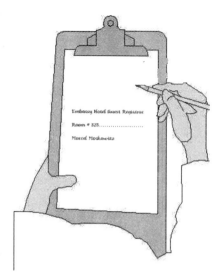

But what exactly took place after this ledger had been completed? Did someone go to Marcel's hotel room with it? Did the members force Marcel to re-analyze every hand? Did they all squeeze into Room 623 at the Embassy? Did they first accost him at the club? The only thing for sure was that Marcel got to see these sheets, and continued his protest with exclamation points next to the bids and plays that he thought were the true reasons for his unlucky results. Did his continued stubbornness and his failure to admit his errors finally provoke one of his partners (or all twenty-one of his partners) to commit murder? Who are these people, forty years later, trying to protect the secret of what happened in Room 623 early the following morning — and why?

I was on the brink of exhaustion as I thought about these issues. One can take only so much mental and physical strain. Preparation for a duplicate can be achieved by a few minutes rest, a little mental exercise, a few seconds of concentration. A tournament where you play day and night requires even more training. Sit-ups in the morning. Correct eating habits. But this was different — to spend a full day and night like the one I had just been through, without falling apart, required the training of a marathon runner, and I was the type of guy who had trouble with the fifty-yard dash.

I turned to Mitchell and suggested that we go back to his apartment for some rest, when I saw a woman approaching behind him in a panic. Too tired to run, I stood there awaiting another battle with the real-life, 1983 version of 'Marie'.

Those heavy meals

When she got within a few feet of Mitchell I heard Little Imp, prancing to our rescue. Like the beautiful sight of an oasis, she appeared, her tail wagging, jumping up on her hind legs. However, she was not biting or scratching our attacker. She was licking her. Then I saw who it was — Zia's redheaded girl friend number two! If I had the strength I would have heaved a sigh of relief.

"Quick," she said. "It's Zia. He's in terrible trouble. She has him in bed, she has him in bed!" Suddenly her compatriot was upon us too. Slower, more sluggish, and out of breath, redhead number one was panting, crying, and shrieking at the same time.

"Aiii. Aiii. Blood! She's got him in bed! You have to come quick! She's got him in bed!"

I felt a chill again. My robe was loose. I retied it and looked at my feet. Good God, I was still wearing Mitchell's slippers too, standing there in the middle of Central Park. I looked back up. Where was Mitchell, and the dog? Almost as if in a dream I heard myself mutter, "So she's got him in bed. That doesn't sound like terrible trouble. In general, that's the place where Zia tries to finish up the night."

The two girls stopped crying and looked at me like I was mad. Then I saw the panic in their eyes. It was not me that they thought was mad. No. Nor was it simple jealous rage that had sent them dashing into Central Park at four in the morning. It was her, — Marie! She was the mad one! And she had trapped Zia into being a part of her mad scheme. A surge of energy from an unknown source sprang up inside me as I thought of the danger my friend was in. I grabbed both ladies' hands and ran to Fifth Avenue.

It took us four minutes to hail a cab. It felt like an hour. I told the driver to take us to the Embassy Hotel, and to make it fast. He told me it looked like I had already had enough that night. While we whizzed down Fifth Avenue and around to Central Park South, the girls tried to explain what had happened.

They had stopped for a drink at Rusty's, a bar and grill on Third Avenue at 73rd Street. They didn't eat anything since they were already stuffed from the feast at the Taj Mahal. When they returned to the Cavendish Club, no one was there. Under normal conditions Zia would have left a message in the lobby for one or both of them to meet him later in his room. However, this time there was no message, at least the kind that they were used to.

When they left the club, they saw some blood on the window of the main entrance. Number two thought it was only paint. In either case, the red markings were '6-2-5'. I recognized it as Zia's room number at the hotel, the room I had left vacant. Perhaps he had just left the room number for the girls' information as he often did. But that seemed foolish since they already possessed keys to the room.

They rushed over to the Embassy Hotel, but there was no answer to their knocking at the door of Room 625. Redhead number two used her key to open the door. They both let out a scream. Zia was gagged and tied to the bed, half-dead or semi-unconscious, they didn't know which. For sure, observed number one, he was not his normal convivial self.

The sound of running water came from the bathroom, but both girls were afraid to go in. A few seconds later, the water stopped and out emerged a woman wrapped in a towel, carrying a razor blade and shaving cream. The two girls jumped into each others' arms in fright. (Redhead number one shuddered at the recollection.)

The woman had a crazed look in her eyes, and that was enough to make them both run out of the room and down the hall. Just as they were about to yell for the cops, they ran into two older men, one in a white summer suit, one in a seersucker (good Lord, not the hit men!), scaring them even more. Strangely enough, the men (one had a German accent) told them that if they wanted to help their friend (meaning Zia, I suppose) they should not go to the police, but instead go to 12 East 97th Street, apartment 10E, and tell a Victor Mitchell what had happened. Now partners, the girls consulted each other, and decided to follow this advice, since both men seemed quite serene and level-headed (said redhead number two).

A taxi brought them to Mitchell's apartment. Not finding him in, the doorman suggested Central Park where Mitchell often walks his pets. Miraculously they saw me and rushed over. Yes, they had also seen a man with a dog, but in the commotion he seemed to have disappeared.

What was most perplexing to redhead number two was how Zia could have been physically overcome, tied and gagged, by a mere girl. Redhead number one agreed, confiding that even with both of them there, Zia often had the strength to remain on top of things. That is, interrupted number one, when he hasn't had too much for supper.

There was no question, I said, that overeating will reduce your physical and mental capabilities. Although I was confident Marie had tricked him into being tied to the bed by some false promises, I was sure that the recently digested curry was also a factor. Duplicate players do it all the time. They eat too much at dinner and lose tons of matchpoints because their physical and mental strength is less than what it should be.

Alcohol and drugs

Not just that, insisted number one, but Zia had been drinking wine. Oh well, said number two, then it was just as well she hadn't spent the night with him. You know Zia when he's had too much wine. Two glasses and he's finished, agreed number one. "I guess it will serve that woman right when she gets finished shaving and hops into bed."

Gets finished shaving! Was Marie doing to Zia what she had done to me? But Zia had no mustache! My whole body trembled at the thought. Poor fellow. He rarely drank and never took drugs. But even two glasses of wine was enough to spoil his fine judgment in bidding a bridge hand. Suddenly, I remembered that he had also been drinking champagne! Good Lord, this time it was not just another competitive auction, it was a matter of life and death.

12 ETHICS

Fighting fire with fire

As we passed 59th and Broadway, redhead number one tapped the driver on the shoulder. "We're getting out here." He came to a halt. "This is where I reside," she said.

The two girls, suddenly fed up with the misadventures of their man, Zia, helped each other out, and proceeded into an apartment entrance, arm in arm. I was shocked to see them abandon Zia when he needed as much help as possible. When had they decided to call it quits and form their own new partnership?

I had no time to reach any major conclusions because we were soon at the Embassy, where I suddenly realized I had no wallet, let alone cash. I did something I had never done before. I told the driver to wait while I went inside to get some money. This was a lie, of course. I got out of the cab and ran around to the back courtyard of the hotel. But what could I do? In matters of life or death, does one stop to be ethical? Sure, I could have waited and tried to explain the whole matter to him, but it must have been close to 4:30 a.m., and that meant Zia (if he was still alive) was about to pose unwillingly as the reincarnated corpse of Marcel Moskowitz.

It was quite dark in the back, but I found the end of the fire escape and jumped up three or four times until my hands hit the ladder. Then I started to climb. I reached the steps, and lumbered up six flights. What I would do when I found Zia, I didn't know. Nor did I have any idea how I would fight off Marie.

When I reached the sixth floor, I realized that I was not at the window of Room 625, for the back of the Taj Mahal was too far over to my right. Crawling across window sills was no easy task, and both slippers fell off. I made it to the fire escape of what I judged to be Room 623, opened the window and slipped in. The bed was empty and waiting, I supposed, for the reenactment of the crime. That meant she still had Zia tied up in his own bed in Room 625.

I went into the hallway and crept up to his door. In the keyhole I could see two bodies sitting up in bed. I put my ear to the door and listened. I heard a laugh! Stunned by the implications of the sound, I decided not to bash in the door, and knocked softly. I heard feet. "Who is it?" called Zia. He was alive and well!

I called back, "It's me, Matthew."

The door opened. "Did you bring any food?" Zia was standing there in a long silk nightshirt with queens-of-hearts patterned around the collar. "Where have you been, anyway?" he continued. "We've solved your bloody case for you." He closed the door behind me, and darted his eyes towards the bed. Was he trying to tell me something? There was Marie wearing Zia's shirt, the top button undone. She was sprawled under the sheets, leaning on some pillows, reading by the lamp.

"Now look at this one," she said, pointing to the paper. Then she looked up. "Oh, it's you." She gave me a curt glance.

Zia got back into bed beside Marie and motioned for me to sit next to him. I was ready to lie down, but less than enthusiastic about doing so on that bed again, with that woman lying there. I could swear she looked perfectly sane at that moment. How long would that last? Was there a razor under her pillow? Zia, however, seemed perfectly all right, and there were no signs of a struggle or any traces of rope.

I sat down carefully at the end of the bed, and Zia took the paper from Marie. "Where?" he asked. She pointed, and I edged closer, resting my legs on the bed and peeking over Zia's shoulder. It was a copy of Marcel's notes. "You see this, you shmigeggie?" Zia said to me. "The Marcel character you love so much was quite unethical."

Trigger doubles are unethical

Exhibit #19   South dealer
Board 7   Both vulnerable

NORTH
♠ 6 4 3 2
♡ 5 3
♢ A K 10 8
♣ Q 6 3

WEST (*Marcel*)   EAST (*Marie*)
♠ K Q J 10   ♠ 9
♡ Q J 10 7   ♡ A K 9 8 6 4 2
♢ Q J 9 7   ♢ ——
♣ 7   ♣ J 9 5 4 2

SOUTH
♠ A 8 7 5
♡ ——
♢ 6 5 4 3 2
♣ A K 10 8

MARCEL	NORTH	MARIE	SOUTH
			1♢
pass	1♠	3♡	3♠
4♡	pass	pass	4♠
DBL	5♢	pass	pass
DBL	all pass		

Opening lead: ♠K
Result: making 5

Here was still another disaster for Marcel. This time he had made a 'trigger double', meaning that he had doubled quickly and loudly. Whether it was intentionally done to stop partner from pulling the double under any circumstance or merely a reflex (to his incredible trump holding) does not matter. It was poor ethics.

This time it backfired. South was able to win the spade lead, and guided not only by the double, but by the volume and speed of it, deduced the 4-0 trump split. He played a diamond to the eight, ruffed a heart, diamond to Marcel's jack and dummy's king, another heart ruff to hand, and a third round of trumps, finessing Marcel again. Declarer discarded a spade from hand on dummy's fourth trump then took his club tricks, conceding two spade tricks at the end.

Make your penalty doubles in a normal voice and in tempo

"Most players," said Zia, "are not aware of how unfair a trigger double is. You've heard of the slow double that partner pulls. Your opponent can protest and have a director or committee adjudicate the result."

"When partner makes a slow double because he's in doubt, you should not even look at your cards," I said. "The only way to stop him from doing that is always to pass, even with a hand where you would normally pull the double."

"Listen to me, shmigeggie. The trigger double is worse than the slow double. Everybody, with six voids up their sleeves, always passes when their partner makes a trigger double, and nobody can call the director and say 'this guy would have pulled the double if it had been in correct tempo.' "

"But he didn't get away with it," said Marie from the other side of the bed. "The declarer played him for every card."

"Yes, that's what I like about this hand," continued Zia. "As a result of his poor ethics, he tipped the hand to the opponents, not just to his partner. Listen. Nobody loves to double more than me, but I always do it in my normal voice and in tempo. There is a sportsmanship matter here that few people understand. If you are about to kill the opponents, you don't do it loudly and flamboyantly. Consider that you've already got them murdered with your trump stack. Then double like a gentleman, for they will feel bad enough when they receive a zero."

Don't huddle, then pass

"Speaking of murder," I said, "I don't see what this proves about Marcel's case."

"It establishes a further motive," said Marie. "Marcel was not only a bad bridge player—"

"Who refused to admit his mistakes," I interrupted.

Marie continued. "He was hated for his poor ethics, too. That's why he had so much trouble getting a partner. Marie was the only person at the club who would play duplicate with him."

"I have news for you," I said. "There was no Marie."

Suddenly our real-life Marie let out a scream. *"Don't say that!"*

"Do me a favor," whispered Zia. "Don't say that."

"Are you nuts?" I whispered back. "I just found out from Vic Mitchell. This Marie character was a cover-up. It was an Individual that night at the club, a seven-round Individual."

"There *was* a Marie, there *was* a Marie," repeated Marie. She stared wildly into space, then back at the notes.

Something very strange was going on. I was suddenly aware of a huge black object next to Marie's right hand, partly covered by the sheet.

"Where's the rope?" I asked. "Your two redheads claim they saw you tied and gagged."

Zia put a finger to his lips. "Button your lip, shmigeggie." Then in a regular tone: "That was a game invented by Inspector Clousseau. It's not for happily married men like you to know of such things." Marie laughed in a voice much too high.

"My wife," I sulked. "Don't mention the wife. On top of everything else I forgot to call her today."

"Your wife is somewhere in Central Park trying to fish you out of the lake," Zia whispered again. "Keep cool, everything's under control. Just don't make any quickie moves."

"Now," he said in his normal voice, "let's get back to business and examine another hand."

"Here's one! Deal twenty," said our delightful detective, her voice less than steady. "Look, Marcel huddled five times, *five times*! And got away with it — the son of a bitch!"

Zia and I cautiously moved our heads over Marie's shoulder. I got a better look at that black thing under the sheet. It was a gun. Good grief, it was a submachine gun! I gazed back at the diagram, my heart beating much too fast:

Exhibit #20   West dealer
Board 8   Neither vulnerable

NORTH (Marcel)
♠ K 5 4 3
♡ A K 6 4
◊ 2
♣ Q J 10 9

WEST   **EAST**
♠ J 9 8 6   ♠ A 10 7
♡ Q 9 2   N   ♡ 5
◊ Q J 9   W   E   ◊ K 10 8 7 6
♣ A K 3   S   ♣ 8 7 6 4

SOUTH (Marie)
♠ Q 2
♡ J 10 8 7 3
◊ A 5 4 3
♣ 5 2

WEST	MARCEL	EAST	MARIE
1♣	pass *5 sec.*	1◊	pass
1♠	pass *6 sec.*	2♣	pass
2◊	pass *8 sec.*	pass	2♡
pass	pass *3 sec.*	2♠	pass
pass	dbl *5 sec.*	pass	3♡
all pass			

Opening lead: ♣K
result: making 4

Indeed, it was a frightening auction. Dr. X., the bridge analyst, had gone out of his way to detail the exact number of seconds for each of Marcel's huddles. This was obviously meant to illustrate to Marcel his poor practice of hesitating with a problem, but never taking action.

Marcel either felt he had already 'bid' via his huddles, or he was such a beginner that he actually did have a problem on every call.

The fact is that he never took a legitimate bid until he doubled, and even that was tempered with a pause which let partner know he also had heart support.

Good Lord, I thought, this is worse than his bad bridge. He simply wasn't playing fairly. Nor was his partner on this hand. She had a questionable two heart balance, and certainly had no business removing the double of two spades. Marcel had done nothing within the context of the game to tell her he was making an optional double with heart support on the side. What he *had* done was convey this message by unethical pausing.

Bend over backwards to be ethical when partner huddles or bids too quickly

"You see this," said Marie, her voice lower and more subdued. We both looked intently. "This is the first hand where Marie does something wrong."

"I don't know what you mean by wrong," said Zia. "If you mean it was wrong for her to pull the double, I disagree. There is a strong case for her three heart bid, since the logic of the auction, East and West each bidding three suits, indicates shortness in the fourth. Her partner, therefore, was marked with heart support. However, if you mean ethically wrong, that's another story."

I wanted to say that it's hard to criticize somebody who never existed, but instead, I prudently referred to Marie as South. "South should be shot — just an expression — for pulling the double. We all agree that whenever partner doubles in a manner suggesting doubt, you must bend over backwards to pass."

Don't put partner in an awkward position

The culprit in a huddle auction is usually the partner of the huddler. We all have problems at the bridge table which require extra thinking time. If we choose to think and then pass, it is partner who must be careful not to take advantage of the pause. Yet, in this case it was the huddler, Marcel, who was blamed. This was because he huddled so many times in one auction without ever bidding his hand. He should have bid something even if he decided it was best to pass, because his informative pauses put too much pressure on his partner.

♠ K 5 4 3　♡ A K 6 4　◇ 2　♣ Q J 10 9

WEST	MARCEL	EAST	MARIE
1♣	pass *5 sec.*	1◇	pass
1♠	pass *6 sec.*	2♣	pass
2◇	pass *8 sec.*	pass	2♡
pass	pass *3 sec.*	2♠	pass
pass	dbl *5 sec.*	pass	3♡
all pass			

Marcel could have done this on his first turn by making an over-call of one heart (technically inferior to 'pass' but better than passing out of tempo). Over one spade, at his second turn, he had little option but to pass. At his third turn, however, he certainly should have backed in with a double. He was short in diamonds (the last bid suit), and had support for the other three suits. Instead he passed, putting pressure on his partner to make a skimpy, and ethically uncomfortable, two heart bid in the balancing seat.

His failure to raise hearts on the fourth round of the auction was unbelievable, holding four-card support to the ace-king and a singleton. Perhaps Marcel thought he had already bid his hand by huddling three times.

Finally, on the fifth round he climaxes with a huddle-double. If he had doubled in tempo it would have simply been a poor bid. But to huddle, then double is to torture partner. After thinking for a while, Marcel should have raised to three hearts, a bid that would cause no headaches for 'Marie'. His double must have put his partner in a state of apoplexy, especially if, as Zia pointed out, South was astute enough to deduce from the auction that Marcel did indeed have heart support.

Was it possible that Marcel had driven this so-called 'Marie' crazy with his destructive huddles? Was this the one piece of evidence that provided a reasonable motive for murder? In legal jargon, was South placed in a state of temporary insanity when Marcel tortured her for the fifth time in one auction? I posed this to my bedmates.

"People who are put in positions like this are bound to do something crazy — I mean, crack up — you know what I mean."

Zia eyed me carefully. Did he think that I was cracking up?

Marie spoke up again, this time with a far-off look in her eyes. "I think we have our murderer. Poor Marie, she couldn't take it any more. Marcel had played horribly all night long and finally brought her to the brink of insanity with this hand. She must have confronted him with these notes in his hotel room early the next morning. They argued over the hands. Oh yes they argued. Marcel became impossible to deal with. Impossible. He deserved to die. There was no other way for Marie to cope with the man who had destroyed the game she loved so dearly."

I could see Marie fingering the gun on her right side during this speech. I wanted to point out that Marcel was not in this room. Suddenly she sat upright. Zia quickly put his hand on her wrist. pretending to fondle her; I believe he was restraining her.

Losing is better than cheating

"Our Marie is right of course," said Zia. "This naughty Marcel character of *forty years ago* (he emphasized) certainly deserved what he got. But didn't you say, Matthew, that he was found dead *without bullet wounds* or other such markings?"

"Yes, that's right," I answered nodding my head three or four hundred times. Marie loosened her grip on the gun.

"Yes," she agreed. "He died of suffocation, pillow suffocation. Somehow Marie must have gained strength in her vexation, in her revenge, in her madness."

"I'd say it was partially her own fault," said the quick-witted Zia, trying his best to get the girl off the subject of murder. "After all, she should have passed two spades doubled, don't you think? This would have been punishment enough for Marcel. I say it was her natural but unhealthy desire to win at any cost that led to temporary insanity."

"She wanted to win, yes," said Marie in a monotone that was far from comforting.

"Ahh," Zia went on, "it is true. The importance you Americans attach to winning is seen every day in all your sporting events. I am not a noble giant, believe me, but I would rather lose than be thought of as a cheater, or even the least bit unethical. But your Marie character — she was bent on success. If she couldn't succeed with Marcel, she should have found a new partner. There's no bloody sense in murdering and smothering people over these things. Don't you agree, my girl?"

"You don't understand," said Marie. "It wasn't just winning. It was the game of bridge that she loved. And look what he had done to it — to her —"

Win or lose, the game can be fun

"Absolutely correct," I chimed in. "Win or lose, that girl enjoyed the game. On the other hand, you are right about Marcel destroying the aesthetics of the game. But on the other hand, each new deal could be a new adventure, the last deal not really being a factor. However, if you think about what her partner did to her on all the other hands, why would it be any fun to pick up another deal? On the other hand, there was no Marie — I know I'm not supposed to mention that — but it certainly is a good reason why she was able to get through the evening, enjoying the bridge competition. For if you don't exist, you tend to have a greater threshold for pain than the average guy. Which really means that the only way you could get through an evening like this is if you were actually many people — which I've been trying to explain to you.

"It was an Individual. Many people played with Marcel, not just one woman named Marie. Many people, therefore, were probably the murderers — just like in the book, *Murder on the Orient Express* — all of them taking revenge on this slob, Marcel. It also explains how he was smothered. There is no way one woman could have done it, and it makes sense then that one woman did not do it, but instead *all his partners that evening!*"

There was silence. I couldn't help but throw in one more line. "Besides which, Marcel was really Morris, the son of a religious bookie who mended clothes in Brooklyn!"

Our young detective shook her head. "There was a Marie. There was a Marie. *If there was no Marie I wouldn't be here!*"

"There *was* a Marie," Zia said elbowing me.

"Okay, there *was* a Marie. She was there too if you like. So now that we've solved the case, let's say we all go down to the local deli and celebrate, huh?"

"*No!*" screamed Marie, jumping up again, this time brandishing her compact submachine gun. "Not until we look at the last hand! I want my report to be complete."

"Agreed, agreed," I said in a conciliatory fashion. "Mustn't leave any stones unturned. One last hand for the road. Good idea, huh Zee?"

"Look," she cried. "Look what he did to her on the last hand..."

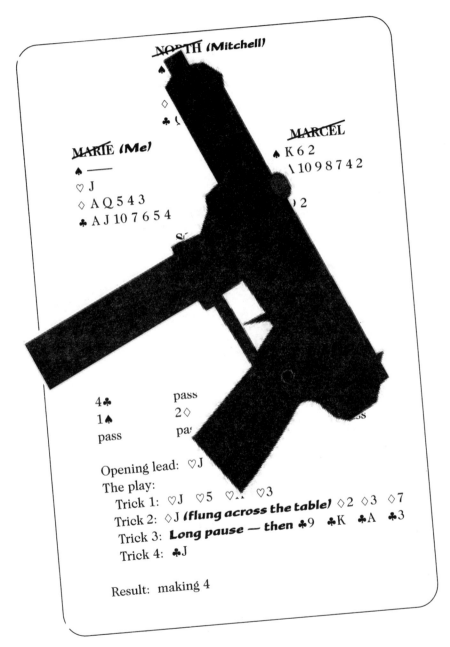

NORTH (Mitchell)

♠
◊
♣

MARIE (Me)
♠ —
♡ J
◊ A Q 5 4 3
♣ A J 10 7 6 5 4

MARCEL
♠ K 6 2
♡ 10 9 8 7 4 2
◊ 2

4♣   pass
1♠   2◊
pass   pass

Opening lead: ♡J

The play:
   Trick 1: ♡J ♡5 ♡.. ♡3
   Trick 2: ◊J *(flung across the table)* ◊2 ◊3 ◊7
   Trick 3: **Long pause** — then ♣9 ♣K ♣A ♣3
   Trick 4: ♣J

Result: making 4

Play your cards in tempo

Exhibit #21
Board 9

North dealer
East-West vulnerable

NORTH (Mitchell)
- ♠ Q 9 8
- ♡ K Q 6 5
- ◇ 9 8 7
- ♣ Q 8 3

MARIE (Me)
- ♠ ———
- ♡ J
- ◇ A Q 5 4 3
- ♣ A J 10 7 6 5 4

```
        N
    W       E
        S
```

MARCEL
- ♠ K 6 2
- ♡ A 10 9 8 7 4 2
- ◇ J
- ♣ 9 2

SOUTH (Dr. X.)
- ♠ A J 10 7 5 4 3
- ♡ 3
- ◇ K 10 6 2
- ♣ K

MARIE (Me)	NORTH	MARCEL	SOUTH
	pass	pass	1♠
2♣	2♠	3♡	3♠
4♣	pass	pass	4♠
pass	pass	dbl *(huddle)*	all pass

Opening lead: ♡J

The play:

Trick 1: ♡J ♡5 ♡A ♡3
Trick 2: ◇J *(flung across the table)* ◇2 ◇3 ◇7
Trick 3: **Long pause — then** ♣9 ♣K ♣A ♣3
Trick 4: ♣J

Result: making 4

I went into a state of shock when I saw the last hand on Marcel's list. Maybe it was the pressure I was under. Maybe it was just the hand, but there were certainly some revealing features in the bridge, the ethics, and the people involved.

First, there was the confusion as to who was sitting East and who was sitting West. Also, North-South suddenly took names of real people. Our detective swung the barrel of her gun towards the sheet of paper and digressed. "You see what Marcel did to Marie? He overtook her heart-jack lead with his ace. Then flung his diamond singleton across the table! You will both notice how honest Marie was not to overtake with her queen. Then the cad took a long pause before leading the club nine — this pause to indicate he had a doubleton club, not a singleton! Marie, oh such a beautiful creature, such a noble woman, won the club trick with her ace and deliberately led back a club to spite the evil man!"

Indeed, if what our mad detective said was true, 'Marie' certainly had learned her lesson from the previous hand. Bending over to the extreme in order to be ethical, she had allowed three tricks to disappear. Had she overtaken her partner's diamond jack with her queen, cashed the ace and given East a ruff, he would have returned a club to her ace for another diamond, overruffed with the spade king. That would have meant three down.

After her actual duck of the diamond jack, she won the defense's third trick with the ace of clubs, and returned a club. Dr. X., the declarer, won in dummy and cashed two hearts, discarding all three of his remaining diamonds. Then the trump finesse secured the contract.

Don't fling out a singleton

While Zia tried his best to placate our increasingly distraught detective by reciting quotations from the works of Mahatma Gandhi, I could not help but notice certain inconsistencies with regard to the players' positions.

For one thing, the names of the East-West players had lines through them, the West position having a 'Me' after it. Secondly, the crossing out of North and South and the addition of Mitchell's and Dr. X.'s names to the list, was a breach of the cover-up used on the other deals. Thirdly, although the ethics used in the tempo of the card play were consistent with Marcel's previous behavior, I doubted very much that such a poor player could suddenly rise to overtaking the lead of a jack with his ace, when staring at the king-queen in dummy. Finally, and conclusively, Mitchell, who was having a bite at Hector's Coffee Shop, admitted he had heard screaming on the round before. He could have returned to the club in ample time to fill in on the last round.

It was obvious that someone had tried to reveal the truthful participants on this deal! The East hand was not relabeled, which shows compassion for the culprit who had played so unethically. The West hand was marked 'Me'. Who else could 'Me' be but Marcel himself, who was last to see the notes, and the last guy in town interested in a cover-up? Was this an attempt to leave a clue as to the murderer? Yet how could it be? Corpses do not leave written clues, especially those who have just been smothered. The notepad was left on the body. No murderer in her right mind would leave a clue like this at the scene of the crime. Did this mean the murderer was mad? Or did this mean Marcel had not been smothered, and had died in some way that allowed him to make these corrections — a last-minute attempt to prove he was ethical, that his bridge game had some redeeming feature?

In any case, I was convinced Marcel was West on the diagram. It was Marcel, not the fictitious Marie who had learned a lesson and bent over backwards to punish a partner for playing cards out of tempo. On the last hand of the evening, the man had shown himself capable of common decency. Yes, some will say, it is easy to be ethical when it can't possibly affect your score. He certainly had nothing to lose at this point in the evening. But still it showed that no human being, no hopeless bridge player, is all bad.

Don't pause with a doubleton

> "To love two women at the same time
> is possible in mind only,
> unless you are young
> and very much in love.

> "Paupers unite,
> kings are taken not only by aces.

> "It is highly unethical to pause
> with a doubleton
> when partner leads from his ace-king."

Zia had run out of quotations, and Marie was not exactly showing signs of mental stability. In fact, she was up on her knees fluffing pillows with her gun, obviously testing to see which pillows would work nicely for a neat little smothering job.

Trying to help, I agreed profusely in my own poetic style:

> "Second hand low, hand high,
> Zia and I are too young to die."

Still my Pakistani friend made no move for the gun. Why should he go for the gun when I could go for the gun? Like good bridge partners passing the auction around to partner, each of us was waiting for the other to initiate an escape. Or was this a case of two exhausted, beaten defenders allowing a mad declarer to claim her contract? All I knew was that Marie was piling up pillows like a stack of tricks, getting ready for the final smother play, and I didn't like it.

The last vestiges of human curiosity still sparked inside me. I had to ask myself if this is how it had been for Marcel Moskowitz — a group of irate, crazy bridge players fluffing and stacking pillows in preparation for the final snuffing of a bridge player's light.

Suddenly, and in a way that has happened to me at the card table under less dangerous circumstances, a vision appeared. It was a beam of light coming through the curtained window that looked down on the courtyard. Perhaps it was dawn, though it seemed a little too early for sunrise. The beam manifested itself in my brain like a realization, a forgotten card, a miscount that might not be too late to rectify.

THE CASE IS SOLVED

Competing to the best of your ability

If Marcel Moskowitz had been mass-murdered by a group of insane bridge players, it is probable that someone would have left a clue. Detective Gardner would have found some evidence — footprints, clothing threads, fingerprints. The fact that he found only a list of bridge diagrams and a few extra pillows indicated that there had been an insidious cover-up.

The most obvious card, or clue, that I had missed since arriving back in Room 625 was that no one had fired bullets with a machine gun. Nor had the murder even taken place in Room 625! It had taken place in Room 623. (6-2-5 is an unusual distribution for a bridge hand. I should have remembered the distinction.)

If our female detective was hell-bent on recreating the forty-year-old murder perpetrated on one Marcel Moskowitz by one fictitious Marie, then she would be compelled to do it with pillows, not with a machine gun. And she would have to get us into Room 623 to do it.

The fact that I was able to think so clearly in such a crisis was remarkable, even if I say so myself. Some players are great bidders, some great declarers. Others are best on defense. But the players who win most consistently are those who can concentrate under pressure and play up to their potential.

Hadn't Zia said there were four heats for a bridge player? Well, it had taken nearly twenty-four hours, but at last I was in top form. I turned to Marie and asked in a direct and firm voice that no experienced psychiatrist could have matched, "What room is this, Marie?"

She looked at me, machine gun in hand, her face white as the pillow covers. "What room? Room six-two-three. The room Marcel must die in."

"No," I said calmly. "Marcel was smothered next door. His favorite number was twenty-three. His player number in the Individual was twenty-three. This is room six-two-five. "

Marie shook her head, then her whole body vibrated violently, the gun waving in all directions. "*Six-two-three! Six-two-three!* This is room *six-two-three!*"

"Six-two-three," repeated Zia. "Six-two-three, you idiot."

"Okay, okay," I said. "Six-two-three." Marie stopped waving the gun. That tactic wasn't going to work, but I still had another suit to shift to.

Confidence

There's nothing like talent and diligence. You can achieve terrific results with either attribute and tremendous results with both. There is a third ingredient for success which is useful no matter where your strengths lie — a dignified and confident table manner.

Confidence is a tremendous psychological advantage, as anyone who plays cards will tell you. If you act the part of an expert bridge player you will sometimes be able to trick the opponents into believing you are one. They may, for example, refrain from doubling you when you have run into a bad trump split. Who would not prefer to compete against a player who trembles a bit than a player who bids and plays his cards like a commanding general?

With this in mind, I rose from the bed, marched confidently

over to Marie and demanded that she hand over the gun. She pointed it straight in my face, and I reached up for it with my right hand.

"*Are you mad?*" screamed Zia.

No, I was not mad. I was simply demonstrating the power of
confidence. Had I been a great jujitsu expert I could have whisked
that gun away from Marie without any chance of it going off. Being
merely a local card shark, with as few credentials in the martial arts
as one could possibly have, I relied on a show of psychological
strength.

"Get back or I'll use this," Marie warned.

"No you won't," I answered in the strongest voice I could
muster. "Marcel Moskowitz died by suffocation, not by gunfire.
That's a submachine gun in your hand, not a pillow." I grabbed the
barrel.

Marie did one better. She grabbed two pillows and sandwiched
the gun in between. "Now it's a pillow. *It's a pillow!*"

I let go, my arm dropping along with my newfound confidence.
If Marie thought her gun was a pillow, I was doomed.

"Don't shoot," I pleaded. "I mean — don't smother."

She raised the machine gun sandwich higher in triumph. I
grasped at straws. "Listen. It has to be done in bed. Marcel was
murdered in bed."

Suddenly a sound came from the fire escape, and the beam of
light I had imagined earlier moved past Zia's face.

Brilliancy versus consistency

Most bridge players prefer consistency in their partners rather than
brilliancy. In the bidding, consistency has the advantage of relia-
bility and trust. It's nice to know partner always has her values for
her overcall. When she bids a suit where you hold enormous
length, she is not psyching. On defense, one prefers to know partner is not underleading aces, or falsecarding declarer at the cost of
misleading you. But when you're dummy, you are no longer
involved in the hand.

Consistency in declarer play is an attribute, but if partner occasionally attempts a bit of brilliancy, at least it will not be at the cost
of leading you astray. Zia is a flair player. He likes to psyche, likes
to underlead aces, and likes to be in the spotlight. When the beam
of light hit him from the window, something brilliant must have

dawned on him as well, for the next thing I knew, he had shut his eyes and slumped over on the bed, grasping the copy of Marcel's notes. To all appearances, the man was dead. I could swear I heard someone mutter in a foreign language outside the window.

Marie put down her gun and pillows, and leaned over Zia. "He's dead," I said, hoping to reinforce the deception that my partner had begun. "I guess that means it's all over."

"But I didn't kill him," Marie complained as she opened his eyelids searching for a sign of life.

"No, I'm sorry," I said, trying to console her. "He died a natural death." I took hold of Zia's wrist and pretended to be checking him for a pulse. "Perhaps, though, you did instigate it. Fear can certainly cause anxiety, which in turn might produce a nasty heart attack."

Tears began to well up in her eyes. Was she crying for Zia? Or was it that her mad scheme, her compelling urge to recreate the scene of the crime, was over?

"You realize what this means?" she said, the tears turning to sobs.

I wasn't sure what she was getting at. But I reached for the machine gun and took it in my arms without a single protest from the girl.

"He died," she continued, "like Marcel. He wasn't murdered, not really."

I leaned over to her and took out the perfumed handkerchief Zia always carried in his shirt pocket. Then I patted her face and gave her the hanky.

"He couldn't stand it any more," she cried.

Suddenly I realized that this sad Marie had stumbled on the real solution. She was suggesting that Zia was a great bridge player who could no longer exist in a world of bad bridge.

"But what has that got to do with Marcel?" I asked, the novice once again.

"Marcel," said Marie in a calmer, quieter voice. "Why, Marcel could not stand bad bridge either."

But Marcel was a terrible player, not like Zia in any way. Oh no, hadn't Mitchell said that Marcel thought himself a great player. So what had happened? Good Lord, the man had read twenty-one hand analyses from the worst-played bridge session in the history of the game. He had been forced to realize that he was himself a hopeless player. Marcel Moskowitz had murdered the game of bridge, and the game of bridge had come back to murder him!

Unable to face life any more, he must have buried himself with remorse, sickness, with a mental pain that no human who loves the game could bear. Surrounding himself with extra pillows in a futile attempt to sleep, he tossed and turned half the night, unable to purge the truth from his soul, and finally died a so-called natural death while clutching to his heart the written evidence of his horrible crimes.

This meant that Inspector Gardner was right; Marcel had not been murdered. There was no cover-up, no Orient-Express ritual. The case was solved... or was it? What about the fictitious Marie? What about the mass assault on Marcel's ego? There are other ways to murder a man than to stick a dozen knives in him.

Hard work versus dumb luck

Victory at duplicate is often, like anything else in life, the result of hard work. The player who concentrates more, maintains partnership discipline, and tries his best on every board is usually the player who wins, in the long run. Occasionally two players who are not particularly talented, nor very studious, will win the afternoon duplicate. That is because, on that given day, few of their mistakes cost, while their opponents presented them with gift after gift. Those of us who work hard at the game must remain philosophical on these unjust occasions, and accept the fact that dumb luck will occasionally triumph.

I heard the window open, and who appeared but none other than Jaggi, the waiter from the Taj Mahal, a flashlight in his hand. "I sleep in a room above the kitchen," he said. "Mister Zia told me to check on him if I did not get a message by six o'clock. What time is it now, do you know?"

I glanced at the clock by the mirror. "A quarter to six."

"I am early then. That's why I waited outside. Sorry. Is Mister Zia okay?" He turned to the bed. "Ah, it is Miss Marie, the detective, and Zia is sleeping. How are you, nice to see you again." He bowed, then saw the machine gun next to me on the floor. "Ahh, the gun. If you don't mind I must take it back to my son, Jonny. Oh how he complained before he went to bed. His mother said no, he may not go nighty with a submachine gun under his blanket. So I let him sleep with his rubber knife and atomic weapon system, which he prefers." Jaggi smiled apologetically, picked up the gun and squeezed the trigger. Water spurted out on the bed directly in Mister Zia's face.

He came immediately to life. "What the hell is this water, eh?" Looking around he asked, "What is going on? Did I fall asleep?"

"You must have fainted," I said, recalling how this act had led me to the true reconstruction of Marcel's death.

"And where've you been, shmigeggie?" he asked Jaggi. "Didn't I tell you to check on me at four o'clock?"

"Oh my goodness, I thought you said six. I am sure you said six. Sorry, sorry. I must go now before Jonny wakes up and sees me gone. His mother is out cold with jet lag. Sorry, I was sure it was six." With that, the inimitable headwaiter exited through the window from whence he came, the toy machine gun under his arm. Marie went into convulsions like (shall I say it?) a child who has had her favorite toy taken away.

"What's going on now?" asked Zia, shaking his head in grogginess. "What have you done to her?"

"Done to her? The girl has held us here for two hours. How was I supposed to know the gun was a water pistol?" I turned to our crying detective. "Now, now Marie, calm down. It's all over."

She looked up at both of us. Color began to rise slowly in her cheeks. She blew her nose in Zia's hanky.

"My name is Evelyn."

"*Evelyn?*" Zia and I looked at each other in shock.

"Yes," she sniffed, "Evelyn Barkowsky. I live in Ann Arbor, Michigan with my parents and brother, Jan, and sister, Leslie. My phone number is 715-6331." Then she started to cry again, this time in normal teardrop volume.

Zia turned to me with an accusing look. "What kind of women do you introduce me to?"

There was the sound of a key in the door. It opened and in walked the two hit men who had followed Marie (Evelyn) and me during the duplicate the night before. They rushed over to the girl. One of them took out something from his breast pocket. I tried to stop him.

If you don't improve, give up the game

I wasn't fast enough. I was hardly able to walk, let alone jump over the bed. No doubt my reflexes were slow, which was not unusual for an ordinary guy who has been through twenty-four hours of amateur sleuthing. Would that have happened to a real sleuth? No way, I thought. A real homicide detective would not tire out on the last board, and I had to give serious thought to the idea of tossing in the towel.

One day and night of this hard-boiled stuff was enough for me to realize I wasn't cut out for detective work. Yet many bridge students go at it for years, and often never improve. My detective days were finished when I couldn't stop an old man from attacking a young woman. Luckily, however, it wasn't a gun or a knife that the hit-man pulled out from his pocket. It was a piece of cotton.

"It's all right," the younger man said. "We're physicians." He took a bottle out of his jacket pocket and gently rubbed alcohol on her arm. Then the older doctor handed him a needle. She started to resist.

"I want my mommy," she called out. "I want my mommy and daddy!"

"You hear thees?" the older one said. "She no longer needs thees injection." The younger doctor put the needle away. "You may all come een, please, come come."

In walked the middle-aged couple from the bridge club, followed by the polite young brother and sister with blonde hair who had been our opponents at table seven the previous night.

"Oh dear, dear, dear Evy," cried the mother as she rushed to her daughter. "My sweet Evy is all better."

"Yes," said the older doctor. "Eet looks good for the moment. But we cannot be sure. Time, Mrs. Barkowsky. Time vill tell."

The father looked at Zia and raised his arm. He jumped off the bed. "I didn't touch her, believe me." Zia pointed at me. "*He's* the one. *He's* the nut who's got me involved here."

"Then I'd l-like to thank *you*, Mr. G-g-gran— and give you a t-ten thousand dollar check for the t-trouble you've been through." The father held out his hand and I held out mine.

You've b-brought my daughter b-back home to Mother and me. You see she had a f-f-fixation. The doctors here call it manic d-d-d—."

"Manic Depressive Impersonata," said the younger doctor. "Just a long name for what has been a nightmare for the whole family. It happened last year when Mr. and Mrs. Barkowsky sent their daughter off to NYU. It was there she took up the game of duplicate bridge."

"Exc-cuse me doctor."

"Sorry. You tell the story, Jinks."

Jinks Barkowsky turned back to Zia and me. "We had p-played only friendly rubber bridge at home, you know. Along with rummy, c-canasta and other good c-card games families enjoy. I c-can't tell you how many years I myself wasted as a youth in a certain b-bridge and chess club, right here in this v-very hotel, b-before I finished my d-degree in c-c-criminal psych-chology.

"Well, the p-point is that this d-duplicate species seemed to change her. I had not p-played for nearly f-forty years, and did not realize how much more work, more s-studying, c-concentration, c-conventions were now necessary. The p-pressure of competing is a far c-cry from the relaxation the game p-provided for her at home with the family on S-saturday nights." Jinks paused and sighed. "The game became more than a d-drug to her. It became her life. Why she even g-got a B in her Astrophysics c-course, didn't she Mother?"

"She's a straight-A student," said Mother proudly, "but likes to take after her father in more ways than one!" She turned back quickly to the comfort of her daughter, her two other children surrounding them on the bed.

"Now, now Mrs. Barkowsky," said the doctor. "It's only natural. You see, it wasn't enough for her to copy the great bridge plays from the books and newspapers she read. A compulsive student like her father, she began to copy the bridge stars' lifestyles as well. She stayed up until the small hours of the morning, watching old movies, drinking coffee—"

"Drinking and cavorting!" Mother said shaking her head in revulsion and glancing over in my direction.

"Not with *me*," I heard Zia mutter. Marie's sister giggled.

"Well," said Jinks, "it s-seemed like just another extra c-c-curricular activity college students have these days. Mother and I p-politicked for Ike you know." Mother blushed.

"But then the girl began mixing reality with fantasy," said the doctor. "For example, if the parents asked her how she had done on her Latin midterm, she would answer that she had had a 72% game. If they asked to see her report card, she produced her convention card and masterpoint record. Things like that tend to make parents concerned. So they sent Evelyn to talk to the college psychiatrist. That was me."

He started to pace back and forth, reviewing the case. "At first she seemed like just another kid with a penchant for reliving the lifestyle of the same-gender parent. When I learned it was the father who had spent his early years as a bridge bum — excuse me Jinks — well, I knew that the case required a second opinion. I consulted with an old professor and colleague of mine from Bellevue." The older doctor was busy taking our subject's temperature, and acknowledged us with a nod.

"Meanwhile," he continued, "Evelyn's condition worsened, I am ashamed to say, under my care." Mother rolled her eyes. "Everything was becoming something it wasn't, sort of like Alice in Wonderland. She thought of us not as doctors but as policemen, grilling her for information. Soon her family entered the realm of conspirators, and one day at the school library she started reading old newspaper columns about bridge, and came across the 1942 editions concerning a man who had died clutching bridge notes to his chest. When she saw the name of her own father as a suspect, something must have snapped. This parental connection was all she needed to complete the elements for a new game her subconscious had devised: that of detective."

"I know that game," I said.

"Well," he continued, "there again was a second link to her father in the duplication of his work as a criminal psychologist. Evelyn knew something of the research procedures necessary for such an investigation. She followed up her library studies with a visit to the microfilm department of the New York City Homicide Squad. There she obtained a copy of the bridge notes found on Marcel Moskowitz's body. Finally, she took on the persona of a detective while using the name of Marie, the corpse's bridge partner." He stopped pacing and pointed to me. "She must have contacted you, Mr. Granovetter, sent you a copy of the news clippings and notes, or perhaps called you on the phone, met you secretively in Greek coffee shops and so forth. She might have even warned you to stop the very investigation she had initiated, a normal subconscious effort to halt her own impersonation in its early stage."

"Yes," I confessed, "and she even reported a fake hand to the *New York Times* which she purportedly played with me at the same hotel where Marcel was murdered. That was not very nice considering my wife would read about it."

"I'm sorry," said Evelyn. Her cheeks were soaking wet. I do believe she really was sorry.

"The d-doctor c-called me in Ann Arbor to report that Evelyn had been missing for three d-days. I flew to New York, and the next thing I knew Mother and Brother and Sis had followed. The doctors c-c-concurred that it would be useless to simply force Evelyn to come b-back with us, and Doctor Xonivitch, whom I knew as a b-boy — by the way — had the b-brilliant idea that so long as no harm could come to anyone, we would let her p-play out the role until the end."

The old doctor nodded. "Ven I learned who was involved — that it vas my old comrade Jinks who brought me coffee on so many vonderful occasions during the var — I vanted to try anything at all to help. Then, ven I found out it vas the very case I vas keebitzing forty years ago, vell, it vas quite fascinating." He pointed to the notes on the bed, a smile creasing his thin lips as his head cocked back and forth. "I wrote those analyses, you know. Not bad for jest a keebitzer, eh?"

I gave Dr. X. a nod of approval. But why had he taken so long to appear? Why did I have to suffer an entire night of frustration and fear? He answered my thoughts.

"It vas my opinion that eef the girl could achieve her goal — vhatever that fantastic theeng may be — then the psychosis could be cured by itself. Eef she could solve the murder of the man you set out to investigate, she vould fulfill her Freudian destiny, the stepping into the shoes of her father, or in thees case, you Meester Granovetti—"

"Granovetter."

"Yes, vhatever." He waved his arms in the air. "It is of no importance. Vat vas important vas that ve do not interfere! Now you see the result." He turned to Evelyn who was smiling amidst dried teardrops, holding hands with Mother. "A healthy and happy young adult, able to cope with the vorld vonce again vithout resorting to changes of identity. Able," (and this time he bent over to tell us in a whispered sneer) "to even vone day perhaps return to the pressures of your insidious game, Granovetti, with its appropriate nomenclature: duplicate bridge."

With that, Dr. X. grabbed a copy of his bridge notes, and sat down on the bed. "Permit me," he said. "I never got to see vat Moskowitz had to say about my criticism."

There was still one piece of the mystery, however, left unanswered. That was the forty-year-old question, "Who was Marie?" Was she a fictitious character placed in the analysis sheets as Marcel's partner simply as a convenient shorthand, rather than the tedious process of writing twenty-one different names? Or was she an actual person? I asked Dr. X. if he ever knew a Marie.

"Vait, vait, it vas forty years ago. Yes, yes, I remember now; it vas Lulu's idea. She had a niece, I believe, named Marie—"

"Let me see those papers!" cried Mother suddenly. She took some of the notes from Dr. X., and examined them. "Well, the nerve of her!"

"Now, now, M-m-mother. I'm sure it was j-just one of Aunt L-lulu's j-jokes." Jinks moved quickly over to his wife's side and put his arm around her.

"Jokes? Jokes, my eye! She introduced me to him when I visited New York. I was just learning the game, and he presumed he could teach me the finer points. I accepted his invitation to play bridge and it was the most awful experience of my life. It was my very first duplicate, you see. There was so little time between hands, and he took every opportunity to embarrass me in front of the other players. Why, I don't care how much experience he had, he couldn't tell an ace from a deuce." Mrs. Marie Barkowsky shuddered at her own recollection. "Aunt Lulu was always trying to fix me up with some horrible bridge player."

"She introd-duced you to me," said Jinks sweetly.

"Oh, Father, I didn't mean you."

A yawn came from across the room. Zia was leaning against the bathroom door in his nightshirt, looking quite exhausted. "Excuse me," he said, "I know how difficult it's been, curing your bloody psychoses and all. But this is the room I've booked, and it is an hour past my bedtime. I suggest you post-mortem the rest of this someplace else, and let me get some rest."

We all apologized, though Dr. X. was a bit peeved, having just gotten into the hands. And, one by one, we left Room 625 to its rightfully registered guest. I'm proud to say, however, that I still had enough wit about me to remind Jinks of the reward he had promised.

"Oh yes, of c-course." He took out his pen and checkbook.

"One second," I said, having had a brilliant idea that might help me get out of some hot water later that morning. "Make the check out to Mrs. Granovetter."

EPILOGUE

```
MICHIGAN STATE BANK
ANN ARBOR, MI                                    J. BARKOWSKY

     Pay to    Mrs. Granovetter          $ 10,000.00

     Amount    Ten thousand dollars

     #2635632365 --14              J. Barkowsky
```

Pros and cons

There are a large number of bridge teachers in the United States who are seen every day at the local bridge clubs playing with their students. This is a difficult chore, since

a) there is little time between hands to explain mistakes adequately, and

b) the student may be embarrassed in front of other players, inhibiting him from fully concentrating on the lesson.

Is bridge the only sport where the teacher actually competes with the student? Shouldn't the student spend more time in the classroom before embarking on competition? Does a music teacher take his student on a concert tour and play duets? Does a psychiatrist practice on his patients at the beginning of his learning process or at the end? These questions began to bother me as I stepped out of the Embassy Hotel. Luckily, a taxi was waiting right at the entrance.

There are also those amateur players, I thought, who play a

strong club game, give advice free of charge, and believe they play like professionals (and could prove it if only given the time to travel and play bridge every day). If there was one lesson I had learned in the last twenty-four hours, it was that there are professionals and amateurs in every field. No matter how successful I was on my first detective case, I was not a pro.

Nor should I be mixing with pros. Yet bridge players don't see it that way. In no other sport or walk of life do we see anything like it — top-class players competing against absolute amateurs. Personally, I enjoy baseball and would love the chance to play a few games in right field for the Mets. As a sleuth, what I wouldn't give to be on a case with a real New York City homicide detective! Alas, I doubt either of these things will ever happen, and rightfully so.

When the cab pulled up to my East 61st Street apartment, I gave a yawn of intense relief. I was a bridge writer — maybe I should stick to what I did best. When I went to pay the fare, the cabbie surprised me by asking for $146.00. Indeed, that's what the meter said! Then I looked more closely at the man. Good grief, it was the same driver I had left waiting at the Embassy Hotel three hours earlier. Dare I tell him to wait again? What could I do? I did have a few dollars in my wallet, and that check from Jinks, but I doubted he could change ten thousand.

So I told him to hang on a little longer, got out, and stepped briskly to the front door. The street was filled with morning sunlight, yet it was only 6:30 a.m. As I searched my trenchcoat for the door key, I spotted a piece of paper sticking out of the mailbox. It was taped along the top and I opened it.

> Dear Matty,
>
> I am at Vic and Jacqui Mitchell's. Don't show up without a damned good excuse.
>
> Yours truly,
>
> Pamela

Experience counts

The greatest attribute of any human endeavor is experience. It takes years to become a truly great bridge player. As well, they say that a second marriage usually works better because of the lessons learned from the first. This, however, was my first marriage, and also the first time I had been away from the wife overnight. I had absolutely no idea what I was going to say — I certainly couldn't tell the truth. Missing for twenty-four hours, most of which was spent with another woman, amateur sleuthing, gunplay in Central Park, and finally an innocent *ménage-à-trois* in a hotel room across town. This might not go over so well. Still, I was too tired to make up a story, and the truth had the virtue of being honest, a trait all wives love in their husbands.

When I got to the Mitchells' residence, the meter had reached an all-time high. Again, I asked the trusting driver to stand by. There was a new doorman, and I had to wait until he buzzed me up. When I got out of the elevator on the tenth floor, I found the door of 10E partly open. I pushed it further ajar, expecting to be pounced upon by an army of huskies. There was not one bark, however. Instead, I was greeted by a wonderful aroma — it was the savory odor of fresh pancakes, bacon, and coffee. I had stepped out of a nightmare into an oasis.

I walked into the living room and nobody was there. So I followed the aroma to the dining area where I found Jacqui Mitchell serving breakfast to her husband, my Pamela, and Harry, the night doorman. There was a growl from under the table. The dogs were all bunched together waiting for leftovers. Victor Mitchell was in his pajamas, and was the first human to greet me.

"Where's my robe and slippers, you thief?"

I told him I was sorry, I had left them at the Embassy Hotel and would retrieve them later in the day.

"There," he said to Jacqui, "you see, I told you he was on a murder case. Now let him sit down and eat."

The wife was not talking to me. I noticed that right off the bat. I sat down between Victor and Harry, and asked her (rather nicely I thought) for the syrup. Jacqui had made it bubbly hot, just like maple syrup was meant to be. The wife passed it without a word, but along with the bowl came a small calling card with the name and address of a psychiatrist, and an appointment written in for that very afternoon.

```
625 West 76th St.
NY, NY 10045
742-4441

        Arnold Moskowitz
        Doctor of Psychiatry


Appointment ___8/23 3:00___
```

I looked up at her, but Victor answered. "A very good doctor. Very handsome son of a bitch too. Looks a bit like Clark Gable. Takes bridge lessons in exchange for fees. At one time he was Jacqui's student. He's the one who recommended my dark glasses."

"There's nothing wrong with me," I insisted. "I just got a little carried away with my investigation. Speaking of which, did you know Dr. X. is a psychiatrist too? And quite an expert in his field."

"Dr. X.?" said Harry. "Why I didn't know he was still ticking? He used to kibitz down at the club. Ain't that right Vic? It was during the war when I was a police officer—"

Jacqui interrupted. "Keep quiet and eat. There'll be no more talk of murder and Dr. X. or any of these insane, fictitious shenanigans that Victor likes to imagine he's involved in."

Harry went back to work on his breakfast. "Dr. X.?" said Victor, swallowing a bit of crisp bacon. "I never heard of a Dr. X."

I turned to the wife. She looked at me and shook her head disapprovingly.

I started to protest, saw Jacqui's face, saw the second helping of pancakes, and rested my eyes downward on the plate. "Okay," I admitted. "I've been a bad boy. But before you send me to analysis, look at this." I handed over my last trump, a check for ten thousand dollars.

The wife read it, looked up in disbelief, then read it again. "This will do for now," she said. "Here, let me pour you some coffee. God, you smell of Indian food."

I ripped up the calling card and ate four more helpings of pancakes. I didn't tell her about the cab waiting downstairs, nor about my adventures in Room 625, but she eventually found out about both. And forgave me.

THE END
(Finito Benito, schmigeggio)

Other bridge titles from Master Point Press

Partnership Bidding   *A workbook* by Mary Paul
0-9698461-0-X   96 pp. PB   Can $ 9.95   US$7.95   UK£5.99

"A wonderfully useful book." *BRIDGE magazine*

There Must Be A Way... *52 challenging bridge hands*
by Andrew Diosy (foreword by Eddie Kantar)
0-9698461-1-8   96 pp. PB   US & Canada $ 9.95   UK£6.99

You Have to See This *52 more challenging bridge problems*
by Andrew Diosy and Linda Lee
0-9698461-9-3   96 pp PB   Can $12.95   US$ 9.95   UK£7.99

"A frustratingly enjoyable read." *ACBL Bulletin*
"Treat yourself to a gem of a book." *Eddie Kantar*

Tales out of School *'Bridge 101' and other stories*
by David Silver (foreword by Dorothy Hayden Truscott)
0-9698461-2-6   128 pp PB   Can $ 12.95   US$9.95   UK£6.99

A Study in Silver *A second collection of bridge stories* by David Silver
0-9698461-5-0   128 pp PB   Can $ 12.95   US$ 9.95   UK£6.99

"Every bridge book by Silver has a golden lining." *The Toronto Star*
"Hilarious." *Alan Truscott, New York Times*

The Complete Book of BOLS Bridge Tips edited by Sally Brock
0-9698461-6-9   176 pp PB, photographs   Can $ 24.95   US$17.95

"The quality of each and every tip is exceptional and we maintain that
the book cannot fail to improve your bridge." *Australian Bridge*

The Bridge Player's Bedside Book edited by Tony Forrester
0-9698461-8-5   256pp HC   Can $27.95   US$ 19.95

"A delightful collection." *Matthew Granovetter, Jerusalem Post*